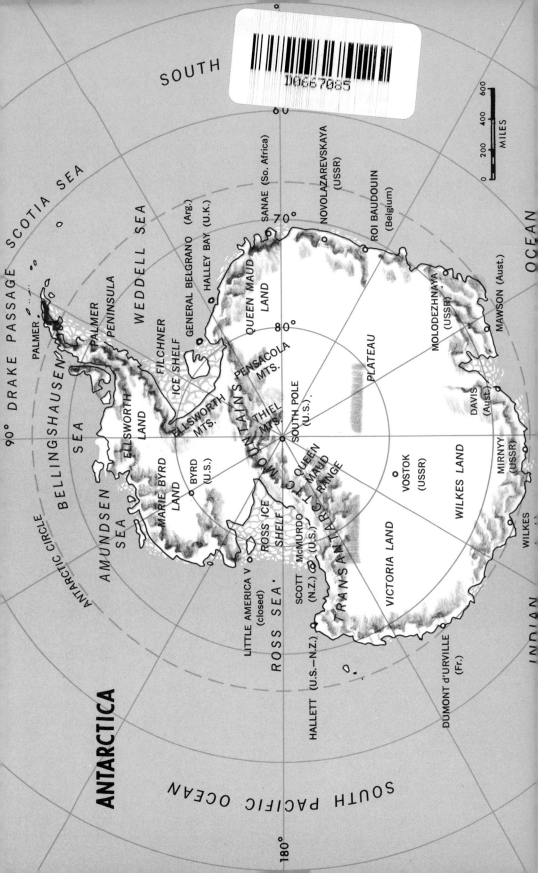

POLAR SECRETS

*A Treasury of the Arctic
and Antarctic*

POLAR SECRETS

A Treasury of the Arctic

and Antarctic

Edited by Seon Manley and Gogo Lewis

Doubleday & Company, Inc., Garden City, New York

We are grateful to the authors, agents, and publishers who have given us permission to reprint the following selections:

"What the Arctic Is: Eskimo Environment and Origins" by Peter Freuchen. Reprinted by permission of The World Publishing Company from PETER FREUCHEN'S: BOOK OF THE ESKIMOS edited by Dagmar Freuchen. Copyright © 1961 by Peter Freuchen Estate.

"How I Learned to Hunt Caribou" from HUNTERS OF THE GREAT NORTH by Vilhjalmur Stefansson. Copyright 1922, 1950 by Vilhjalmur Stefansson. Reprinted by permission of Harcourt, Brace & World, Inc.

"Time of the Poppy" from SPRING ON AN ARCTIC ISLAND by Katharine Scherman. Copyright © 1956 by Katharine Scherman Rosin. Reprinted by permission of Little, Brown and Co.

"The Mammal from the Permafrost" from EXOTIC ZOOLOGY by Willy Ley. Copyright © 1951, 1959 by Willy Ley. Reprinted by permission of The Viking Press, Inc.

"Arctic Ghost" by Felix Riesenberg from TOLD AT THE EXPLORERS' CLUB. Copyright 1931 by Albert & Charles Boni, Inc. Reprinted by permission of Albert & Charles Boni, Inc.

"A Novice and His Dogteam" from MY WAY WAS NORTH by Frank Dufresne. Copyright © 1966 by Klondy Nelson Dufresne. Reprinted by permission of Holt, Rinehart and Winston, Inc.

"We Reach the Pole" from THE NORTH POLE by Robert E. Peary. Reprinted by permission of Marie Peary Kuhne.

"Flight Over the Pole" by Richard E. Byrd. Reprinted by permission of G. P. Putnam's Sons from EXPLORING WITH BYRD by Richard E. Byrd. Copyright 1937 by R. E. Byrd.

"Nautilus 90 North" by Commander William R. Anderson, U.S.N. with Clay Blair, Jr. Reprinted by permission of The World Publishing Company from NAUTILUS 90 NORTH by Commander William R. Anderson, U.S.N. with Clay Blair, Jr. Copyright © 1959 by William R. Anderson and Clay Blair, Jr.

"What the Antarctic Is: Land of Ghosts" by Thomas R. Henry from THE WHITE CONTINENT. Reprinted by permission of William Morrow and Company, Inc. Copyright © 1950 by Thomas R. Henry.

"The Southern Ocean" by R. B. Robertson. Reprinted by permission of Alfred A. Knopf, Inc. from OF WHALES AND MEN by R. B. Robertson. Copyright 1954 by R. B. Robertson.

"Antarctica: The Urgency of Protecting Life on and Around the Great Southerly Continent" by Robert Cushman Murphy. Reprinted by permission of Natural History.

"The Antarctic: A Laboratory for Men Under Stress" by Captain Finn Ronne, U.S.N.R. From ANTARCTIC COMMAND. Copyright © 1961 by Finn Ronne. Reprinted by permission of the publishers, The Bobbs-Merrill Company, Inc.

"Alone" from THE HOME OF THE BLIZZARD by Sir Douglas Mawson. Reprinted by permission of THE MAWSON INSTITUTE FOR ANTARCTIC RESEARCH and Lady Mawson.

"The End Is in Sight" from THE HEART OF THE ANTARCTIC by Sir Ernest Shackleton. Reprinted by permission of J. B. Lippincott Company.

"The Last March" by Robert F. Scott. Reprinted by permission of Dodd, Mead & Company, Inc. from SCOTT'S LAST EXPEDITION by Robert F. Scott. Copyright 1913, 1941 by Dodd, Mead & Company, Inc.

For Seth Agnew
who knew the secret
and strength of friendship

Acknowledgments

We would also like to thank the following persons, agencies, libraries, museums, and businesses who contributed to various aspects of this book:

Alaska Department of Economic Development; Alaska Airlines; Douglas G. Allan; the American Geographical Society; the American Museum of Natural History; the Barrett Bookstore, Stamford, Conn.; Susan L. Belcher; the Bellport Memorial Library, Bellport, N.Y.; Robert A. Carter; the Donnell Library Center; the Encyclopaedia Britannica Educational Corporation; John Ernst; the Ferguson Library, Stamford, Conn.; Webster C. Givens; the late A. H. Greenley; the Greenwich Library, Greenwich, Conn.; Mrs. William W. Kuhne; Carolyn Lewis; Sara Lewis; William W. Lewis; the Library of Congress; Robert R. Manley; Shivaun Manley; the Mariners Museum, Newport News, Va.; Mr. and Mrs. D. R. Matthews; Donald Matthews; the Mawson Institute for Antarctic Research; Mary McCabe; Dr. and Mrs. Robert Cushman Murphy; the National Archives; the National Science Foundation; the New York Public Library; Office of the Assistant Secretary of Defense; Office of the Canadian Consulate General; Mrs. Harry Palevsky; the Patchogue Library, Patchogue, N.Y.; Mr. and Mrs. George Pederson-Krag; Steven Rowan; Mrs. Carolyn Royal; Grace Schiro; the Scott Polar Research Institute; Mr. and Mrs. Robert Sheffield; Herbert Shrifte; Evelyn Shrifte; Sou'wester Bookshop, Bellport, N.Y.; Anne Takashige; the Thompson Bookstore, Seacliff, N.Y.; the United States Fish and Wildlife Service; the United States Geological Survey.

Our personal thanks to Lady Mawson.

Because this collection contains many rare historical pieces, the editors have chosen to leave the original writings in their original state in terms of punctuation and capitalization.

Contents

THE MYSTERIOUS ARCTIC

THE LURE OF THE NORTH POLE

THE MYSTERY OF THE ANTARCTIC

Illustrations

This is the way Frank Dufresne learned to travel ("A Novice and His Dogteam"). COURTESY OF THE NATIONAL FILM BOARD OF CANADA

A chart of the discovery of the Northwest Passage ("Arctic Mutiny"). CONTEMPORARY CHART OF HUDSON'S DISCOVERIES IN 1610–11 BY HESSEL GERRITZ

View of the Arctic seas from the mouth of the Coppermine River ("Nightmare at Fort Enterprise"). FROM SIR JOHN FRANKLIN'S NARRATIVE OF A JOURNEY TO THE SHORES OF THE POLAR SEA, 1819–1822

Some of Sir John Franklin's Officers ("Nightmare at Fort Enterprise"). FROM THE "ILLUSTRATED NEWS" OF SEPTEMBER 13, 1851

Following page 240

Dr. Elisha Kent Kane who led an expedition to investigate the mysterious disappearance of Sir John Franklin ("First Lessons from the Eskimos"). A CONTEMPORARY PORTRAIT

Members of the Lady Franklin Bay Expedition ("Three Years of Arctic Service"). A CONTEMPORARY PHOTOGRAPH

Long and Jens killing a bear ("Three Years of Arctic Service"). A CONTEMPORARY PRINT

Fridtjof Nansen ("Adrift on the Polar Seas"). A CONTEMPORARY PORTRAIT

Nansen's ship the Fram leaving Bergen ("Adrift on the Polar Seas"). A CONTEMPORARY PHOTOGRAPH

Robert E. Peary, the first man to reach the North Pole, on the deck of his ship Roosevelt ("We Reach the Pole"). COURTESY OF THE LIBRARY OF CONGRESS

Amundsen greeting Byrd and Bennett after their flight over the North Pole ("Flight Over the Pole"). COURTESY OF THE LIBRARY OF CONGRESS

USS Nautilus, the first ship to pass under the Arctic ice cap ("Nautilus 90 North"). OFFICIAL U. S. NAVY PHOTOGRAPH

Trans-Polar route of the USS *Nautilus* ("Nautilus 90 North"). OFFICIAL U. S. NAVY PHOTOGRAPH

Lenticular clouds in the Antarctic ("What the Antarctic Is: Land of Ghosts"). COURTESY OF THE NATIONAL SCIENCE FOUNDATION

Mountains of granite five degrees from the South Pole ("What the Antarctic Is: Land of Ghosts"). COURTESY OF THE NATIONAL SCIENCE FOUNDATION

Whaling in the Southern Ocean: the killer ship; the factory ship; flensing the whale ("The Southern Ocean"). COURTESY OF THE MARINERS MUSEUM, NEWPORT NEWS, VA.

The bird that walks like man ("Antarctica: The Urgency of Protecting Life on and Around the Great Southerly Continent"). COURTESY OF THE DEPARTMENT OF THE INTERIOR U. S. GEOLOGICAL SURVEY

Antarctica today: a U. S. Geological Survey base camp ("Antarctica: The Urgency of Protecting Life on and Around the Great Southerly Continent"). COURTESY OF THE DEPARTMENT OF THE INTERIOR U. S. GEOLOGICAL SURVEY

Isolation today: the scientist in his laboratory ("The Antarctic: A Laboratory for Men Under Stress"). COURTESY OF THE NATIONAL SCIENCE FOUNDATION

Roald Amundsen, the first man to reach the South Pole ("The Serious Business of Exploration"). COURTESY OF THE ROYAL NORWEGIAN INFORMATION SERVICE

Mawson of the Antarctic: a portrait; Mawson emerging from his makeshift tent; the half-sledge used in the last stage of Mawson's journey ("Alone"). COURTESY OF THE MAWSON INSTITUTE FOR ANTARCTIC RESEARCH AND LADY MAWSON

Sir Ernest Shackleton, the Antarctic explorer ("The End Is in Sight"). COURTESY OF THE AMERICAN MUSEUM OF NATURAL HISTORY

Captain Robert Falcon Scott and members of his expedition at Amundsen's tent ("The Last March"). COURTESY OF THE LIBRARY OF CONGRESS

THE MYSTERIOUS ARCTIC

What the Arctic Is: Eskimo Environment and Origins

PETER FREUCHEN

Peter Freuchen, the Danish explorer, lived among the Eskimos of the Arctic for over two generations. The Eskimos themselves long ago unraveled some of the secrets of polar living. Freuchen felt that everything about the Eskimos from the way they live to the way they look and the way they think and feel is largely determined by the arctic conditions under which they live.

THE ESKIMOS have for centuries been the object of much interest and admiration from all peoples of the civilized world, and the reason for this is obvious: Alone of all primitive people, they live permanently in the inhospitable arctic zone, and have there established a way of life and an economic culture independent of many things millions consider necessary for survival. To put it briefly, the Eskimos possess an extraordinary hardiness which enables them to live where nobody else can.

It is true that there are other people living in the Arctic, as for instance the Samoyeds and Chukchi of northern Siberia, but these are seasonal dwellers who live on the arctic tundras and coasts in summer, but retire to the forests of the temperate zone in winter. Only the Eskimos confine themselves to the Arctic the year round, and they alone have adapted themselves completely to it.

It might be useful to make it clear what the Arctic is. Perhaps you have been told that it is that part of the globe which is north of 66½° north latitude, and is the realm of the midnight sun. At best, this delineation is only a very rough one. Consider, for example, that it would divide such a typically arctic region as the Greenland icecap in two, and that it would include northern Norway, which is, generally speaking, temperate because of the passage of the Gulf Stream.

The demarcation generally accepted now, therefore, is a July mean temperature of 50° F. This division works out well, because it classifies as Arctic a number of regions that are similar in climate, plant life, and animal life: Greenland and the North American archipelago, the Hudson Bay coasts and the Barren Grounds, the northern coasts of Canada, the northern and western parts of Alaska, the northern coast of Russia, with the islands that are a part of it, and the island group of Spitzbergen.

Climatically, the Arctic is characterized by two features: short cool summers and a small amount of precipitation. The winters vary in rigor and darkness from the low-Arctic to the high-Arctic regions, but although the sun is in the sky through all or most of the summer, it does not give much heat because of its low position. There is less than two months between the last spring and the first fall frosts, and the mean temperature is above the freezing point for only three or four months. Cold air has a lower saturation point for water vapors than warm air; therefore the small amount of precipitation consists mainly of snowfall. This is also the reason why large areas of the northern Arctic are quite bare of snow in winter, so much more so as the violent arctic gales often sweep the landscape clean of what snow may have fallen and deposit it in drifts behind the rocks or the pack ice.

There are three main types of landscape in the North American Arctic: the permanent glaciations called icecaps, of which the Greenland icecap is by far the most extensive— there are several smaller ones on Baffin and Ellesmere islands; then we have the rocky coasts and plains of Greenland, the North American archipelago, and Alaska; and thirdly, the vast rolling plains around Hudson Bay and the region northwest of it, the Barren Grounds.

There are no trees in the Arctic, for the simple reason that the limitation of the arctic zone, as we have defined it, coincides in general with the northern tree limit. In other respects there is remarkably rich plant life in the low-Arctic zone. The precipitation here can be as much as twenty inches annually, but this still would not be sufficient to sustain plant life if it were not for another arctic phenomenon, the permafrost. This is the thick layer of permanently frozen ground which we meet a few feet down, even at the height of summer. This frozen layer prevents the water from the ice and snow which melt in spring from sinking deep down, and causes it to remain in the upper layer of soil, creating extensive stretches of clay and bogs. Here we get the type of vegetation known as *tundra*, typified in the Barren Grounds. On the low, rolling hills and flat plains, cut through by lakes and small streams, we find low heath, mosses, and grasses, and, in the more sheltered places, even low shrubs like willow and dwarf pine. Where the soil is thin or too exposed to the arctic gale, the plants are low and so scattered that the bare underground becomes dominant. This type of vegetation, often called rock-desert, is the most common in the northern Arctic. Finally, as we come to the rocky ground and coasts of northern Greenland and the islands west of it, lichens become the only plant form that can exist.

The animal life of the Arctic, on the other hand, is abundant, and it is characterized by sea mammals: seal, walrus, and whales that live on the fish, clams, and krill in the waters. Other special species are the polar bears, the arctic fox, the snow hare, the caribou, and the musk ox. It is upon these animals that the Eskimo has based his material culture; he feeds on their meat, he makes his clothes, his bed, his boats, and his summer tent from their skins, and most of his utensils from their bones and teeth. And let us not forget the millions of sea birds and waterfowl that in summer inhabit the cliffs and islands along the arctic coasts.

But no description of the Arctic is complete without the seascape. The Arctic Ocean is in winter completely frozen over, and the ice reaches a thickness of three feet or more along the coasts. This ice forms the smoothest road for dog-sled driving, and without it the extensive Eskimo migrations would not have taken place. In summer, the ice breaks up all along the polar shores. The ice drift follows the south-going ocean currents, particularly the East Greenland Current through the Denmark Strait and the Canadian Current through Baffin Bay and Davis Strait. To the drifting ice floes are added the thousands of icebergs that are continually being produced by the glaciers in the fjords of Greenland.

Conditions all over the Arctic are pretty much the same, but the scenery varies considerably, and while it is a rugged and severe world, it has a majesty and haunting beauty all its own. To think of it as "the white desert" can only be correct in reference to the icecap, that is the only completely lifeless desert in the world. Personally, I have always thought that as a tourist country the Arctic is greatly neglected, and I can think of no place more beautiful than a Greenland fjord in summer. The sun remains low in the sky, coloring it red and yellow, while the black and bottomless abyss of the still water reflects the glowing colors, while the floating icebergs break the rays into blue, green, and blinding white.

Although the Eskimos live in a world where even the smallest deviation from the usual—as for instance, a change in the trek of the seals—can spell catastrophe, a world where danger and death are daily companions, they think it is a beautiful world. They pity greatly those people who live far south, where there is no ice to drive a dogsled on, and where it is too hot for comfort.

The superior techniques of the white man have greatly improved the living conditions of the Eskimos in recent times, but basically they have changed nothing in their culture, which is so admirably suited to the severe conditions of the Arctic. Almost everybody who has visited the Arctic has felt himself obliged to write a book, or at least an article, about The Extraordinary Eskimos, and many have done so without knowing them very well. You may therefore well ask what are my qualifications for writing about the Arctic and especially about the Eskimos.

My first trip to Greenland was in 1906, when I went there as a stoker on board the *Hans Egede,* a little steamer which transported a team (of which I was also a part) whose task it was to prepare for the "Danmark" Expedition to northeastern Greenland. On this trip I fell in love with the country and its people forever. I participated in the "Danmark" Expedition 1906–08 as a regular member, and when I returned to Denmark I got to know the very famous explorer Knud

Rasmussen, who was then forming a plan to establish a trading station at Smith Sound, among the Polar Eskimos.

At that time, Smith Sound was unclaimed territory. The rest of Greenland had since 1721 been colonized and civilized by us Danes, but for some reason or other, probably because of the rough traveling conditions around Melville Bay, connection with the Polar Eskimos had not been kept up. Their existence was known, but only vague and mysterious tales circulated about them among the Christian Eskimos.

The first record we have of the Polar Eskimos is from the English explorer Sir John Ross, who tells about a brief meeting with them in 1818. Admiral Peary used them on most of his expeditions, taking advantage of their superior traveling technique, and training them for his fantastic journey to the North Pole; four of them went there with him in 1909. But the first Danish contact was the so-called Literary Expedition in 1903, which got its name because its purpose was to look into the material and intellectual culture of the Greenlanders. Participating in it were Mylius-Erichsen, who later headed the "Danmark" Expedition, the physician Alfred Bertelsen, the painter Harald Moltke, and the young Knud Rasmussen. The latter, in particular, spoke of the Polar Eskimos with love and enthusiasm, and now he was talking of going to live among them. He suggested to me that I go with him, and that we establish ourselves as traders. I was all for it!

But it didn't seem possible to arouse much interest for Knud's plan in Denmark. Following the attainment of the North Pole in 1909, Peary indicated that he would no longer visit the Polar Eskimos. It could therefore be anticipated that they very soon would lack the many wonderful implements of the civilized world to which Peary had introduced them. Further, the Norwegian explorer Otto Sverdrup was working on a plan exactly similar to Knud's. This last circumstance, in particular, caused a few men of vision to give Knud their support, and, although lacking the blessing of the government, we got off to a good start in 1910. In the same year we arrived in North Star Bay and established our station. We called it Thule!

For eleven years following this, I lived among the Polar Eskimos, trading with them but also living like them, and

I married an Eskimo girl. I am the last one to have seen these people in their virgin state, and that (mainly) is what I want to write about.

The Polar Eskimos are but a small tribe, less than 300 in number, but they are generally considered to be the noblest strain of the Eskimo race. At any rate, I came to love them as my dear friends. Since, as we say in Denmark, every child whom one loves has many names, you may variously find them called Polar Eskimos, Smith Sound Eskimos, Thule Eskimos, or North Pole Eskimos. Only 900 miles from the North Pole, they live north of everybody else in the world, under the most rugged conditions that any human beings can tolerate.

You will also find occasional references to the Hudson Bay Eskimos, whom I visited as a member of the Fifth Thule Expedition 1921–24, the Danish expedition to Arctic North America under the leadership of Knud Rasmussen.

One of the purposes of the Fifth Thule Expedition was to throw some light upon the riddle of the origin of the Eskimo race, which had been puzzling scientists for years (and actually still is). There are several conflicting facts to consider.

First, we must wonder at the complete uniformity of Eskimo culture, all modern influences disregarded. Although the Eskimos are spread over a huge area and relatively few in number, their instruments and hunting techniques as well as other cultural elements have—in spite of local adaptations—maintained distinct resemblances. It can therefore be concluded that the Eskimos developed their unique traits in one certain locality and through the centuries undertook extensive migrations, facilitated by the dogsled. This original locality was probably not a coastal area, for many Eskimo implements appear to have been developed for coastal ice hunting from implements used inland at rivers and lakes. Also, many of the ancient tales of the Eskimos show traditions that must stem from an inland culture.

When we try to relate the Eskimos to other races, we meet difficulties all along the line. Nothing in their economic or intellectual culture points to other peoples of the world. Their language resembles none other. Like many Indian languages, it is polysynthetic—that is, words or word roots are chained together in composite words forming meanings that in European-type languages would be expressed in whole sentences. But the scientists cannot classify it as belonging to the Indian language group, though a vague kinship to the Ural-Altaic group has been seen. The Ural-Altaic languages comprise such widely different tongues as, for instance, Finnish, Hungarian, Turkish, Samoyed, Kalmuck, and Mongolian. The most probable explanation seems to be that the Ural-Altaic languages, the Indian languages, and Eskimo have developed from a common ancient Asiatic root.

Racially, the Eskimos differ from the Indians by having much more Mongolian features, such as high, broad cheek-bones, small noses, and often slanting eyes, and their babies are born with the blue Mongolian spot at the base of the spine. However, they are taller than the Mongolians, and they are long-skulled where the Mongolians are short-skulled, a point too important to be overlooked. As far as can be divined, their nearest relatives are the palaeo-Asiatic people of north-eastern Siberia. The palaeo-Asiatics comprise several small groups, such as the Yukaghir, the Chukchi, and the Koryaks, and are actually the remainders of an ancient people, small dark men of a type approaching the Mongolian. These people followed the retreating ice north after the last ice age and occupied the forests and tundras of northern Siberia, but were later almost completely wiped out by another immigration from the south, that of the Samoyeds and the Tungus-Man-churians.

Then, in 1917, a bit of the veil that covered the Eskimos' mysterious past was lifted quite by chance at no other place than our Thule settlement. Captain Comer of the Crocker Land Expedition, which was then ice-bound, began out of forced idleness, to dig in our kitchen midden. It was slow work digging in the frozen earth, but when we saw what he found we appropriated one half of the midden and started digging ourselves. We also appropriated some of his glory, for the place went down in history as Comer's Midden, while the old Eskimo culture that here was unearthed for the first time was named the Thule Culture.

One of the purposes of the Fifth Thule Expedition was

to determine the extent of the Thule Culture. We excavated all of the old house ruins we found, which were many, and our eminent archaeologist, Therkel Mathiassen, concluded that the Thule Culture had extended all along the coastline of the Canadian Arctic.

But another and maybe even more important clue was found when the expedition visited the Caribou Eskimos, who inhabit the tundra between Back River and Chesterfield Inlet. Theirs is the most primitive Eskimo culture in existence, and they were also the poorest people I had ever seen. They didn't own a fourth of the hunting tools that we knew from the Eskimos of West Greenland. They did not have winter houses, but lived in snow houses when their caribou skin tents couldn't be used. They hunted caribou in summer and fished salmon in winter, and thus had no blubber for heat and light. Their houses were sparsely lit by a lump of caribou tallow with a wick of heather in it, and even with many people present the temperature was usually around zero.

Their women were robust, for their life and work were so difficult as to mark them completely. They did their cooking by heather and twigs. This was not so bad in summer, when the ground was free of snow and they could collect their fuel in big bundles, carry it down to the tents, and make festive cooking fires. But in winter it was worse; then the women had to go out and scrape aside the snow to get to the heather, and since they did not have many skins and had to save their mittens, they pulled the heather loose with their bare hands. Imagine what that meant at a temperature of forty below! Their hands were completely malformed, black, hard to the feel as if made of wood, and full of frost scars. Besides, they let their nails grow very long, so that the general impression was that of sinister bird claws. When they came home in winter with their fuel, they couldn't burn it under the open sky, for that would use it up too quickly. Cooking wasn't possible in the snow house either as the snow would melt, and, also, the smoke would bother the master of the house. So adjoining the house they would build a small, low hut with a hole in the roof, and in there the woman would lie down to do the cooking. She had to blow on the fire continually to keep it going, ashes would fly around her face, hair, and shoulders, and her eyes were always red and watering, so that the tears made deep grooves of bare skin down over the otherwise dirt-covered face. You can easily understand that such a woman looked old and decrepit before she was thirty.

The caribou hunt took place twice a year. First in the spring, when the herds migrated north; the caribou were lean, but the Eskimos were hungry and gladly ate the tough meat. Then in the fall the herds would return south to the forests, fat from the grazing on the tundras. In between, the Caribou Eskimos lived on salmon, a poor diet in the cold climate, and they were often starving. But it didn't occur to them to follow the caribou herds or to make deposits for the bad seasons.

It became apparent that their primitive culture had originated in the interior. Not only did none of their implements show signs of their ever having stayed by the sea, but their religion was a typical inland religion, very different from that of the coast dwellers in that there was almost no observance of taboo. Their relatively few taboo rules and simple birth and death customs made it clear that they lived under conditions that were traditionally indigenous and natural to them, and that as long as they could obtain sufficient food, they always felt secure in their surroundings.

The reasoning behind this conclusion is that those Eskimos who came down to the sea to live came upon something that was quite unknown and strange to them, and in their primitive fear and insecurity it gave rise to intricate precautions in the form of taboo rules and more complicated religious ideas.

The late Professor Steensby of Copenhagen had already put forth his widely publicized theory that the Eskimos had originally been an inland people who had come out to the sea from the great lakes in northern Canada, and there adapted their lake and river culture to the requirements of the sea. It would seem that the Caribou Eskimos were living proof of his theory, since theirs seemed to be a remnant of the original Eskimo culture, from the time when the transformation to a coast culture had not yet taken place. It would also seem that the kind of tundra landscape they lived in was

the Eskimo's original habitat. Their old tales were—in substance
and form—much the same as those we already knew from
Greenland and had met in all the Eskimo tribes we visited,
thus again demonstrating the puzzling uniformity of all Eskimo
cultures.

But all this did not explain the presence of the Thule
Culture, nor did it explain the presence of an even older
culture which previously had been excavated at Coronation
Gulf and in South Baffin Land, and which had been called
the Cape Dorset Culture.

Some years later, remains of a later phase of the Thule
Culture were found in northeastern Greenland, but it became
quite obvious that—nonetheless—the Thule Culture was akin
to that of the Alaskan Eskimos! The next step in this
exciting detective mystery would, then, be excavations in Alaska.

In the years 1939–50, American and Danish scientists excavated along the coasts of Alaska, and they came up with
some pretty gratifying results. They found a layer corresponding to an early phase of the Thule Culture; they found layers
corresponding to the Cape Dorset Culture; and they found
traces of a stone-age culture that became known as the Cape
Denbigh Flint Complex.

To look even further into the past, let us look upon the
other forms of life in the Arctic, the plants and the animals.
They show a difference from those of the rest of the world
by being distributed in both the western and the eastern
hemispheres. While America and Europe as well as Asia show
great differences in the native flora and fauna of their temperate
and tropical zone, the arctic zone is characterized by the
uniformity of species throughout. Most species of animals and
plants are distributed around the Pole, very few being confined to either the New World or the Old World. To explain
this we must go back to the ice age, which actually was a
series of glacial periods during which the northern parts of
the European-Asian and American continents were covered by
huge icecaps. In between were interglacial periods during
which the ice retreated and the climate became approximately
like it is now. The last glacial period ended about 25,000

years ago, and we may very well be in an interglacial period.

During the last glacial period, the ice covered northern Europe and most of Siberia, and the biggest icecap was that of Greenland and the North American continent, reaching as far south as the fortieth parallel. However, except for some smaller icecaps, eastern Siberia was ice-free, and so was the greatest part of Alaska. Since the sea level there was much lower than it is now, as so much water was tied up in the icecaps, the two continents were landfast at that point, and in geology the country thus formed is called Beringia. Also, the continental shelf of northeastern Siberia is low and stretches hundreds of miles out into the Arctic Ocean. No doubt this shelf was also dry land and connected with Beringia. In this and other glacial refuges, plants and animals survived and developed special traits which enabled them, with the retreating ice, to move in and occupy all of their natural habitat, the Arctic.

With all these facts in mind, I should like to put forth a theory of the Eskimos' origin and development which may seem daring at some points, but which can be defended biologically and archaeologically.

No traces of man from before the last glacial period have been found in Beringia. Yet this would seem ideal as the home country of the Eskimo culture. Particularly the northern plains of the dry continental shelf would provide the kind of tundra landscape that seems to be the Eskimos' ancient habitat, and there were probably great herds of reindeer there. It would also provide the degree of isolation in which the Eskimos—then, as later, the object of the most merciless selection of nature—could develop their peculiar racial, cultural, and linguistic traits. Maybe some development to a coastal culture already took place, as the Arctic Ocean advanced after the ice age. The Eskimos have, in their old tales, traditions of a flood. In all primitive peoples, such traditions have signified the sudden or gradual inundation of formerly habitable country. The flood the Eskimos tell about had never been placed anywhere; could it be in northern Beringia? For my part, I cannot help imagining that the traces of the original

Eskimo culture lie hidden north of northeastern Siberia, under the ice-filled waters of the Arctic Ocean!

Be that as it may, it has been fairly well established that the Eskimos, probably under pressure from migrations from the south, left Asia and crossed the Bering Strait to the American continent about 6000 years ago. A branch of them spread to the Aleutian Islands, off the southwest coast of Alaska, and established their own special culture that is still, in language and traditions, closely related to that of the Eskimos. An Eskimo culture developed on the Alaskan shores of the Bering Sea, and the *kayak*—that important hunting aid—was in full use there.

But it is my contention that the bulk of the Eskimos migrated inland, through the tundras of northern Alaska and northern Canada right over to Hudson Bay. Since the migrations of the caribou herds are roughly north-south, these early Eskimos may even have entered the forest belt. But here they clashed with another population wave, that of the Indians.

The Indians had already before the last ice age arrived in America from Asia in several groups and migrations, and they had the continent pretty well populated. With the retreating ice—or rather, with the subsequent advance of the forests—they moved north into Canada and Alaska. It may well have been under pressure from them that the Eskimos moved right out to the arctic coasts. At any rate, we have—both from historic and prehistoric times—stories and sagas of clashes between the Eskimos and Indians, massacres that even the most blood-curdling fantasies cannot match. Even as late as this, our twentieth century, the cry of "Indians!" in an isolated southern Greenland settlement could throw the inhabitants into a state of senseless panic, and this was true even though the word had lost its meaning to them hundreds of years before!

The Eskimos could not match the Indians in cruelty and warfare and had to retreat. It may also be that they simply followed the migrations of the caribou out to the coast. They occupied the coasts between Coronation Gulf and Boothia Peninsula, and their implements underwent adaptation to ice hunting. We are now on surer ground, since this is the period of the Cape Dorset Culture. The Eskimos spread east to Baffin Island and west right to Alaska. But the broad belt of boggy tundra west of Hudson Bay kept the group known as the Caribou Eskimos back in the interior, and preserved it as a remnant of the original inland culture.

In the region around Point Barrow, Alaska, under the influence of ever richer whale and walrus herds, a new Eskimo culture evolved, based upon the hunting of aquatic animals from *umiak* and *kayak,* and it passed through a period of unequaled prosperity. This new, vigorous, and wealthy culture was the Thule Culture. It spread to the coasts of the Bering Sea and even crossed the Bering Strait to reoccupy a corner of the ancestral home, Siberia. And it spread, through several waves of migration, eastward through the Northwest Passage to Hudson Bay and Labrador, north to Baffin Island, and right over to Greenland. One wave went along the east coast of Greenland and settled northeastern Greenland, but due to worsening climatic conditions that population died out, maybe as early as the year A.D. 1000. Several waves passed through Thule (we counted three layers in our kitchen midden); and the western and southeastern coasts of Greenland, with the rich sealing, became one of the true homes of the Eskimo race. The last migration wave probably overran the dying-out Norse settlers in the fifteenth century.

But in the Hudson Bay area, the Thule Culture was later wiped out by a new migration wave from the interior, probably as recently as the fifteenth century. The tribes we meet, for instance, on the central north shore of Canada, the Iglooliks around Fury and Hecla Straits, the Netchiliks of Boothia Peninsula, and the Copper Eskimos at Coronation Gulf, are descendants of these late immigrants. They have more taboos and more complicated religious systems than any other Eskimos, all of which indicates that they have been the last to reach the strange habitat of the coast and adapt to it. The Netchiliks have, in their traditions, many tales about a strange people called the Tunrit who occupied the country before them, but who moved away without protest when they came. They tell about the Tunrits' great skill at hunting, and no doubt they were the people of the Thule Culture. What actually happened to them? Well, there are some indications that they had degenerated and succumbed, others that they all moved to Greenland. One little pocket of Thule Culture

survived on Southampton Island in the strange tribe of the
Sagdlermiut, who in many respects seem to have resembled the
Polar Eskimos. But they were all wiped out by an epidemic in
1903.

At present, the Eskimos are divided into three groups: the
Eastern Eskimos, which are the eastern Greenlanders, the
western Greenlanders, and the Polar Eskimos, and whose cul-
ture descends from late phases of the Thule Culture; the
Central Eskimos, whose culture is a recent adaptation of the
original inland culture (with the exception of the Caribou
Eskimos); and the Western Eskimos, which consist of the
Mackenzie Eskimos, the Alaskan tribes, and the Yuit of Siberia,
and whose culture is a development of an early phase of the
Thule Culture.

Of course, this would not be apparent in places like southern
Greenland where the Eskimos—during the last decades—have
been emancipated into a fully modern civilization. The Central
Eskimos seem to be the weakest group. The census figures for
Eskimos look approximately as follows: Greenland, 25,000;
Canada, 10,000; Alaska, 16,000; and the Yuit 1500.

Not all of the Eskimo migrations took place in prehistoric
times. At Thule, I got a first-hand account of the last migration
into Greenland from my wife's grandfather, old Mequsaq. I
should like to tell about it, not only because it is one of the
great sagas of the Arctic, but also because it demonstrates how
cultural elements were dispersed throughout the Eskimo world.

Mequsaq's original home was at Admiralty Inlet in the northern part of Baffin Island. He was only a little boy when his
tribe was hit by misfortune. The weather was continually bad,
the game animals stayed away, and starvation threatened. The
wise man of the tribe was the great Kritlaq, the greatest sha-
man in man's memory, said Mequsaq. He understood all
things, and he could ask stones in running brooks and interpret
the answer. Urged by him, and under his leadership, the tribe
broke up and started the long trek north over Devon and
Ellesmere islands to Greenland. They stopped at several places,
and the trip took several winters, but Kritlaq urged them on.
His power was so great, it was said, that when he drove ahead

of the other sleds in the night, fire and flames could be seen shooting out from his head!

Several expeditions that were in the area at the same time have reported meeting this strange little group, and they fix the time of their crossing to Greenland as 1864.

Mequsaq told me that, when they had arrived, his father thought it best to find out if they had traveled far enough. So he went bear hunting and drove as far as snow and ice would permit. He went all the way to Thom Island in Melville Bay. And there he discovered that he had absolutely no desire to continue his travels!

But the Smith Sound area was well inhabited by the Polar Eskimos, and it wasn't easy for the new group to fit in. After a few years in the new country some of them, among them Mequsaq's family, decided to return to the homeland. On the way they had terrible snowfall with bad driving, and since they as travelers had no winter depots, and the hunting was bad, starvation began to ravage them. They ate most of their dogs, but they had to keep some so that they could eventually continue their journey. There were two men in the company, Minik and Mattak by name, who were the strongest and always took bigger parts of the game than they were entitled to, because they were very hungry and didn't know how to comply with their people's customs and be content with what was theirs.

They became more and more savage. And one day, when Mequsaq's father was hunting with the other men, they entered the house, intending to kill them all. Mequsaq's older brother defended himself well, but the two boys had to see their mother and their sister stabbed to death and carted off to be eaten! They tried to get Mequsaq also, and they cut one eye out of him, a knife landed deep in his neck, another in his back, and for the rest of his life he had deep scars from the fight. But he saved his life.

When the father returned and heard this, he decided to set out after Minik and Mattak to revenge his wife and daughter. But his dogs were too weak from hunger, and he didn't have much strength himself, so he gave up this resolve. The rest of the party now moved together into one large igloo to defend themselves better against the two cannibals.

One night, some time later, they woke up as they heard sleds arrive outside the igloo. It was Minik and Mattak again. But when they saw that the men were home and ready for defense, they didn't try anything. They hung around for a while, and nobody dared leave the house.

It turned out that the two cannibals had seen tracks in the snow showing that some had died from hunger and been buried in the scree, where there were loose stones to build graves from. It was seen that the two men went there and returned with two corpses which they put on their sleds and drove away with, to eat them. After that time Minik and Mattak were never heard from again.

But even when the light returned and hunting became better again, it was still feared that the two men would return. Asayuk and his sister Itusarssuk were children then, and they were always put behind the skins covering the walls of the igloo when the men went out hunting. There were no women to stay at home with them, since Minik and Mattak had killed those who had survived the hunger. Asayuk often told me how he sat together with his sister behind the drapery so as to be out of sight in case wicked men should enter.

But when they had been sitting there for a long time, they felt their hunger very keenly, so they crawled out and ventured outside the house. He remembered clearly how they looked around them for the cannibals. When they saw the sleds far out on the ice, they became afraid and ran back in to hide behind the skins.

When their father, Krumangapik, came nearer, he saw that the snow block that had closed the igloo had been thrown aside. He feared that his children had been abducted and killed. He ran inside quickly and saw that they were still there. Then they all laughed a lot at his fear, and that was the first laugh they had had in a long, long time. He had come home with game, and the hunting stayed good thereafter, so that they regained their strength and kept their dogs alive.

But since they didn't have any women, they didn't feel any desire to travel for several winters in order to get home, and they knew that there were better chances of getting women in Greenland. So they crossed again from Ellesmere Island to Etah. And they stayed there ever since.

There was, however, some strife before a regular family life could be established in the new country. A circumstance that helped them was that the Polar Eskimos did not have any kayaks or any bows and arrows. By one of those strange mishaps of the many wanderings between regions of different nature, they had lost the use of these things. Thus they could not hunt in the summer when there was no ice, and their winter depots were few and small and usually used up too early.

Therefore, when the darkness was at its deepest these people went into the houses, lay down and covered themselves with skins, and moved as little as possible. They had no blubber for their lamps, they had nothing! And they didn't go outside and never ate before the sun came up over their middens, when they could see to go out hunting. By that time they were usually so weak that they could barely reach those seal blowholes that were nearest to the settlement. Only after they had eaten for some days did they regain strength to hunt as usual. Their dogs were usually dead except for a few strong ones which had perhaps sustained themselves by eating the others.

Mequsaq's father and his group taught these people the use of the kayak for hunting seals and walrus, and the use of the bow and arrow for hunting caribou in the mountains. For this they were held in respect, and when we came to Smith Sound, the Baffin Islanders were thoroughly integrated, and the Polar Eskimos were a wealthy people who always had plenty of skins and lots of good things to eat in their houses.

Knud and I had to try to adjust to this rugged world. You might like to know exactly what our new surroundings looked like. We built our station on the rocky south shore of North Star Bay, also known as Thule Fjord. In this fjord are two islands, of which one, Saunders Island, was the biggest bird cliff in Greenland. The fjord was surrounded by mountains, behind which the icecaps could be seen. Three glaciers went down to the fjord and filled it with icebergs, which provide the Eskimo a supply of fresh water. We didn't have much real snowfall, yet we often had spectacular snowstorms, when the wind was such that it swept myriad ice crystals off the top of the icecap and carried them out over the coast.

Average temperature at Thule during the winter was ten below zero, that in the summer just above the freezing point. The ice broke up very late in spring, and the drifting ice and the icebergs filled the waters all through the short summer. Melville Bay, while it formed a beautiful icy road to southern Greenland in winter, was notorious among navigators as the worst waters in the Arctic in summer. Only for a few weeks in July and August could ships get through to us, and we had to rely on one ship a year to supply us with all the things we needed.

For three months of the winter, from November to mid-February, we didn't see the sun. On the other hand, it didn't leave the sky for the three and a half months from May to mid-August, and we had brilliant, though cool, summers.

This severe and beautiful country became my home; with all my heart and soul I came to love it and its people.

How I Learned to Hunt Caribou

VILHJALMUR STEFANSSON

*"Stefansson will stand for all time as the Great Interpreter of the North,"
said Dr. Isaiah Bowman, former Director of the American Geographical
Society, about the Canadian explorer Vilhjalmur Stefansson who explored
arctic islands and polar seas and who uncovered many secrets of keeping
alive in the Far North. Stefansson attempted to live off the land as the
Eskimos did and learned to trust his own experience and knowledge
rather than some of the misinformation about the Arctic that was once
so prevalent.*

APART from the islands actually discovered by my expedition,
there is no known country in the northern hemisphere that
has been so little visited as Isachsen Land, in north latitude
79°, west longitude 103°. We feel sure that no Eskimos ever
saw that island. From the beginning of the world to our
own time it had been visited only once—by Captain Isachsen
in 1901. Isachsen made a hurried sledge trip round the island.
The journey took him about a week. In one place he saw some
caribou tracks, and I think he may have seen some caribou at
a distance, but he did not try to hunt them. The next visitors
were my sledge party in 1916, and on that occasion we saw
no caribou and had to feed ourselves and our dogs entirely on
seals.

My second visit, and the third visit of human beings to the
island, was in 1917. We were then on the most dangerous
adventure that has ever fallen to our lot. By the road we had
to travel we were some five hundred miles away from the
nearest Eskimos and six hundred miles away from our own
base camp. Four of us had been on a long journey out on the
moving sea-ice to the northwest. When we were more than a
hundred miles northwest from Isachsen Land two of my three

companions were taken seriously ill. We turned toward shore immediately, and it was a hard fight to make land. When we got there after a struggle of two weeks we found ourselves with one man so sick that he could not walk, another who could barely walk, but was of no use otherwise, and with two teams of dogs that were exhausted with hard work and so thin from short rations during the forced march toward shore that they were little more than skeletons. It had been my pride through many years never to lose a dog. Furthermore, I was exceedingly fond of every one of these dogs, for they had worked for me faithfully for years. I was concerned for their safety, and still more concerned for the safety of the sick men. By that time, however, my confidence in our ability to make a living in the Arctic had become so strong through eight years of experience that I felt more worry for the lives of the men on the score of illness than for fear they might actually die of hunger.

But the first day on Isachsen Land was a depressing contradiction of my hopes and expectations. The one man in good health and the two men who were sick had to make their way as best they could along the coast while I hunted inland parallel to their course. I walked that day twenty miles across one of the very few stretches of entirely barren land that I have seen in the Arctic. Under foot was gravel without a blade of grass. Much of the land was lightly covered with snow, as in other typical arctic lands in winter, and I looked in vain in the snow for track or other sign of any living thing.

That evening my men were depressed, partly because of their illness and also because it looked as if we had at last come into a region as barren as many people think the polar countries generally are. It was clear that if we saw game the next day we should simply have to have it. Where game is plentiful you may lose one chance and soon get another; but where it is scarce you must not allow any opportunity to slip through your fingers.

I am telling this particular hunting story rather than any other to illustrate the principle of how you must hunt caribou in the polar regions if it is essential that you should get every animal you see. It certainly was essential in this case, for I wanted not only to stave off immediate hunger, but to secure

meat enough to enable us to camp in one place for several
weeks and give the sick men a chance to become well.

On our second day at Isachsen Land, the men again followed the coastline with the sledges, cutting across the shortest
distance from point to point, while I walked a much longer
course inland. I had gone but a few miles when I came upon
the tracks of a band of caribou. You can seldom be sure from
the tracks of the minimum number in a band if there are more
than ten animals, for caribou have a way of stepping in each
other's footprints. There are always likely to be more animals
in a band than you have been able to make out from the
tracks.

The trail showed that these caribou were traveling into the
wind, as they usually do. There were only light airs, and the
snow had on it a crust that broke underfoot with a crunching
noise. Under such conditions the band were likely to hear me
four or five hundred yards away. The country now was a
rolling prairie—not barren gravel as yesterday. It was impossible
to tell which ridge might hide the caribou from me, so instead
of following the trail ahead I went back along it for about half
a mile, studying the tracks to see just how fast they had been
moving. They had been traveling in a leisurely way and feeding here and there. I estimated that their average rate of
progress would not be more than three or four miles per day.
I could not rely on this, however, for a wolf may turn up any
time and begin a pursuit which takes a band twenty-five or
fifty miles away. Should a wolf pass to windward of them, so
that they got his smell without his knowing about them, they
would be likely to run from five to ten miles.

When I had made up my mind that these caribou were
moving slowly I went to the top of a neighboring hill and
through my glasses studied the landscape carefully. With good
luck I might have seen some of them on top of some hill, and
the problem would have become definite. But I watched for
half an hour and saw nothing. Clearly they were either feeding
in some low place or else they were lying down, for caribou are
like cattle in their habit of lying down for long periods. I now
commenced a cautious advance, not along the actual trail, but
crisscrossing it from high hilltop to high hilltop, hoping to get
a view of the animals while they were at least half a mile

from me and while I was beyond the range of their eyesight, for they cannot see a man even under the most favorable conditions farther off than half a mile. Under ordinary conditions they would not see you much beyond a quarter of a mile.

Finally I saw the band lying quietly on some flat land. There was no cover to enable me to approach safely within five hundred yards, and that is too far for good shooting. I thought these might be the only caribou in the whole country. We had thirteen hungry dogs and two sick men, and now that I had a large band before me it was my business to get enough food at one time to enable us to spend at that place two or three weeks, while the men had a chance to regain their health and the dogs to regain their flesh and strength.

On a calm day, when caribou can hear you farther than you can shoot, there is only one method of hunting. You must study their movements from afar until you make up your mind in which direction they are going. Then you must walk in a wide curve round them until you are in the locality toward which they are moving and well beyond earshot. This takes judgment, for they usually travel nearly or quite into the wind, and you must not allow them to scent you. You therefore have to choose a place which you think is near enough to their course for them to pass within shooting distance, and still not directly enough in front to enable them to smell you.

On this occasion, the glaring light on the snow had been so hard on my eyes that I did not feel they were in perfect condition, and no one can shoot well if his eyes are not right. Unless there is a change of wind, caribou are not likely to turn their course back along the trail by which they have come. I accordingly selected a hill across which they had walked that morning and half a mile away from where they now were. On the top of this hill, where I could see them, although they could not see me (because my eyes were better than theirs) I lay down, covered my head with a canvas hunting-bag to keep the sun away, and went to sleep. Sleeping is the best possible way of passing time, but my object now was not only to pass the time until the caribou began moving, but also to get my eyes into perfect condition.

When you go to sleep at twenty below zero, you have in the temperature an automatic alarm clock. My clothes were warm enough to keep me comfortable while I was awake, but I knew that when I went to sleep my circulation would slow down. This reduces the body temperature, and the same weather that will not chill you when you are awake will chill you enough to wake you from a sleep.

In this case, the chill woke me in about half an hour to an unpleasant situation. A fog had set in, and I could not see the caribou, nor had I any means of knowing whether they were still lying down or whether they had started to move. If this had been a good game country, I might have taken chances on advancing through the fog a little, but I was so impressed with the possibility that these were the only animals within a hundred miles that carelessness was not to be considered. At this time of year we had twenty-four hours of daylight. The fog was bound to lift sooner or later, and whenever it did, I would commence the hunt over again.

The fog did lift in about two hours, and I did have to commence the hunt all over again, for the caribou were gone. I was to the north of them, and I felt sure that they had not gone by near me; so they must have gone east, west, or south. I was probably so near them that I could not with safety go on top of any of the adjoining hills, so I went back north half a mile and climbed a high hill there. From that hill I saw nothing, and went half a mile to one side to another hill. Then I saw the caribou. They were now feeding half a mile south of where they had been when the fog covered them up. In the meantime the breeze had stiffened, so that now there was no longer danger of my being heard. I did not, therefore, have to circle them and lie in wait in front, but could follow up directly behind.

Eventually I got within about three hundred yards. But I wanted to get within two hundred, so I lay still and waited for them to move into a more favorable locality. During my wait an exceedingly thick fog bank rolled up, but with it the wind did not slacken. Under cover of this fog I felt safe in crawling ahead a hundred yards, for I knew that I could see through the fog quite as well as the animals, and that they could not hear me because of the wind. The reason I had not approached them in the previous fog was that the weather then had been nearly calm and they would have heard me.

At two hundred yards I was just able to make out the outline of the nearest caribou. I did not dare to go closer, and, of course, I could not begin shooting with only one or two animals in sight when I wanted to get them all. I had before now counted them carefully. There were twenty-one, which I estimated would be enough to feed our men and dogs between two and three weeks, giving them a chance to recuperate.

After about half an hour the fog began gradually to clear, and in another half hour I could see all the animals. I was near the top of a hill and they were in a hollow, the nearest of them about a hundred and fifty yards away and the farthest about three hundred.

In winter the ground in any cold country will split in what we call frost-cracks. These are cracks in the frozen surface of what in summer is mud. They are ordinarily only half an inch or so wide, but I have seen cracks four or five inches wide. These cracks form when the mercury is dropping and with a noise that resembles a rifle shot. Under the same conditions, the ice on the small lakes cracks similarly. These loud noises are so familiar to the caribou, and the report of a rifle is so similar, that the mere sound of a rifle does not scare them. Of course, we have smokeless powder, so they cannot see where the shots come from. What does scare them is the whistle of the bullet and the thud as it strikes the ground. It is instinctive with all animals to run directly away from the source of any noise that frightens them. It is another instinct of caribou when they are alarmed to run toward the center of the herd. A band that has been scattered while feeding will bunch up when they take fright. When you know these two principles it is obvious that the first caribou to kill is the one farthest away from you. On some occasions when I have been unable to get within good shooting distance of a band, I have commenced by firing a few shots into a hill on the other side of them, hoping that the noise of the striking bullets would scare them toward me. Frequently it works. On this occasion, however, I merely took careful aim at an animal about three hundred yards away. It dropped so instantaneously that although the sound of the bullet striking it induced the other caribou to look up, they recognized no sign of real danger.

They were, however, alert, and when they saw the second caribou fall they ran together into a group and moved somewhat toward me. I now shot animals on the outer margin of the group, and as each fell, the others would run a little away from that one. Their retreat in any direction was stopped by my killing the foremost animal in the retreat, whereupon the band would turn in the opposite direction.

It would not have been difficult for me to kill the whole band alone, but I was not shooting alone. From a point somewhere above and behind me I could hear other shots, and some animals I was not aiming at were dropping. Without looking round I knew what this meant. My companions traveling along shore on the ice had seen the caribou, and had waited for some time until they began to fear that I might have missed the band. The two sick men had then been left behind in camp, while their Eskimo companion had come inland to try to get the caribou. When he got near he saw that I was approaching them, and very wisely did not interfere. There is nothing so likely to spoil a caribou hunt as two hunters whose plans conflict. Even when they have a chance to consult at the beginning of the hunt, two men are less likely to be successful than one. For one thing, caribou may see a black dot on the landscape and take no warning from it, but if they see two black dots and later notice that they are either closer together or farther apart than they were a moment before, this makes a danger signal which they understand. That is the main reason why I always hunt alone. If there are two hunters to go out from the same camp on any given day, they should go in opposite directions. In this way, they double the chance of finding game, and each has a fair chance of getting the animals he does find.

On our journeys, we never kill more animals than we need, but in this case we needed the whole twenty-one. The Eskimo and I went down to the ice with my hunting-bag filled with the tongues of the caribou. This gave the sick men a more appetizing meat than they had had for a long time. The dogs had to wait for their food until we were able to move camp right to where the caribou had been shot. Although they were thin and tired, they became so excited at the smell of the fresh-killed caribou which they got from our clothes that they pulled toward shore as if they had been well fed and of full strength.

On the hill from which I had shot the caribou, we pitched camp. During the next two weeks the invalids rapidly gained in health. We called the place Camp Hospital. Few hospitals have ever been more successful. When we left it three weeks later, the dogs were fat and the men well.

Time of the Poppy

KATHARINE SCHERMAN

The Arctic is not all snow and ice: In the spring and summer, the tundra swarms with life, sparkles with color. From the poppies to the butterflies and bees, from the lemmings to the abundant bird life, the Arctic has a magic of its own, which has been beautifully captured by Katharine Scherman. Mrs. Scherman is a New Yorker "in love with the wilderness" who went with a scientific expedition of eight Americans to Bylot Island, four hundred and fifty miles above the Arctic Circle.

SUNDAY, July Fourth, was hot, bright and mosquitoey. The temperature was forty-two degrees in the shade and much higher in the blazing sun, reflected back at us from snow and ice. We were now so well adapted to the cold that this weather felt like midsummer. We peeled off several layers of our many-tiered clothing, got out the 612 and resigned ourselves to an uncomfortable day.

We had come to the north prepared for a terrible invasion of mosquitoes. But, as an optimistic Eskimo poet wrote, "Cold and mosquitoes, these two pests, come never together—and such is life." To our relief, we found that the country was too cold and dry to support many mosquitoes. The earth of northern Baffin and Bylot islands is called "dry tundra." (What, we often wondered, sinking to our knees in wet, mossy ooze, is "wet tundra"?) Very few mosquitoes found it to their taste, and they bothered us only on the few warm days. They were *Aëdes;* the word means "odious" and the mosquito is a carrier of yellow fever in the tropics. But these northern *Aëdes* were not very efficient. They were slow and clumsy, and many of them did not bite at all. That was because they were mostly males. They were swarming, preparatory to breeding, and they didn't feel like eating.

I sat outside the tent in the bright sun doing laundry. As I hung the tent lines with a colorful festoon of dripping, soap-smelling woolen clothing, the wavering sound of children's voices singing hymns floated over the still Sunday air. I left the chores and went to Idlouk's tent. Opening the door a crack, I peered in, afraid to interrupt. Idlouk and Kidla, with immediate delighted hospitality, invited me to join the service. The white tent was hot under the high morning sun and the six children sat in a solemn row on the sleeping platform, dressed in clean, neat clothes. Kidla quietly nursed Susanna, and Idlouk, facing the family, read the morning service with serious devotion. At the end of the long service, replete with prayers, responses and hymns (all verses), Idlouk handed me a beautiful English Bible. Then he read a chapter from his own dog-eared Eskimo Bible, explaining the verses carefully to Kidla and the children as he went along. They were eagerly attentive; not a child was bored or fidgety during the whole hour and a half.

When it was over, I tried to explain to them, through Leah, what the Fourth of July meant to Americans. It was uphill work. They did not understand what it meant that one country "owned" another, or the meaning of revolution. Men fighting one another over the taxes did not enter into the Eskimo scheme of life. The Bible was easier than politics—the strong, archaic stories in the Old Testament had a spiritual similarity to their own solemn, earthy tales of the creation.

No work was done on Sunday in the Eskimo tent. I stayed a little while longer to give Leah a music lesson on the tin whistle (we had advanced to "Frère Jacques"), then blew smoke rings for Nua and played finger games with Rootay. "This Little Pig Went to Market" and "Here Is the Church" were familiar to the two year old, and her mother repeated them in Eskimo for me. While I played with the children Panilu, Idlouk's seventeen-year-old son, bounced the naked baby Susanna on his stomach. Susanna's skin was white and her face sallow, like all the Eskimo babies we had seen. The Eskimo race is not dark-skinned, though the adults are brown-faced. Born pale, their cheeks turn bright red as soon as they are big enough to be out of their mothers' protective hoods. Later their faces and hands become dark brown from constant exposure to the burning sun and ice and the bitter winter winds.

The baby laughed as she bounced, and suddenly she began to whimper. Quickly her mother took her and sat her on an empty coffee tin. Eskimos begin toilet training at birth, and for occasional accidents inside the hood there is a wad of dry, absorbent moss more efficient than a diaper. This early training obviously does not warp the children's personalities—because no sense of strain or punishment is attached to it.

Idlouk's tent was clean, and as neat as a small tent could be with nine people living in it. On the sleeping platform were caribou hides and a confusion of faded quilts and clothing, many times mended and patched, and all clean. The shallow, blackened seal-oil cooking lamp was in its proper place, on the left as one entered. Along its straight edge a wick was laid, roughly spun of arctic cotton (a sedge grass gone to seed. We had seen a meadow back of Pond Inlet white with the tufts, like a cotton plantation). Over it hung a rack of black cooking pots. When Kidla cooked, her fuel was provided by a large piece of seal blubber which was suspended from this rack, slowly melting, drop by drop, into the lamp. But the low flame was not burning this day; bannocks and seal meat had been cooked the day before for Sunday eating. Bannocks, an Eskimo staple, were heavy dry cakes made of flour, baking powder, seal oil and water and cooked slowly in a frying pan over the feeble flame of the lamp wick. Their only virtue was that they wouldn't freeze and kept practically forever. The seal meat looked equally unappetizing, dark gray and soft from at least twelve hours of cooking.

The ground was covered evenly with clean small pebbles which the children had collected on the beach. When Idlouk and Kidla smoked, they used an empty peanut tin as an ash tray—nothing was thrown on the floor. The only smell in Idlouk's tent was the familiar rich smell of seal oil and animal skins. That was so much part of our lives now that we did not notice it. A small stuffed doll of wool plaid, made from one of the boys' old shirts, was pinned to the tent wall. The sun shone warmly through the white canvas; fat gay Rootay pounced on one big brother after another; Idlouk whittled at

a piece of soapstone; Kidla sang quietly to her baby; and
Leah plaited wool for a belt. It felt like Sunday.

I looked at Idlouk's carving. He was hollowing a little dish,
a replica of the big cooking lamp. The soapstone was porous
and soft, and could be shaped with an ordinary pocketknife
more easily than wood. Idlouk fitted a ridge of narwhal tusk,
carved into dainty miniature teeth, into a slot along the straight
sides of the dish. He looked up at me as I watched, and
indicated that the ivory ridge was an imitation of the flame
along the wick of the real cooking lamp. Then he smiled and
handed it to me.

"For you," he said.

I was touched by his gracious gesture, and thanked him in
Eskimo and English. Kidla, smiling, helped me with my pro-
nunciation, while the children giggled softly.

After lunch, Axel and I walked inland. As we topped the
hill above our camp, the northwest wind met us like a sudden
burst of high summer, hot, strong and sweet with the smell of
young plants. The dry wind came from the interior of the
island; it baked the hilltops and made the valley bogs and
puddles retreat. In the eleven days that we had been away,
the tundra had quite changed. Most of the snow was gone,
and the new moss was thick, lumpy, and bouncy—we felt as if
we were walking on pillows. Everywhere was the sound of
running water, of small streams finally freed from winter ice.
It was difficult to judge up and down and level on the tundra
because of the sameness of color and lack of landmarks, and often the quick little brooks seemed to run surrealistically uphill
from moist, boggy depressions. Over all was the deep roar of the
tremendous Aktineq River, rushing down from its inexhaustible
glacier and taking the mountains with it into the sea.

The earth was still moist from recent snow, but it was so
warm that one could walk barefoot on it. A profusion of low,
many-colored flowers gleamed like stars through last year's
yellow grass. This, the time of warm, wet earth and constant
sunlight, was the period of the tundra's most enthusiastic
flowering, and the blossoms of high spring were bigger, bolder,
and brighter than the modest blooms that had graced the cold
earth two weeks before. Daisy fleabane (no relation to our
daisy) grew in clumps, its delicate white petals sharply thin,

its center shining yellow. Avens, wide-eyed, very pale yellow with a deeper yellow center, clung close to the ground and stared straight at the sun. The thick red mosslike foliage of arctic bell heather now bore blossoms, tiny white bells, like lily of the valley.

Most beautiful of all were the arctic poppies. Their fragile pale yellow blossoms nodded gracefully on long slender stems, and bent to the ground with every breeze. This frail-looking offspring of the tundra can grow only in the Arctic and on high mountains in the Temperate Zone—it does not like an effete climate. We found the dainty poppies blooming hardily on the tops of the windiest and coldest ridges, amid sand and pebbles, where nothing else would grow.

When I remember the arctic springtime, I see first this tender flower, unfolding sun-colored, like hope, in a cold land.

Beetles crept through miniature jungles of arctic heather and willow, spiders scuttled over the rocks, mosquitoes and flies hovered in clouds over stagnant pools. Rick had set insect traps up and down the tundra hills, together with thermometers, to determine differences in species and populations at different levels and temperatures. He found that populations and species were fairly constant at all levels, and that the insects of the tundra were, like the birds, more generalized than those found in the Temperate Zone. Those with special needs and tastes had dropped out on the way north, and here were found insects similar to those of high mountain areas of America and Europe, which can live on practically anything.

The commonest spider was *Tarentula asivak,* a big, ugly, gray wolf spider (not poisonous to man). The commonest beetle was *Curtonotus brunnipenis. Tarentula asivak* fed contentedly and almost entirely on *Curtonotus brunnipenis,* wrapping it in a cocoon for safekeeping. There was an odd spider, the ant mimic, whose relatives dwell mostly in the tropics. It seemed misplaced in a land totally devoid of ants. But, we learned, it resembled an ant, not to catch prey, but to deceive birds which don't like the taste of ants but *do* like the taste of spiders. Many of its predators came from latitudes where there were ants. There were crane flies, long-legged and delicate-appearing, which also breed in water or moist soil in high mountains of the Temperate Zone. There were springtails, primitive, wingless insects whose larvae helped to aerate the earth and which, in adult form, leaped easily about the tundra by means of caudal appendages folded beneath their abdomens. There were a few butterflies, among them the sulphur butterfly and the black and orange *Boloria frigga,* which helped to cross-pollinate the plants. The butterflies did not have the range in size of our butterflies, but were uniformly medium-sized—about one and a half inches of wingspread.

Insects were difficult to transport and had a tendency to bite, so we did not intend to take any this day. But on the way home I saw two beautiful *Boloria frigga.* They were mating and paid no attention to me, so I picked them up and laid them carefully in a matchbox. They continued their honeymoon undisturbed until I got them back home to Rick and the ethyl acetate bath. At least they died happy.

The month of June is called by the Eskimos *Erniwik* ("the young are born") and all over the tundra, infant life had begun during our absence. Tundra-colored birds' eggs in shallow open nests were so frequent that we had always to watch where we stepped. A white-rumped sandpiper crept away from us, barely keeping out of the way of our feet. She trembled, fluffed her feathers, dragged her wings, and uttered distressful little bubbling cries. I sat down to watch her while Axel walked away, hoping that she would be unable to count and would think we both had gone. I sat quiet as a rock. In a few minutes, she walked delicately toward me, showing no sign of fear. About seven feet away she stopped, then settled on the ground, fluffed her breast feathers, and wriggled herself domestically into a comfortable position. We had not seen the nest although we had walked right over it. I inched slowly toward her, not rising. She regarded me without curiosity and gradually I moved my hand over the nest. But not until I actually touched her did she finally, reluctantly, leave her eggs and creep off, dragging her wings and crying. The nest was shallow and open, carelessly lined with a little dry grass. Four dun-colored, irregularly speckled eggs lay in it, invisible unless you knew they were there. I picked them up and held them in the palm of my hand. Daintily the bird walked toward me, looked the eggs over thoroughly, as if she were counting them, then retired a few feet away and waited patiently for me to give them back.

A little further on, a female golden plover showed us where she had her nest. Her display was a creeping run with all feathers spread out, accompanied by an incessant, thin, high crying. After a few feet she stopped and lay flat on the ground, spread her wings wide and beat them slowly, looking piteously up at us. "See, I'm helpless," she seemed to say. Suddenly she saw her beautiful mate on a nearby knoll. He was making the same display, trying to distract our attention from the nest. But he only succeeded in distracting hers. In a flash she gave up her pose and dived at him. When she had driven him off she came back to us and tried again to lure us away. In the meantime we had found her nest; two large eggs lay in it, almost as big as hens' eggs. Brown, spotted unevenly with darker brown, they were part of the tundra. As we left the nest, she accompanied us, simply walking, as if she were on a leash. She stayed close to us for some fifty feet and then she saw her mate again, standing innocuously on a hill. With an angry cry she was in the air, darting at him. This ungrateful behavior was apparently a product of frustration. Unable to get rid of us, but feeling an irresistible urge to drive *something* away, she picked on the nearest live object.

The tundra birds inevitably showed us where their nests were by their creeping and wing-dragging displays. The weasel, an intelligent mammal with a taste for eggs, uses the same reasoning we did to find nests. Seeing a bird displaying, it follows, then waits unmoving until the bird returns to its nest. Most eaters of birds' eggs, however, are not so clever. The only small-birds' nests we found destroyed during our six weeks' observation of sixty-five nests were two snow buntings' and one American pipit's—a weasel had got all three. In spite of the shortage of lemmings, the small birds were not much disturbed by other predators. Either they could not find the flat nests which looked like tundra or else the birds actually succeeded in luring them away with hurt-pretense.

The psychology behind this display of ground-nesting birds is a puzzle. Some say it is an undirected instinct born of fear which makes the bird tremble, crouch, and cry, showing every sign of intense shock. Others think it may be a sign of elemen-

tary reasoning ability. Josselyn told us that now the most widely
accepted theory is that it is neither blind fear nor pure reason
but a sharply directed instinct. The bird shows these signs of
shock and distress *only* when she thinks her nest is threatened,
never if she herself is threatened—in that case she simply flies
away. As soon as the intruder is a safe distance off or the bird
is satisfied that he is not dangerous, the tactics cease.

This is one more instance of the astonishing specialization
of birds, which are much more highly developed than any
animal in the class of mammals. Not only have they keenly
directed instincts, which have reached a high degree of variety
and precision, but their physical structure, too, is delicately
adapted to their role. Birds which do much flying, for instance,
have hollow bones so they are light in the air. And their
wings act as a bellows, forcing muscular contractions of the
thorax, so they actually breathe more easily while flying than
while perching. We humans, in comparison, are sloppy, im-
perfect creatures. Nothing of us works quite right. Our instincts, though strong, are few, misty, and vague, and our
physical structure leaves a great deal to be desired. The human
brain, developed to a remarkable extent, has apparently grown
at the expense of other functions, which have been retarded
and in some cases have deteriorated. This dulling of instinct,
however, has resulted in an extraordinary freedom of action
and thought, exclusively human. We cannot envy the birds the
set and narrow paths of their uncompromisingly efficient lives.

Way back on the tundra, on the high plateau that rose
slowly toward the Aktineq Glacier, the land was bone dry
and tenantless. We walked, entirely alone, over the unblooming
ground, and suddenly two long-tailed jaegers screamed out of
the sky, attacking us. Again and again they dived, almost
touching our heads and uttering squeaky little cries, quite
unsuited to their powerful and frightening figures. Clearly
they told us that they had a nest nearby, and we found it
easily—not a nest at all, but the barest depression in the
ground, containing one fat, mottled, brown egg. We tried the
same trick which had worked with the sandpiper. Axel walked
away while I sat quiet, trying not to notice the mosquitoes
which immediately settled on my face and hands. But these

birds were evidently more intelligent than the songbirds and
shore birds we had observed earlier. They knew well that I was
not a rock and they assumed that my intentions were dis-
honorable. They were not going to rely on any feeble wing-
dragging ruse but intended to drive me away by force.

I did not move, and after a long time, they retired to a
small hill about a hundred yards away. There they sat hope-
lessly, close to each other, waiting for me to go. Every now
and then one of them flew around me again, calling in its
high-pitched, wailing voice. Finally, apparently, the female
worried about her egg. She favored me with one more shrieking
dive, then landed close to the nest. Very slowly she approached
it, not taking her eyes off me. She settled gently, her two black
tail feathers arched with slender grace, her dusky wings and
white breast seeming to melt into one another. But still she
watched me, and at the click of the camera she was in the air
again. We left them alone. I had never thought I would feel
sorry for a jaeger, which is a bird that clearly can take care
of itself.

As we descended over the low hills and sharp little ravines
we noted the interesting effects of mud motion, known as
solifluction—the movement of moisture-laden earth over a hard
surface. The permafrost, hard as cement, acted as a smooth
slide for the surface soil, and the hills of Bylot Island were
slipping toward the sea and falling over themselves in folds, the
mud hanging over deep ditches like cake frosting. Along the
damp lower edges of the mud frosting, arctic heather grew thick
and rich, its tiny bell-like flowers looking like sugar. The steady
downward flow of earth was partially held back by the shallow
roots of grass and willow, but they could only slow, not stop, the
inexorable slide. On the flanks of the hills were flat, upended
rocks, like tombstones, and we seemed to be walking through
a vast, open graveyard. The slow downward stream of heavy
earth had probably, with the help of frost action, pushed these
huge rocks upright over the centuries.

Most of Bylot Island's tundra hills were crowned with big
rocks, where the mud had oozed off completely, leaving the
bones of the earth exposed. These hilltop rocks were the richest
areas of life on the tundra. There snowy owls and jaegers had
perched, attracting the orange lichen *Caloplaca*, which played

its part in crumbling the rocks into soil again. There, under the rocks, foxes had their burrows. The food leavings and droppings at the entrances to their lairs attracted rich vegetation, which in turn attracted lemmings, which were then eaten by the foxes. When the lemmings began to come back after the lean years, they made their first burrows on these fertile hilltops, and the slower-reviving foxes came after them, to start the chain again. Geese had made their nests in the lush grass, mosquitoes swarmed and bred there, beetles were attracted and in turn brought spiders, who ate the beetles.

The rock crowns, created by permafrost, mud motion, and the rhythmic thawing and freezing of the surface soil, were microcosms of arctic life. Victim and predator lived there in uneasy balance; organic and inorganic forces played their own slow game of destruction and creation.

In the boggy lowlands near the shore we looked for a clean pool in which to bathe. But most of the inland waters were clouded with algae, swarming with mosquitoes and edged with thick red mud. The color was caused by bacteria which drew iron from the water and oxidized it into rust. (The Eskimos say it is blood, and they have an extraordinarily vengeful and earthy legend to account for it.) We finally came across a puddle which looked deeper and cleaner. On its shore were stones, in its middle was a dark gray miniature iceberg. There we took baths—real ones—with the pale sun shining on our backs and the cold water sparkling darkly. The mountains gleamed, enormous, beyond the white highway of the Aktineq Glacier and the white sea ice was covered with a network of thin dark blue cracks, like a giant cobweb. The land was pure and awesome in its loneliness—yet the small life we had watched, so visibly swarming on its surface, made it seem friendly.

Josselyn, Bill, and Mary had, during our eleven-day absence at Button Point and Pond Inlet, found about thirty birds' nests within a quarter of a mile radius of the camp, and were following their fortunes every day. The ravines and hillocks had received poetic names: Phalarope Pond, Golden Plover River, Lark Gully, Snow Bunting Creek. These names were signposts, not affectations, and they had grown naturally. It was impossible, we found, to give accurate directions. The tundra all looked the same, and one rock, hill or ravine could just as easily be another one half a mile away. "I saw two black-bellied plovers courting near the pond where we first saw the red phalaropes" or "If you go up the gully where we found the first lark's nest you will come to a creek with a snow bunting nest in its left bank" were our only ways of indicating landmarks—so the names grew.

Every day the round of the nests was made by two or more of us, and Mary kept a running record of the number of eggs in each nest, the date of the laying of each egg, as near as we could determine it, the date of the pipping, and the length of time until the nestlings left home. So far as we knew, the nesting of arctic-breeding birds had never before been followed from start to finish in one spot. We would probably see the entire breeding cycle of many of them, from their first arrival on the bleak, snowy coast in June to the flocking on the warm, flowery tundra for the southward migration at the end of July.

The birds, for the most part, had little fear of us. Their instinctive display tactics were perfunctory and very quickly the females would hop delicately back on their nests and pose for pictures. They disliked leaving the nests—the eggs would chill soon in the cold northern air—and sometimes we had to push them away to count the eggs and look for cracks.

In the late afternoon of that July Fourth Axel and I accompanied Josselyn on the nest round. Mary had found a horned lark's nest the day before and had told us that there were young, probably hatched about ten days previously. "Try and find them," said Mary.

Our first difficulty was in finding the correct little white stake that marked the nest. It lay on a slope, named by Ben "Stake Heaven," popular with all the scientists because of its abundant life and its nearness to home. Everything, including nests, was marked with little white stakes, and we trod carefully through a maze of them, trying not to step on anything vital. Rick had planted his insect traps here and marked their locations with stakes. His thermometers, some buried in the ground, were also fastened to stakes. Bill's mud-motion stakes

marched up the hill, wavering slightly where the slowly moving
ooze had given them a push. The outlines of his snow patches,
long since melted, were marked by a nightmare network of
stakes. Even I had added to the confusion, by planting a stake
next to a clump of pure white poppies for Bill to collect if he
was interested in anemic poppies (he wasn't—said they were
as ordinary as pale blondes among humans).

Finally we found the stake with the proper hieroglyphics on
it. We looked directly at the ground about a foot below the
stake, where the nest was supposed to be. There was no nest.
But a little circle of ground was heaving gently. Looking closely,
we distinguished the breathing mass from the unbreathing
tundra. The baby larks, a random mottling of brown, pale
yellow and grayish white, fitted neatly into their nest in a
circle of soft feathers. Somewhere there were beaks the color
of dark horn, invisible unless you put your nose in the nest.
Josselyn touched the wad of breathing fluff. Suddenly it all
came apart and five tiny creatures scattered in every direction,
running competently. Josselyn picked up one and put it in a
pocket for his collection. We quickly gathered the others and
stuffed them back into the shallow nest, but they kept coming
out between our fingers. Finally Josselyn had them quiet by
approximating a mother lark's breast with his hand. The mother
bird, which had been unusually shy, turned up at the last
moment when everything was rearranged and flew in low
circles around us, cheeping wildly, much disturbed.

One Baird's sandpiper nest, the first that had been discovered, had already graduated. Although the youngest was
less than twenty-four hours old all four were out of the nest
and making their way, wobbly fluff balls, over the tundra
toward the beach. Sandpipers, in common with many shore
birds, are precocial—they walk out of their shells with all their
feathers on, almost ready to support themselves. They looked
like bits of tundra come alive. Their red-brown backs were
patterned with delicate threads of black and pale gray-green
splotches so much like *Stereocaulon* that they seemed actually
to have lichen growing on them. Their small black-rimmed
faces were as pale as the whitened pebbles of the beach, and
on their heads were soft reddish caps like pieces of old moss.
Only their black beaks marked them as birds—miniature sand-

piper beaks, long and strong and pointed for digging in marshes and wet beaches. A pair of nervous and worried parents tried to guide their random progress, but the babies gave them a bad time. The adults fussed constantly, uttering small chirping cries, like crickets, while the little ones went off in all directions and teetered and fell and sat down to rest.

A pair of Lapland longspurs had from the day of their arrival fed domestically in our backyard garbage hole. They had made a nest in an abandoned lemming hole under a bank about fifty feet from the cook tent. It was deep and carefully constructed, woven of coarse grasses and lined with white feathers. Today it held three young ones just born and a fourth in the process of hatching. These birds were not precocial. They were pieces of raw meat with a little fluff stuck to them here and there and shards of eggshell glued on their backs. They looked as if they should not have been born yet. (But within nine days they had all their feathers and were out of the nest.)

We found no more young. Most of the arctic birds were very late breeders—for the simple reason that it was too cold for eggs and nestlings any earlier. As a compensation their young matured quickly. By the end of August there would be hardly a bird left on the tundra.

Every day some strange new product of the tundra was found. This evening it was a *Dreikante,* a sand-carved stone. Ned had found the small, smooth, perfectly triangular rock half buried in the earth on top of a high ridge. The tundra had held it viselike for many years, while the strong, constant east wind had carved with geometric precision, using sand as its tool.

After supper Ned analyzed our drinking water under his little microscope. We could now add to our richly varied menu a kind of filamentous green alga (a low form of plant life), some large shrimplike creatures and numerous little worms, called nematodes. I shuddered at the worms. But Bill reassured me. They were the commonest and most numerous worms. If you could take away the entire contents of the earth except nematodes there would still remain the shim-

mering outlines of everything, in nematodes. (He did not add
that some nematodes cause trichinosis.)

Josselyn skinned his baby lark. Inside out, with its skeleton
exposed, the tiny creature looked like a half handful of nothing
at all, and its soft skull was flattened under Josselyn's fingers.
Delicately he scraped the brain out, removed the infinitesimal
eyes, filled the skull with cotton and turned the skin right side
out, while we held our breaths. We were sure that the little
head would go to pieces and that all the tender, downy fluff
would come off. But it turned out a real baby bird, dark beak
as large as its head, new soft feathers fluffed out. It could almost be put back in the nest, except that Mama would wonder
how it had got its feet tied together.

Then he turned his attention to a murre egg we had
wheedled out of Panipookoochoo and brought back from Button Point. It was about four inches long, a giant egg for
such a small bird, pointed at one end, wide at the other, and
of a lovely pale green unevenly spattered with black spots. It
looked like a Russian Easter egg.

"We should open it, and find a scene with snow and huts
and angels."

"Well, you can't tell what we may find in here," said Jose-
lyn carefully as he drilled a small hole in the side. He blew
out the contents with a glass tube. A seemingly endless stream
of yellow egg came out, but no huts or Russian peasants—
not even a murre. Then he sucked a little fresh water into his
tube and blew it into the egg to rinse it out, like a good
housewife. He tucked the clean, empty egg in layers of moss
and lichen and laid it in his big trunk, which already held
trays of carefully packed birds resting on beds of cotton and
mosquito netting.

About nine in the evening some of us gathered in the cook
tent for tea and hot chocolate. These evening sessions usually
developed into full meals, and they got longer and longer as
we became more and more timeless, like the Eskimos. This
evening the talk turned to Bill's digging and the underground
patterns of frozen earth he had found in the course of it. The
earth was thawing rapidly under the spring sun and the warm
wind, and every day the holes were filled with water and he
had to dig deeper. Would he ever reach permafrost we asked.

"I don't know," he answered. "No one knows how deep permafrost may be in any particular area. It may be hundreds of feet underground or it may be only six or seven feet. When you hit it you know it. The permanently frozen soil has an entirely different construction from the soil that freezes and thaws every year. What I am hitting now is only annual frost."

"*Annual Frost*," murmured Josselyn, who had been out of the conversation for a long time. "Sounds like a faculty party." And the serious discussion fell apart as if it had been blown away by the northwest spring wind.

Around midnight we began drifting off to bed. Axel and I heard voices and laughter in Rick's tent and walked over to see what was happening. In his tiny dwelling, three by six feet and only high enough to kneel in, Rick was entertaining Panilu, Kidla, and Rootay. A primus stove was humming noisily and they were all drinking tea. Panilu and Rick were exchanging a rapid conversation above the small roar of the stove, though neither knew what the other was talking about. It was like a scene from *Alice in Wonderland*.

We walked down the beach and admired the sunset. Every evening one unconsciously expected the sun to go down and the sky to turn flaming red. But the sun never quite made it, and the suspenseful moment was prolonged all night long. There was no dust to color the sky and the low sun shone through air as thin and clear as outer space. Tonight the mountains across Eclipse Sound, forty or fifty miles away on Baffin Island, were exceptionally high and sharp-etched; one could almost step over to them. Tiny clouds floated high in the sky, the wispy cirrus clouds which were made of ice crystals. Our iceberg was sharply white against the pale pink ice. Although it retained its outlines it was growing noticeably smaller. I wished that it would one day go over with a tremendous crash, or drift majestically down the sound out to sea. But like everything else in the north it was patient and undramatic, and bided its time.

The Mammal from the Permafrost

WILLY LEY

Once the province of the explorer, the Arctic today is the laboratory of the scientist, in particular the archeologist. The ice and permafrost, the perpetually frozen ground, hide many secrets of the past that include the bones of ancient men and the carcasses of strange animals of other ages. Here Willy Ley tells the fascinating story of the great animal that once roamed over the world—the mammoth.

OF ALL the animals of the past, none is better known by name to a wide public than the woolly elephant of the Pleistocene: the mammoth. And of all the animals of the past there is none which has so persistently intruded on human history as this very mammoth. The resurrections of other extinct animals, like the gigantic dinosaurs of the Atlantosaurus beds of Wyoming, or the fish-shaped ichthyosaurs of the German and English Lias, were purely intellectual adventures, requiring an advanced science to accomplish. But the mammoth was always part of human history, even when people had no conscious idea of its existence. Because of that ignorance, it sometimes appeared in strange disguises. Or it cropped up in a curious roundabout manner. Or it appeared in places which were so far outside the realm of normal activities that even professional geographers had to consult maps to identify the strange place names with which it was associated.

At first the relationship between mammoth and Man was simple and direct. Primitive men of the type we now call Neanderthal men hunted it. It must have been a difficult and dangerous hunt, but no other animal rewarded success with such mountains of meat and fat. A less primitive type of Man which came somewhat later, the small and graceful Aurignac people, not only hunted it, they also left its portrait on cave walls. There is no disagreement about the reasons for these paintings; they figured in ceremonial rites which were to assure hunting luck in days to come. The animal which had been "captured" in a picture would not escape in the flesh. But it is quite difficult to date these paintings, even ignoring the obvious fact that they certainly are not all of equal age. A reasonably well-founded estimate for the best of these artistic efforts seems to be 50,000 B.C.

But from then until modern historical times, there is an enormous gap in the direct relationship. When the famous Cro-Magnon men appeared in western Europe, the mammoth apparently was no longer there, although another race of mammoths still inhabited the tundra of northeastern Siberia. The successors of the Cro-Magnon, the ancestors of the modern peoples of Europe, never knew the mammoth.

Yet they were haunted by it all through recorded history. When a river changed its course, large bones were likely to come to light. The people in the vicinity presumably kept quiet about the occurrence and avoided the spot for a while until erosion had done its work and made the bones disappear again. But that was not always easy; often there were too many witnesses present. A king ordered a palace built, and large bones were found in the ground when the foundations were put down. Monks broke the ground for an addition to the monastery and their shovels struck big bones. Many an abbot was faced with deciding whether these bones deserved Christian burial, or should be quietly thrown away, or should be saved.

But not only large bones came out of the ground as mysterious reminders of something past and unknown. Many an old chronicle or description of a town or landscape contains a remark about fossilized hands of monkeys. If some accounts did not include pictures, or if the "stone hands" themselves had not been saved, we could never puzzle out just what the chronicler meant. The stone hands were mammoth molars, found separately because the jaw bone in which they had grown had eroded. The strange designation was caused by the fact that such a mammoth molar had several roots, often five, which were taken to be the fingers.

And then there was, of course, the *unicornum verum*
which was found in the ground and which was the ultimate
remedy for any sickness. That it was also mammoth tusk was
not yet known.

But then there came a time when large bones found in
the ground no longer frightened people, when it was considered doubtful whether those things that looked like stuffed
gloves were actually fossilized monkey hands, and when the
remaining specimens of *unicornum verum* began to gather dust
in dark corners of old pharmacies because both doctors and
patients had lost faith in their remedial value.

Just at this time, the mammoth began to appear in a new
form, this time coming from the east. In 1611, a British traveler,
Josias Logan, returned to London, bringing with him the tusk
of an elephant. That would have been commonplace if Logan
had been in India or Africa. But he had been in Russia,
and the tusk was not a hunting trophy, but had been bought
from Samoyed tribesmen who lived near the shore of the
Arctic Ocean (more precisely the Barents Sea) at the mouth
of the river Petchora. It was not the tusk itself which was
marvelous, it was the climate of the area from which it had
come.

Almost precisely a century later a Dutchman, Evert Ysbrands-
zoon Ides, came with a similar tale. He had journeyed across
Siberia and a member of the party, a Russian, had told him
that he had once found the frozen head of an elephant and
also a frozen elephant's foot, which had been taken to the
village of Turukhansk on the Yenisei River. From more recent
and better-authenticated experience one may conclude that
the find was probably made on the banks of the Yenisei
itself.

There followed confused reports about ivory found in
Siberia and large bones sticking from the frozen ground. The
reason these reports were so confused is now easy to explain:
mammoth and walrus were mixed together and described as
one and the same animal. But the tribesmen, mostly Tunguses
and Yakuts, not only failed to distinguish between the two
animals, which had in common only that they both furnished
ivory, they also added their own reasoning. When they came
across one of these beasts it was always partly in the ground.

And it was invariably dead. Their conclusion was that the animal lived underground like a gigantic mole, burrowing all its life. But sometimes it burrowed up instead of down, or it came out on the bank of a river. When it saw the light, it died.

The hodgepodge of several sets of facts and native legends was not accepted in full by the scientists of the Western countries. But it did indicate that there was something large and interesting in Siberia. A name had filtered through too. It was *maman, mamont,* or something like that. Englishmen, Germans, Frenchmen, Dutchmen, and Swedes decided that it had to be a Russian word. The fact is that it isn't, at least not originally. It was the name given by the tribesmen and just possibly means something like "large," though it is probably safer to say that the meaning is unknown. The reason the word was believed to be Russian was that the Russians, in referring to the indubitably existent Siberian ivory, had adopted the name in a Russianized version and called the ivory *mamontova-kostj.* The last syllable means bone as well as ivory, but when used in such a construction it usually refers to ivory.

In 1722, a Swedish officer, Baron Kagg, colonel of the Royal Swedish Cavalry, returned home from Siberia, where he had been not as an explorer but as a prisoner of war. One of his fellow prisoners, Philipp J. Tabbert von Strahlenberg, had spent whatever time he had in inquiring about those rumors of a large ivory-bearing creature, possibly of subterranean habits, and had found a Russian who claimed to know about it and who drew him a picture such as is reproduced here. It was this picture which von Strahlenberg handed to Kagg to take with him to Sweden, where it is still preserved in the library of Linköping. It is hard to decide whether the Russian who drew this clawed and twisted-horned supercow was sincere in his belief or whether he was indulging in a heavy-handed joke on his imprisoned enemy.

Baron Kagg obviously believed in the picture. Scientists didn't.

Nor were the Russians themselves too sure about those Siberian rumors. Czar Pyotr Alekseyevitch, known as Peter the Great, had sent a naturalist, Dr. D. G. Messerschmidt, to

Siberia, for general exploration but with the injunction to keep his eyes open for those supposed elephants. The Czar knew about Ides' story, for Ides had been a member of his own ambassadorial party to China. Doctor Messerchmidt was lucky. A mammoth had come to light in the steep banks of the river Indigirka in eastern Siberia and he came in time to examine it before wolves had devoured all the fleshy parts and the rapid decay of the hot Siberian summer dissolved what even the wolves did not want. He reported on the large bones and on big pieces of skin with long hair, resembling the fur of a goat, if different in color. Messerschmidt ended his report: "No doubt this is the animal mentioned in the Bible as behemoth."

Since the biblical behemoth is actually the hippopotamus, Dr. Messerschmidt very nearly succeeded in adding a third ingredient to the mixture that already included an extinct elephant and the living walrus. That danger was avoided mostly because few people then believed in the identification of the behemoth and the hippopotamus. But another confusing element was added by a generally very reliable man, the German explorer Peter Simon Pallas, who traveled through Siberia in 1768–74 at the expense of Catherine II of Russia. In 1771, Pallas came across an incomplete skeleton and large pieces of heavy fur of an animal which had thawed from the banks of the Vilyui River, a tributary of the Lena River, a number of miles to the west of the village of Vilyuisk. The fur consisted of thick woolly hair, "of conspicuously dark coloration." Protruding from this woolly hair there were bunches of stiff bristles, about three inches long, almost black in color. On the head of the animal the fur was reddish brown and in places a brownish-black. But this animal—and it did not need Pallas's training and experience to recognize it—was most certainly a rhinoceros.

The one thing which prevented Western scientists from giving up in resignation was the fact that they could find the same animals on their home grounds, in Germany and France. The Siberian finds were superior in producing whole carcasses which had frozen when the animals had succumbed in treacherous muck or broken through thin layers of new snow covering rifts in the ice. In Germany and France, the dead animals had been covered by sand and had decayed, so only bones and teeth were left. But they had some advantages just the same. They were not 4000 miles away. And one did not have to carry a shovel in one hand for the work and a rifle in the other for the wolves.

The first European rhinoceros bones had been collected from Pleistocene deposits in England in 1701. They had been turned over to Professor Nehemiah Grew, who had recognized them for what they were and put the case on record. But since he was a botanist, he had not pursued the matter any further. Precisely half a century later, in 1751, a similar collection of bones was handed to Professor Samuel Christian Hollmann of the University of Göttingen. They had been found at Grubenhagen near Herzberg in the Hartz Mountains. Professor Hollmann saw quickly that they, too, were rhinoceros bones and described them in detail. But he also refrained from drawing conclusions. That was left to his younger colleague, Johann Friedrich Blumenbach, who became professor of medicine at the same university after Hollmann's retirement.

Blumenbach began to collect large bones from the sand pits, which were a special kind of sand that later received the name of loess. Some of the bones were certainly rhinoceros bones, just as Hollmann had said. Others just as certainly were not. They were elephant bones, but not quite the same as the bones of the two living types of elephants. In 1799, Blumenbach felt that he had his evidence complete and he announced that there had once been a kind of elephant in Europe which was different from the living types. And it was also, obviously, much older. Hence he proposed the name of "first" elephant, or *Elephas primigenius*. The name, we now know, was a bit enthusiastic—the mammoth was by no means the "first" elephant. Blumenbach also could not know that it had had a heavy fur. But he traveled around and looked at various "giant's bones," preserved in churches, castles, town halls. All *Elephas primigenius*. He ferreted out old pieces of *unicornum verum*—*Elephas primigenius*, too.

Then he turned his attention to the rhinoceros bones. They, too, closely resembled those of living species of rhinoceros, but again were not quite the same. By 1807, Blumenbach was sure that this was a species apart and he named it the "old rhinoceros," *Rhinoceros antiquitatis* (now *Tichorhinus antiquitatis*). A little later a second type of extinct rhinoceros was identified; in honor of Goethe's friend, the privy councilor, writer, and literary critic Johann Heinrich Merck, this was named *Rhinoceros merckii* (now *Coelodonta merckii*).

Meanwhile another mammoth had thawed from a river bank in Siberia, in the delta of the Lena River. This was found in 1799, the same year in which Blumenbach proposed the name *Elephas primigenius*. A Tungus ivory collector, Ossip Shumakhoff, saw it first, but he did not know at once what it was. It looked like a small dark-colored icy hillock. But it also looked unusual, so that Shumakhoff returned to the place in the following year. He still could not be sure. But one year later, in 1801, one of the tusks protruded from the ice. Shumakhoff was much less happy than one would think. The Tunguses think nothing of picking up tusks which they find lying around by themselves. But to find a whole *mamont* is, for some reason, bad luck. Indeed, it prophesies the death of the finder and of all his family. And Shumakhoff actually fell sick; he had worried himself into a psychosomatic condition of some kind. But matter triumphed over mind in his case, and he recovered, from his illness and also from the superstitious fear. He had not died, in spite of everything people always said. Now for some money.

There was a Russian in a neighboring village, one of the men who traveled through Siberia for the purpose of buying *mamontova-kostj*, and also furs on occasion, from the tribesmen. The Russian, whose name was Boltunoff, followed Shumakhoff to the place which the latter had kept carefully secret. During the third summer, the carcass had really thawed. The two men pried the tusks loose and then Boltunoff handed the tribesman fifty rubles. He also made a drawing which a few years later was acquired by Blumenbach, was seen in Blumenbach's study by Cuvier some time prior to 1812, and later belonged to Ernst Haeckel. Blumenbach made a notation at the bottom of the picture which reads (translated): "*Elephas primigenius*, which in Russia is called *Mammut*, dug up with skin and hair in 1806 at the mouth of the Lena River at the Ice Ocean. Badly drawn, just as it was found, mutilated and all dirty."

The date 1806 refers to the year when a special expedition under Professor Adams reached the place to salvage the whole skeleton and much of the pelt. The drawing itself does look funny, most because there is no trunk and the tusks are in an impossible position. But one should not judge too harshly. Boltunoff most likely had never seen an elephant and the mammoth's trunk probably had been torn away by wolves before Boltunoff got there. Presumably the whole face had been torn away, because Boltunoff placed the eyes of his drawing in what must be the ear openings. There were probably no ears left—the mammoth had rather small ears anyway—and the remaining holes looked as if they might be the eye sockets. I believe that Boltunoff was as careful as he could be under the circumstances, because above his picture he placed a sketch of the grinding surface of the mammoth's molar.

This find, often called the "Adams mammoth," converted Blumenbach's "first elephant," assembled from bones only, into the "woolly mammoth." The skeleton which Adams had salvaged was mounted in the museum in St. Petersburg (now Leningrad) with the skin on the feet and a number of tendons still attached to the skull. Cuvier printed a picture of this mammoth in his large work on fossil bones. With that picture, the mammoth finally and definitely entered the world of science.

Nevertheless, there was still some feeling of uncertainty. Thanks to Mr. Boltunoff of Yakutsk and Professor Adams of St. Petersburg on the one hand, and Professor Blumenbach of Göttingen and the Baron de Cuvier of Paris on the other hand, the woolly mammoth was nicely nailed down. So was the woolly rhinoceros, thanks to Pallas and Blumenbach. The other rhinoceros, which had been named after Goethe's friend Merck, was summarily taken to be woolly too. From all we know now this was a mistaken conclusion, but what applied to the one was logically thought to apply to its contemporary too. The question was, why had they been woolly? By then, scientists had good pictures and descriptions of the elephants and rhinoceri of Africa and India, and many of them were even in a position to visit the steadily improving and growing zoological gardens where they could see these animals alive. The modern animals were not completely hairless: the rhinoceros had some few hairs on face and ears; the elephants had some around the mouth, on the trunk, and on the tail. The Indian domesticated elephant even has something like a sparse baby fur which does not last long and of which the few hairs one can see later are the remains.

All of which showed that it was not impossible for an elephant or a rhinoceros to grow a fur. The living types just happen not to; the extinct types, as was established beyond any doubt, had done so. Why?

To this question, a troublesome Frenchman added another. It was now known that the mammoth had, without being recognized, intruded on human history as far back as there were records. This Frenchman, Jacques Boucher de Crèvecœur de Perthes by name, claimed that at one time in the past Man had intruded on the mammoth. Monsieur de Perthes, in his younger years a diplomat in the service of Napoleon I, later economist, playwright, novelist, and self-styled archeologist, had dug up things fashioned of stone. They were really just pieces of flint, chipped around the edges. Such things were no novelty in themselves. They had "always" been found, and the population had called them "thunderbolts" and many other names. Oh no, one didn't know what they were. One had to admit that they did resemble some implements which travelers had brought back from certain backward tribes beyond the seas. Monsieur de Perthes insisted that they were tools and weapons of a primitive race of Man which had once inhabited France. Maybe so, maybe so, but he certainly went too far. He said that those primitive men, our own ancestors, had hunted mammoths with such weapons!

Of course not! That was just the kind of idea one could expect from a man who had written novels, not even using a pen name, a man who had written stage plays and probably even associated with actors and actresses. What Monsieur de Perthes apparently did not know was that the mammoth and the woolly rhinoceros and primitive Man (whatever *that* term was supposed to mean) had not been contemporaries. More, that they could not have been contemporaries, because the mammoth and the various European rhinoceri had lived during the preceding geological period. In that period, there had been no men because men belonged to our period.

The name most frequently quoted in all attacks on Boucher de Perthes' *chimères* was, quite naturally, that of Cuvier. Cuvier had said that he had never found a fossil animal in more than one period. Sometimes similar forms, yes. The mammoth had existed in one period, while the Indian and the African elephants lived in another. They were similar. But they were not the same. And most especially, Cuvier had emphasized that no fossil man had ever been found. This was not true, as was learned later, but the Cro-Magnon skeleton found by Dean Buckland in 1823 was then believed to be the skeleton of a British lady of the Roman period.

Boucher de Perthes kept quiet. He was not looking for a professorship anywhere, he had some income, derived in part from those novels and plays that were cited against him. He went on collecting his chipped flint implements, meanwhile resolved not to believe in Cuvier's worldwide catastrophes. Johann Wolfgang von Goethe in Germany did not believe in them either, but he was another playwright and novelist and one did not have to believe his scientific reasoning even though he also held a high position in society and in politics. But somebody else who did not believe in them was Sir Charles Lyell in England, a professional geologist. He collected all the geological evidence he could find. But he could not find any evidence for worldwide catastrophes. Tectonic forces built mountains; rains and rivers washed them away again. Rivers filled seas with sediments and made them shallower and shallower. On the other hand the surf nibbled at coastlines and slowly moved them inland. Wherever Lyell looked, he saw only those forces which are still operating, day and night, day after day and night after night, through weeks, months, years, centuries, and millennia.

There was no longer any reason for disbelieving that a species of animals or plants had survived from one geological period into another. In fact later on scientists began to look very avidly for such "living fossils." There was no longer any reason why the mammoth should not have survived into the present geological period (then called the Alluvium). Conversely, if the mammoth had died out with the end of the Pleistocene there was no reason why Man should not have lived *then*. Sir Charles Lyell himself considered this not at all improbable. And one day, in 1859, old Boucher de Perthes, living reasonably contentedly at Abbeville in the beautiful valley of the Somme, received a visitor, an English gentleman by the name of Sir Charles Lyell. He wanted to see the stone implements which Monsieur de Perthes had collected. After that, he wanted to see where they had been found. He checked carefully, not saying much. But when he did open his mouth he began with the words, "Monsieur de Perthes, you are correct."

With that, one of the two questions which had been answerless in 1830 had been disposed of. Theoretically, at least, man and mammoth could have been contemporaries. It took the remainder of the nineteenth century to show that they actually had been, and also that they had lived in the same place at the same time. This was not as easy as it sounds nowadays. Fossil remains of man not only had to be found, which in itself was mostly a matter of luck, they also had to be established as unmistakably fossil. That took time, and many people did not want to go along with these new ideas. Not only that, some individual scientists, being human, were reluctant to abandon theories which they had treasured as valuable property. They were even justified in being skeptical; skepticism is a prime requirement in scientific work. To us, who see everything brightly illuminated in the light of after-knowledge, some of the skepticism looks exaggerated, stubborn, and blind. All that was the case on occasion, but essentially the skeptics were merely wrong.

I'll just touch upon a few cases. When the first skull of Neanderthal Man was found, the eminent medical authority Professor Rudolf Virchow tried to show that its differences from a modern skull might be explained as individual pathological differences, caused by battle wounds in youth and by *arthritis deformans* in old age. It was nonsense, but as long as only one such skull was known the possibility existed. When a place where ancient man had obviously eaten mammoths was discovered near Předmost in Bohemia, the Danish zoologist Japetus Steenstrup said that this still was no proof for contemporaneous existence; the men might have found frozen carcasses, as Tunguses and Yakuts still do. When the first cave paintings came to light in France, they were suspected of not being genuine. But fossil Man, or his modern champions, won all along the battleline.

Before that victory could be complete, something fundamental had to be learned, which had to do with that other question already posed: why had the mammoth been woolly? The Siberian finds indicated a fur from six to nine inches thick.

It was a question about which one could think in circles for any length of time. If one took the fur to be a special adaptation to Siberian conditions, from the example of the Siberian tiger which has a heavier fur than his Bengal brother, one got into the dead-end problem of why the mammoth no longer walked the Siberian tundra. If one did not take the fur to be a Siberian specialty, one had to assume Siberian climate in Europe, all the way from England to Bohemia. There was one suspicious indication in Switzerland, relating to the glaciers, which became a tourist attraction after the invention of the railroad simplified travel. A glacier is essentially a slowly flowing river of compacted snow. When rocks are dislodged by the glacier itself, or by other causes, they are carried by the glacier. If it should at some later time melt faster than it can advance, these rocks are left as a telltale mark, called a moraine. But a glacier not only carries rocks on its back, it also moves them with its sole, scraping another telltale mark into the rock over which it flows. Nobody who had looked at the evidence could doubt that the glaciers of Switzerland had been much larger in the past. In 1829, Goethe himself, after looking at them, stated thoughtfully, "For all that ice [of the larger glaciers] we need cold. I hold the suspicion that a period of great cold has passed at least over Europe."

But the scientific world did not pay too much attention to the Swiss glaciers. It had another and geographically larger puzzle on its hands. All over North Germany and the corresponding areas of Poland and Russia one found large blocks of stone, from pieces a man could still move to boulders weighing hundreds of tons. They were scattered without rhyme or reason over a landscape which was largely sand, with bedrock hundreds of feet below the surface. Nor did that bedrock correspond to the boulders on the sand. Geologists comparing rock samples had established something at least as surprising as the presence of the boulders themselves. Their material perfectly matched the mountains on the Scandinavian peninsula. How did large pieces of Scandinavian mountains get to Pomerania and Poland?

Lyell's answer, incorporated in his big work, seemed to explain all this nicely and was fully accepted for about half a century. Let's assume, he began, that all of Europe north of the Alps was lower by a certain and comparatively small amount. Then a shallow sea would cover the plains of Germany quite far inland, at least to the Hartz Mountains. The Scandinavian glaciers would then have flowed directly into the sea. When a glacier flows into the sea, its end breaks off periodically to form icebergs. Drifting southward, these icebergs, probably smaller to begin with than the monsters which float down into the Atlantic from Greenland, would slowly melt. The rocks they had scooped up as glaciers would drop to the bottom. As the European mainland slowly rose, the sea became shallower and shallower and simultaneously iceberg production in the north would stop because the Scandinavian glaciers no longer reached the shoreline.

Building on the foundation of that theory, one could even explain the larger size of the Swiss glaciers. If the sea was that much larger, a lot more water could evaporate from it, causing more snow in Switzerland in winter and thereby increasing the size of its glaciers. That that sea apparently had not covered France was somewhat awkward, but France did not seem to have any of those boulders from Scandinavia, so obviously it had not been flooded.

Any doubts anybody might have harbored could not be voiced for lack of evidence. But in 1875, there was a meeting of the German Geological Society in Berlin. Among the invited guests was the head of the Swedish Geological Survey, Otto Martin Torell. Torell did not just come, deliver a speech, and rush home again; he made a few excursions, looking at boulders from Scandinavia resting in the rye fields in the vicinity. And there is a place named Rüdersdorf, about an hour's train ride from Berlin, where bedrock actually breaks through the sand and forms very modest mountains. The bedrock is Muschelkalk. Torell had to see that. When he did, he also saw the typical glacier scrapes which he knew so well. (Later a boulder from Sweden was placed near that spot as a memorial.) The same night Torell spoke to the assembled geologists. Europe had not been covered by a shallow sea with icebergs from the Scandinavian glaciers, he said. Europe had been covered by the glaciers. Wherever there was bedrock at the surface their marks would be found.

Goethe's forgotten remark of more than forty years before about the period of great cold that had passed at least over Europe suddenly seemed prophetic. The idea of a large portion of a continent flooded by a shallow sea was not a rare concept to geologists. Europe had been flooded like that during the Jurassic and Cretaceous periods. And during the Cretaceous at least, the North American continent had been split in two in the same manner by a shallow sea extending from the Gulf of Mexico through the central plains to Hudson Bay.

It was a different proposition to be asked to imagine large portions of a continent buried under glacier ice. That concept could not be assimilated quickly, not just because it was new, but because it seemed to involve a very profound climatic change. You could imagine a sea breaking through from the Gulf to Hudson Bay, or one connecting the North Sea with the Adriatic Sea, without a climatic change at the outset. Of course the presence of the sea, once it existed, would influence the climate. "But for all that ice we need cold." Something like relief resulted when Melchior Neumayr published a calculation which said that the whole Ice Age could be explained by a reduction of the average year-round temperature of from 8° to 10° Fahrenheit. If every day and every night, Neumayr said, were 8° cooler than it is now, the snow and ice of winter would fail to melt away as completely as it does now. The snow line of the mountains would be lower, for one thing. Next winter more ice and snow would accumulate in these places. If this went on for a sufficiently long time the glaciers could grow large enough to cover all of Europe.

Meanwhile the glacier scrapes which Torell had so confidently predicted had actually been found. Once geologists knew what to look for, it seemed a wonder that they had ever been overlooked. From a mass of data maps were made, showing the extent of that past glaciation. There was one large area of which so little was known that one could not tell. That happened to be Siberia. We still don't know about Siberia, but that expedition under Roy Chapman Andrews established definitely that the ice shield did *not* reach the Gobi and the high land of Tibet. But from the Ural Mountains west, the picture was quite clear. The glaciers had covered Russia to points south of Moscow, Poland to south of Warsaw, and Germany to Berlin and beyond. From there on the "glacier line" ran through Belgium, crossed the Channel, cut across the southernmost portion of England to the vicinity of Bristol, and then ran westward through the Irish Sea. Everything north of that line was covered by the ice shield, including all of Ireland. That is the reason there are no snakes in Ireland. Probably there were some before, but after the glaciers which had killed them had melted away, no snakes could get back.

In the Western Hemisphere, the glacier line began at the shore of the Atlantic Ocean somewhat south of the fortieth parallel, ran west south of the Great Lakes to the Dakotas, turned north there, and then followed approximately the present United States–Canadian border to the Pacific Ocean. Naturally it was not quite as straight as that political boundary. Here in America the areas not covered by the ice shield were comparatively large, including everything south of Pennsylvania in the east and everything south of the state of Washington in the west. In Europe, the Mediterranean countries and all of France had escaped. So had the extreme south of England, much of the area of the English Channel (then probably dry land), western and southern Germany, southern Poland, and southern Russia. Austria and Czechoslovakia had not been reached by the Scandinavian glaciers. But the Alps, as Swiss guides had pointed out to the visiting Goethe, had produced large glaciers of their own.

The evidence seemed to leave little room for early men and mammoths, but there was an ameliorating factor. It was a pardonable mistake of the geologists to have thought at first that there had been just "the Ice Age." Then they discovered evidence that two glaciations had successively gone over the same spot, with an interval during which plants grew there which can now be found in Italy. With eyes sharpened once more, they continued to search, finally arriving at the conclusion that there had been about four glaciations, with "interglacial periods" between. The "glacier line" first established belonged to the time of the maximum glaciation, the third. The others had been of somewhat lesser extent; it is hard to say just how much less. For easier reference the glaciations have received names which as names mean very little, because they are actually just the names of small rivers. In chronological order, the names are Günz, Mindel, Riss, and Würm, and the majority of the experts believe that the last of the four, the Würm glaciation, had two distinct phases.

How much the glaciers receded during the warmer interglacial periods is an especially hard question to answer. Since the first of these warmer periods was quite long in duration one may be justified in thinking that the glaciers had receded to at least their present status, which leaves only the extreme north of America, Greenland, and the Siberian rim still in the Ice Age. As for the recession in the other warmer periods, almost any guess will do, but it must have been a good deal, because one can clearly see that each time a fauna geared to a somewhat warmer climate moved in. When the glaciers advanced, spreading tundra and cold steppes ahead of them, coldproof mammals appeared on those tundras. The mammoth itself. The woolly rhinoceros. The heavily furred musk ox. The reindeer. The gigantic cave bear. Wolves.

When the glaciers receded and the steppes warmed up, forests spread and with the forests came a different group of animals. There was the "old" elephant, the majestic *Elephas antiquitatis* with its long tusks. (Because it was not particularly old, scientists later referred to it as the "forest elephant," in spite of the meaning of its Latin name.) There was Merck's rhinoceros, most likely a hairless form. There were bears, lions, lynxes, stags, fallow deer, deer, and wild hogs.

This seesaw between a temperate forest fauna and a cold-resistant tundra fauna had started with a fairly stable condition in the late days of the Tertiary period. At that time the area which was to be invaded by the northern cold had a fauna which, if anybody saw it now, would make him think that he had been transported to Africa. In fact, in a manner of speaking he would have been transported to Africa's fauna, except that it was not yet on African soil. The north European fauna of the late Tertiary, leaving the slowly cooling continent, largely escaped via the Balkan peninsula (which had somewhat different geography then) into Africa, where they survived with comparatively little change. During the time when the first glaciation was slowly building up there were only a few apparently more hardy forms left.

A species of hippopotamus was still around for a while and so was a rhinoceros which is called the Etruscan rhinoceros. There was a large elephant, called the "southern" elephant (*Elephas meridionalis*). There was a type of moose which is considered to be the direct ancestor of the living form, and another which was the ancestor of a form that flourished all through the Pleistocene and became extinct in very early historical times; it seems to have survived longest in Ireland. There was a very large beaver which has been named in honor of Cuvier and there were large numbers of a wild horse, possibly zebra-striped.

In putting down these names, I am relying on a list prepared by Professor Wolfgang Soergel of Chirotherium fame. Professor Soergel had long been interested in a specific problem. Because of animal bones burned in fires, large bones split open for the sake of the marrow, and lots of similar evidence, everybody was sure that primitive Man had been largely a hunter. The problem which busied Soergel was no longer *whether* the men of the Old Stone Age, the Neanderthalers and the later men of the small Aurignac race, had hunted. The problem was *how* they had hunted their game. But that problem, in turn, rested on the question of what kind of game was available. By about 1910, when Soergel started his work, enough material had been amassed to enable him to draw up tables showing which animals had occurred when. Some ten years later he brought his tables up to date once more. An adaptation of his second table appears in the Appendix, with my own translations of some of the scientific names.

These tables show clearly how that "temperate forest fauna" which was to become so typical for the interglacial periods moved in during the first of them. The earliest known fossil of a man, the so-called Heidelberg jaw, indicating a six-footer of the Neanderthal type (the later "true" Neanderthalers were a good six inches shorter), is also dated as belonging to the first interglacial period. During the second glaciation, the mammoth's ancestor (*Elephas trogontherii*) appeared on the scene, along with the reindeer, an early form of the cave bear, and so forth. The transition from the remains of the Tertiary fauna which somehow managed to hold on for a while to the fauna that "belongs" to the Ice Age was complete.

Man did not have easy hunting in these surroundings, which he could endure only because of his possession of fire. There was much competition from carnivorous mammals, some of them of considerable size. The hunter often enough became the hunted. Even more often he must have lost to wolves game which he could not kill at a stroke.

And, as the remains of his meals show, he was handicapped in other ways too. We do know that the forests of the interglacial periods, as well as the tundra and steppes fringing the glaciers during the glaciations, were inhabited by many small mammals which, being rodents, were probably numerous. There were also flocks of birds, many of them types still living in the nothern countries. But in the refuse heaps of ancient Man the bones of small mammals are a great rarity, and there is not a single well-established case of bird bones as remains of a meal. This seems to indicate at least that Man in the Old Stone Age had not yet learned how to build traps and snares, and that he had no missile weapons—slingshots, bows and arrows, etc.—with which he could kill a bird. He probably relied entirely on what are known as impact weapons: spears, clubs, and related armament which required a close approach. Small animals were difficult to approach and not worth the trouble. With equal effort the hunter could kill a reindeer or a horse.

Anthropologists have often tried to give helpful hints to paleontologists by pointing out the methods of hunting used by primitive tribes in comparatively recent times. They have told how natives use brush fires to stampede animals in a certain direction so that they are forced to jump down steep cliffs. They have told how natives, armed with several spears per man, isolate a single animal from the herd, corner it, and then dispatch it either by means of throwing spears or by using the spears as close-range weapons.

Such hints are helpful, but whether or not they are applicable is another question. The so-called fire-drive requires not only fire (and a suitable locality), but also large numbers of hunters. The anthropologists who told about such hunts stressed that hundreds and sometimes even thousands of natives took part in them, with enough yield for every hunter and his family. But primitive Man, at least during the Old Stone Age, simply was not numerous enough to conduct such hunts. Later, in Cro-Magnon times, the fire-drive was probably used; in fact, there is one place in France where everything speaks in favor of the theory that herds of animals (especially horses) were stampeded over a cliff, not just once, but many times. Neanderthal Man, however, did not live in tribes, in our meaning of the word. There were just large families; maybe two or three families getting together on occasion. They were not numerous enough to stampede herds, either by means of the fire drive or by plain noisemaking.

Separating a single animal from a herd and cornering it was probably practiced, but what weapons they used was another problem. Those primitive tribes about which the anthropologists told had already acquired iron; their spears were tipped with pointed and sharp blades of considerable size and fatal power. Stone blades of equivalent deadliness were a late invention. A German archeologist, Otto Profé, borrowed a number of stone artifacts which were indubitably "Neanderthal," attached them to wooden handles in a manner probably superior to anything Neanderthal men could have managed, and then tried to "kill" a freshly butchered calf with these weapons. Try as he might, he could not even penetrate the thin skin of the belly. Only where the skin was underlaid by strong muscles did the flint implements break through the skin at all. Even if wielded by a powerful man, these weapons could not have inflicted fatal wounds. They were just not sharp enough.

It was a different matter to use the Neanderthal implements to cut the carcass apart. For operations like separating the skin from the flesh, splitting the flesh off the bone, and even for cutting the tendons from the bone, these stone knives were almost as effective as modern tools. One could not cut across the muscle, but Neanderthal man probably did not care whether his meat was sliced into steaks or roasted as chunks. Profé concluded from this experiment, and Soergel agreed with him, that the stone weapons were not hunting weapons at all, with all due respect for Boucher de Perthes' pioneer work. The stone weapons were household tools. They may have been weapons of war, where the situation is different, but they were useless for hunting.

Then what was used for hunting? A weapon was needed which would penetrate deeply with relative ease, causing a wound that did not permit the animal to get far away. Soergel concluded (in 1922) that Neanderthal Man's hunting weapon was probably a spear not tipped by anything. Just a straight stick, either a straight branch or more likely a sapling tree, with the tip hardened by fire and then sharpened. Such a spear would be effective in a more or less individual hunt on reindeer and horse and animals of similar size, and with luck even on larger game. Soergel's prediction was borne out in 1948 when such a wooden spear was actually found near the Aller River in northwestern Germany. It was broken into ten pieces, but nothing was missing. It had been eight feet long, fashioned of the tough and heavy wood of the European yew (*Taxus baccata*), and examination of the tip showed that it had been hardened by fire. It was pointed and showed no traces of having had anything attached to it, but clear traces of the strokes of stone knives that had been used to sharpen it.

The spear could be dated as having been made and used during the last interglacial period, and it was found imbedded in the rib case of a forest elephant. Nearby a dozen flint scrapers lay about. The whole effect was precisely like that of a hunting method still in use in Africa by the pygmy tribes of Cameroon. There, a solitary hunter, armed with a spear longer than himself, carefully approaches a solitary feeding or dozing elephant from behind. If his approach fails to be noiseless enough, the elephant usually just moves on. If the hunter does succeed in getting close, he pushes his spear into the elephant's abdomen from below and behind. The animal, fatally wounded, rarely seems to turn around for an attack on the hunter but races away in terror and pain. Finally it breaks down exhausted, often a considerable distance away.

It worked that way with the African elephant in the last century; it worked that way with the forest elephant during the last interglacial period in Europe.

But it could not have worked that way with the mammoth. The skin of the elephant, while thick, has soft spots. So, presumably, did the skin of the mammoth. But the long hair protected those softer areas. Before a spear could touch the inch-thick skin it had to penetrate some eight inches of wool. And under the skin there were some six inches of fat. A high-powered rifle bullet would be needed to get through all this to the vital organs. No spear could ever do it; no man could put enough driving force behind it.

The only thing we can think of now—and primitive man certainly thought of it too—is the pit. That had always seemed the most likely method, but it was one about which quite a number of archeologists were very skeptical. They said a pit large enough to catch a mammoth was impossible for primitive man to make. The only digging tool Neanderthal Man could have had was the so-called digging stick. It would take a whole tribe many weeks to dig a large enough pit.

It sounded like a very strong argument, but in view of the evidence it had to be wrong. There were several answers. One was that the men would not have dug the entire hole; they would have started with a natural hole of some kind. Another was that it was not necessary to make a hole into which a full-grown mammoth would disappear; it was enough to render it helpless. If only the forelegs or the hind legs were caught, even a mammoth could be clubbed to death by incessant attack. I may add here that I personally doubt very much that the digging stick was the only digging instrument of Neanderthal Man. He dealt with fairly loose sand, and for such material, nature provided a ready-made digging tool: moose antlers. They may be somewhat awkward to handle, but I can testify that they work in loose sand.

Still and all, the mammoth probably was exceptional game which was hunted only under special circumstances. But there was Předmost in Bohemia, where, as mentioned earlier, Man had evidently eaten mammoths. This place, like so many such finds, was an accidental discovery. The ground belonged to a Czech landowner who could not help noticing that his farm hands quite often came across large bones. To the mind of the landowner there was just one use for old bones: he had them ground up as fertilizer for his fields—until one day somebody who knew better saw what was going on and screamed for help, invoking the Academy of Science, the police, the Ministry of the Interior, and everybody else he could think of in a hurry. The practice of fertilizing fields with mammoth-bone meal was stopped and an investigation started.

There were numerous remains of people. There was also numerous remains of mammoths. And the people, it could not be denied, had had some sense of order. Here was a pile of shoulder blades, there was a pile of leg bones. Over there some skulls. Since nobody could tell how many bones had been ground up there was immediate disagreement on the number of mammoths that had been eaten there. First estimates said "at least a thousand"; that was revised downward to about half in the course of time. Soergel, on the other hand, at first refused to believe in a number higher than about 300, but doubled his estimate later on, so that we can't be far wrong in saying that the Předmost site contained the remains of about 600 mammoths.

As I mentioned, the Danish zoologist Japetus Steenstrup (justly famous for other work) held that all these mammoths had just been frozen carcasses, such as had been found in the Lena delta and along the Indigirka River. If he had stopped at that point we would now say, "Old Steenstrup was a good judge." But he elaborated on the case, "proving" that primitive Man had never hunted or killed a mammoth. Very soon afterward overwhelming evidence that primitive Man had hunted and killed mammoths was found in many places. Steenstrup's reputation collapsed, he was ridiculed, and those who had originally sided with him kept very quiet about it. Primitive Man was acclaimed as a great hunter.

But it is now accepted that in the specific case of the Předmost mammoths what primitive Man actually did was to stuff himself with the flesh of dead animals. No doubt he could kill 600 mammoths in time. But he could not have dragged the heavy bodies to the same place. And if he made a mammoth trap of some kind near Předmost, the animals would not have patiently walked into the same trap year after year. Obviously something, probably a blizzard of unusual severity, had killed the mammoths there. Only a natural catastrophe can account for the presence of 600 mammoth carcasses in one place.

Six hundred elephants, however, is a very large herd. And that naturally brings up the question of how numerous the mammoth was. It cannot have been rare. The teeth (molars) of more than 200 individuals have been found in a most unlikely spot: they were dredged up with oysters from the Dogger Bank in the North Sea. In the German state of Württemberg alone, remains belonging to about 3000 individuals have been found during the time interval from 1700 to 1900. The number of remains from Austria and Czechoslovakia must be about the same. And the total of the tusks found so far in Siberia, where the mammoth lasted longest, points to 50,000 individuals.

As to the appearance of the mammoth, there are absolutely no doubts left. We have numerous complete skeletons, we have the Siberian specimens preserved by what engineers now call "permafrost" (permanently frozen ground), and we have, almost more important, the very lifelike drawings left by men of the later Stone Age. These show something one could not have deduced from the skeleton: the mammoth had two humps, like the Bactrian camel. These were indubitably humps of fat for the foodless season. One of these humps was placed above the shoulder blades, as one should expect; the other, strangely enough, was on top of the head. These two humps, combined with the long fur and the enormous tusks which apparently never were put to any use, made the shape of the mammoth quite different from that of living elephants. The color of the fur looks quite red now, but it is supposed that it has faded, so that in life the mammoth was probably clothed in reddish-black. One special adaptation to the cold climate, revealed by the Siberian finds, is worth mentioning. The mammoth carried, at the root of its tail, a strange skin flap which protected the anal opening against the cold. Its tail was quite short and the ears were small, smaller even than those of the small-eared Indian elephant.

And not all mammoths were of "mammoth size." There is really only one type to which this word would properly apply:

the race or subspecies which occurred in Württemberg and which has been named after Professor Fraas. "Fraas's mammoth," as it may be called, stood a full three feet taller than the largest African elephant known. And that measurement disregards the hump, which may have added another foot or two. The most common type was somewhere between the African and the Indian elephant in size, and the Siberian species was smaller than the Indian elephant, just half as tall as the mammoth's ancestor, the admittedly enormous *Elephas trogontherii*. Whether that Siberian species—named *Elephas beresovkius* for reasons which will quickly become apparent—is to be considered a degenerate version of the European species is an unanswered question. But it probably was.

It is usually said that the European mammoth "died out" at the end of the glacial period. But it is more likely that it did not die out but moved out. As soon as the last glaciation in Europe had come to an end the forest moved in again. And apparently the mammoth just did not like the forest. It probably behaved much the same as did another typical animal of the glacial periods—the reindeer. The reindeer also just moved away, with the one difference that it stayed alive in the extreme north and the mammoth did not. One may imagine, therefore, that the mammoth, like the reindeer, stuck to the cold steppes and tundra, following them northward as they receded, and then going east, to Siberia, where conditions were still most like those to which it had adapted itself.

How those Siberian permafrost mammoths which started all the excitement had found their individual end became clear in 1901. During that year the Russian Academy of Science in St. Petersburg received news from Yakutsk that another mammoth had come to light, this time in the extreme northeast, near the Beresovka, a tributary of the river Kolyma. Because of an old ukase originally issued by Peter the Great, the Czar had to be notified about the find and he ordered an expedition to go after the mammoth. The leader of the expedition was Dr. Otto Hertz.

When the expedition arrived, wolves and dogs had already done their work, and much of the skull was bare of flesh. But it was still a virtually complete mammoth, since everything but the head was still solidly frozen. The decayed portions of the flesh emitted such a terrible stench that the scientists more than once felt that they might have to give up. But they always succeeded in persuading themselves to stand it for a few more days. And as the work progressed, their professional enthusiasm dulled their noses, to the great benefit of science.

The mammoth apparently had been feeding in freshly fallen snow which covered a deep crevasse in its path. When it fell in it was fatally injured, having broken both the right foreleg and the pelvis. It is quite probable that it struggled for some time in spite of the injury, pulling down tons of loose snow under which it finally died. There was still food in its mouth, and from the frozen stomach the scientists extracted twenty-seven pounds of chewed but undigested food. Botanists could still classify the food: it consisted of larch, fir, and pine, some ground-up fir cones, sedge, wild flowers of various kinds, wild thyme, and two kinds of moss. Except on the head and one foreleg, the fur was complete, consisting of a thick yellowish undercoat and a thick mass of guide hairs, up to fourteen inches long. There were manelike patches of long guide hairs on cheeks, chin, shoulders, flanks, and belly. The fat layer under the skin was pure white and on the average four inches thick. The meat was dark red, suggesting horse meat, and marbled with fat. The dogs ate it avidly; the men could not quite steel themselves to try it too. Some of the dark frozen blood was saved; a serological test made later indicated the Indian elephant as the closest living relative.

The scientists who did the work were not only hampered by the stench of the decayed parts, but after they had skinned the mammoth and cleaned up the skeleton they were faced with distance. It took ten sleds to carry what they had salvaged, for a 2000-mile journey over a snowy landscape, ending with the city of Irkutsk and the Trans-Siberian railroad. Both skeleton and skin were finally mounted in the museum in St. Petersburg, the skeleton in normal position, the skin in the half-sitting position in which the animal had died.

The mammoth was an American animal too in its time. Together with other elephants, it had crossed over from Asia into Alaska and found its way south. But it was not very numerous in the Western Hemisphere, much less so than the

American mastodon which, in spite of early guesses to the contrary, was probably a hairless type.

For a long time there was a rumor that the woolly mammoth might still be alive in Alaska. Nobody knows just when or how that rumor originated but it is more than a century old. And every once in a while something happened to strengthen it. One of the most widely believed props of the rumor was a piece of fiction describing the "killing of the last mammoth," which appeared in *McClure's Magazine* in 1899 and was taken seriously by a large percentage of the magazine's readers. Obviously it is an appealing idea that the mammoth of the Ice Age, unwilling companion of Man since the earliest days of recordless prehistory, is still alive somewhere. Unfortunately it is not true.

But there must be mammoths in Alaska—frozen mammoths, undisturbed in permafrost like their Siberian kin. A tiny one was found some years ago and made the journey to New York in a deep-freeze unit. It is a promising beginning. Scientists are eying the frozen muck of Alaska. Somewhere in it there must be specimens which will teach us a lot about the mammoth in America—and possibly about early Man in America too.

Arctic Ghost

FELIX RIESENBERG

To the Eskimo, the Arctic is populated with good and bad spirits. The haunting quality of the cold and ice, the desolation of the landscape, often play strange tricks on the mind—the effect is even stronger on the minds of explorers from more temperate zones. Felix Riesenberg, for example, relates his own experience with an arctic ghost.

IT SEEMS to be a principle, if there are principles other than those conjured by imagination, that quick existence, if I may so qualify it, is possible only between the poles of birth and death. But we do know that there is pre-extension of these limits so far as birth is concerned, but just where does this begin? We do definitely know that life starts before parturition, that intention, of some kind, precedes conception, and that a marvelous complication of circumstances leads to the event called life. We may also conceive of a continuation of the result of this elaborate beginning, following the sudden snuff-ing-out of material motion. The hereafter, yes—but still here if we only knew. Why should things that take so long to start end with sudden abruptness? Do the things that are absolutely not of the flesh, such as the conscience and the will, do these things evaporate in an instant, or before the dissolution of their earthly shell? Is memory a thing of mud? Is love a mere assemblage of cells? Is one skull exactly like another? Can we assay the value of a brain by weight or size? There must be something other than the burial of the body to attend the cessation of life. This process is not completed in an hour, or in a day, if there is such an entity as time in the realm of ghosts.

Such speculations are disquieting in the growing gloom of an approaching polar night. And under such conditions there were naïve arguments between us as to the vitality of such things as bones, or entire skeletons, once most intimate parts of living men. In other words (if those more fit to discuss this will permit) do the preserved remains carry with them an allegiance of the spirit? Do mummies, tortured and distorted, still demand attendance on the part of their life principle? Is not the flesh and bone an equal, or let us say, a necessary partner with the soul? Is one *nothing* and the other *all?* The ancient Egyptians seemed to think so. And what are a few centuries, or a thousand or more years, in the scale of all time? May not the spirit cling to the bone and play havoc with weak mortality, adjacent in the living, shivering flesh? Even the stoutest might hesitate to sleep among the headstones of a cemetery through an interminable night.

Fear is as great as faith. The mind, grown out of mystery, unable to pierce the unknowable, totters on the brink of chaos when we revolve it on an inward orbit, searching secrets. Even with all of our jumbled heap of practical learning, how little do we know!

One might hesitate to tell the whole truth in matters of unusual moment, even if it were possible to achieve complete expression or to reveal emotion too poignant for words. Who can convey the utter terror of a small child screaming in the dark at the apparition of a shadow on the wall? Perhaps that child is voicing something only a young soul is tuned to fear. And here it may be said that I do not believe in ghosts—I have repeated this to myself over and over again.

Well, this is the beginning, or at least it is the explanation, or the excuse, for the story to follow. Still there is something more to be added before the matter is set forth. If the departed come back, we must be certain that they were there, and suffered, and sinned, and served, and died. Even the most willing mind can hardly conceive of a virgin planet peopled with ghosts.

I spent the dark months of a polar winter prisoned in a little house just beneath the eightieth parallel of latitude on Danes Island, off the shores of the northern archipelago of Spitsbergen. Our square, stout little house was built on an

ice-encrusted knoll, the timbers of the floor resting on protruding breccia strewn at the base of a steep cliff. The shore-
ward ends of the timber had been bedded by hewing into the
ice, and the ends facing the sea were supported on piles of
stone to level off the floor. The wedgelike sides and front
foundation wall were built of loose rock, calked with reindeer
moss. To make this solid cellar proof against the wind, the
rude masonry was later on plastered with ice and banked with
snow.

This snug little house stood opposite to the relics of a camp
once occupied by Andree. In this camp were intimate reminders of the gallant Swede, reminders vibrant with the last
moments of this determined, earnest man. But it was a camp
haunted only by memories, for no material or actual part of
the travelers remained. If the camp held an element of death,
it was only that of the last contact with men before disaster,
hundreds of miles away. But on every point of the horizon
were headlands and mountains and glaciers familiar in the
annals of polar suffering and discovery. Here came William
Barents and John Cornelius Ryp in 1596—Barents, the ice
pilot and discoverer, destined to perish in Nova Zembla, far to
the south.

And here, too, past the Pyramids and the great Cape of
Hakluyt, sailed the indomitable Heemskerck and the able
Hendrik Hudson, also to perish in frozen seas. But the names
of those who sailed north to die fill a scroll of ample length.
In 1620, the track of the Dutch discoverers was followed by a
blaze of fortune that, for a time, transformed the wastes of the
north into a place of turmoil. The waters were thick with the
black flukes of leviathan. The wide lanes between the pan ice
spouted continual jets of vapor. Fifteen thousand seamen came
to those northern shores in the short summer months. Close to
the little house on Danes Island, on an adjacent level plain,
stand relics of the abandoned city of Smeerenburg, the most
remarkable settlement of all time. It once held shops and
bakeries, and lodgings, inns and drinking booths, and brothels,
for the whale fleet was followed by women and the whalemen
held carnival when they drove their barbs into the huge,
fat fishes spouting near the shore. The smoke of the trying-

kettles rose upward in thick columns, standing in the summer calm, the trembling black plumes on an unearthly hearse.

This ancient killing (and how tremendous is the killing of a mighty whale!) went on amid the rendering of thousands of tons of fat and the carousing of reckless men and women, smeared with blood and blubber and profligate with life and treasure. It was a time of fabulous fortune spouting golden streams of gore and oil taken from the cold blue sea. Two hundred and sixty Dutch ships visited the Spitsbergen whaling ground in the few months of a summer season, first fighting and besetting the English ships of the Muscovy Company, for, wherever free treasure was to be had, fighting and license held sway. All of this ancient killing and rendering of fat and roistering of flesh went on shamelessly beneath the unwinking sky of continual day. There was no dark intermission of night to cover them. Thousands left their bones to bleach upon the arctic shores. Countless rude coffins of oak, often fashioned from the staves of casks, lay in shallow graves amid the stones, the ground too hard for deeper burial. The whales were killed off and all this terrific life departed, this summer life of a brief score of years, centuries ago. Never did human beings survive the night; the few who wintered perished.

Then came an interval of a hundred years and still more adventurous prows forced past the site of Smeerenburg and the headland of Hakluyt. The *Racehorse* and the *Carcass*, commanded by Phipps, with young Horatio Nelson, a midshipman, in the steerage of the *Racehorse*, sailed by the gruesome souvenir of graves. These were followed by Buchan and John Franklin and Parry, by sailors who dragged heavy boats over hummocks, rupturing themselves in the hopeless battle with the ice, breaking hearts by inhuman labor on the polar field. These, too, left their corpses on those shores to join the great colony of perpetual bones, for in those regions there is no decay. Then followed Nordenskjöld, Malmgren, Fabvre, Leigh Smith, Wellman, Nobile, Amundsen, continuing the struggle northward, leaving their trail of death and hopes behind.

Three sailors left in this bleak surrounding were simple men. One was the veteran of many winters in the polar seas and one was only a sailor, a far voyager who believed the things he saw and knew and who had heard many things he could not understand. The first, Paul Bjoervig, bearded, bent with years, was sturdy and uncomplaining. The second, Morten Olaisen, was more voluble and uncertain, for to him the creeping on of the arctic night came with grim precision, each darkening hour casting deeper shadows across his mind. I was a youth, but with a fair record of sailing, long miles of sea spun out in the wake of my experience. I was the navigator, the officer, and in charge. Upon me devolved the command, the responsibility, in the changing world slowly sinking from light and life.

For a time we busied ourselves by tasks, setting our house in shape amid the increasing powderings of snow—piling driftwood and lighting huge bonfires on the dim line of the beach, taking cheer from the crackling flames, noting the shooting of blue-green tongues of light, catching the alternating waves of heat and cold that circled about the flames of driftwood in a world of endings. Always the fires left us more cold. Once, as the blaze burned low, a ghastly knob protruded from the ashes, a grinning skull burned black, the eye sockets filled with glowing coals of wood. This was our last fire. Morten muttered something about smoke in his eyes; then, too, the deepening snow buried the driftwood. Our conversation became less buoyant; small things took on sinister importance in our evasive contemplation of the long black months ahead.

And then we began to talk of the dead.

"Did you see it?"

"What?"

"The coffin," Paul whispered, bending over his pipe, slowly puffing, while Morten worked at the kitchen stove. Pungent smoke filled the small kitchen.

"No. I piled the wood. The rocks and wood are gray. It's getting dark. You can't see so well. No, you can't see."

"It rolled over."

"It rolled over—hot—red-hot."

"The dogs ran."

"Yes, they ran."

"I went back. It's gone."

Fragments reached me. I was determined to be cheerful. Further fall of snow prevented fires; the subject was dropped.

The silence came very close as November shaded into a monochrome of gray, blackening toward the night of inky gloom. The birds left the cliff, and the snow, constantly falling, gave an illusion of upward motion; one could feel the friction of impalpable flakes scratching the ether. It was the silence of interstellar space, of complete insulation in the midst of an enormous cemetery draped in white.

So much had happened in that world of close, deceiving snow. So much was bound to happen again. Silence hung over us like a threat. Often I would wake from deep slumber startled by a dream in which I found myself far aloft, high over the black side of Smedburg's Mountain, with its cap of ice, looking down into the valley to the shore where stood the house, a nub of white almost buried. Once I noted its strange resemblance to a small headstone; a shudder came over me, I seemed to see the mound heave up as if from the struggle of three men buried alive. Everything for many hundreds, and for a thousand miles, was absolutely dead. I would have these dreams during periods of moonlight, for by December the curtain of polar night had drawn its fold across the midday skies.

Once the dream came when the moon was gone. I jumped up in the cold and stole to the small double window and saw a strange light without. Cautiously opening the outer door, having thrown on a heavy robe, I saw a vault of sky covered with waving plumes of fire—the aurora. I ran back to my bunk and prayed, shivering for an hour until sleep came.

That night the only black thing in a world of ghostly white was the moving shadow cast by a curious stone on Deadman's Isle, the great Sarcophagus Stone, standing above the snow where the Isle lifts from the plain of the frozen sea, like the mound of a mighty grave. And it was a grave, a gruesome grave holding the bones of a company of ancient sailors under the snow, graves revealed in ghastly bareness in the lazy summer when the ground is clear and lidless coffins show their skulls and skeletons bleaching in the sun.

If you could look to the north over the festering tidal crack, groaning in the calms with unearthly mutterings, noises that sometimes sound like uncouth words, great mumbling words and moans given back again by the distant glacier fronts and cliffs, if you could look across the smooth white sheet of Dane's

Gat to the mound of Deadman's Isle and see the Sarcophagus Stone lifting above the place, the fantastic light of polar winter playing its pranks with the things that are, you would sometimes also see wreaths of mist above the ice. You, too, would see things moving where nothing should move. Graves are thick on Deadman's Isle—and also the shore where stood the house sheltering three sailors.

Once in the night, night by clocks rather than by any change in the complexion of the sky, a shiver ran through the solid little house, the timbers creaked for a moment and all was silent again. For many days before, the growing gloom carried with it an increasing sense of melancholy, a gradual burdening of the spirit as the mounting depth of snow lifted to a level with the eaves of the house, buried completely but for a hollow scooped out by the scouring wind, a providential trench that bared the narrow windows. It was then that old Paul Bjoervig began to talk of his dead comrade, Bentzen, Brent Bentzen who lay dead in the snow hut in Franz Josef Land while Paul slept alongside the corpse of his companion, in fulfillment of a mutual promise that the one to survive, in the event of death, would not cast out his shipmate to the prowling bears.

Bjoervig was constantly talking *with* Bentzen, talking with him in his sleep, and denying the conversation when awake.

Morten Olaisen became a man of monosyllables. His brows lowered with a haunting frown as his eyes sought the face of Paul, always smoking, smoking and grave. The wind whined over the top of Smedburg's Mountain, crashing down the valley in harsh gusts, screeching across the ice-crusted tar paper on the roof of our house, whirling the metal Jack-in-the-wind that topped the chimney. These winds seemed to suck the heat from the fire, to drain off the vitality of the little house, as if some force without was determined to extinguish all alien life clinging amid the snow.

"Was you awake—last night, sir?" Morten ventured the question after a day of silence.

"You mean the house?"

"Under the house." Morten nodded to the bare floor. Paul, pipe in mouth, looked in from the kitchen door, his face serious, his eyes troubled.

"Only the snow bearing down—timbers adjusting." I had plenty of explanations.

"But the voice. Paul heard it, too. It spoke."

"The voice?"

The house seemed so much colder than before. The weak, asthmatic fire coughed, its consumptive splutter burning up precious coal, with no return in heat. Then, too, the oil lamp seemed so dim, and the wind—it was blowing a gale from the northeast—backed into the valley, recurving down on the little house in violent counterblasts.

"Perhaps it was the dogs. You know they howl. It might have been the echo coming down the chimney. You hear lots of things in the calm. It was calm last night. The wind began at four, according to the anemometer." I pulled on my finskoes and, slipping into a gabardine, left the house, picking a rifle from the rack and murmuring something about "bears." Anything to get outside of the house—away. I stepped into skis and slid to the lee side of a large hummock a quarter mile away. Two dogs followed. I was glad. Of course it was not a voice, it was merely a sound, a human-sounding sound. I had thought it the voice of a woman. But it was *not* a voice, certainly not a woman's voice.

For days nothing was said about this happening—if it was a happening. The sky had cleared and the aurora smothered us under a covering of flashing beauty, painfully vivid, like leaping blood gushing over a milk-white breast. It was an overpowering brilliance that caught us, looking upward into the magnificence and mystery of the polar night. Was the truth so utterly gorgeous? Why? I wondered, why? With eyes wide open, our puny minds were blind.

For a time we could not sleep. We hung awake, tired, with staring eyes and agitated minds. We crept into bunks and tossed through sullen hours devoid of rest. Every moment seemed laden with significance. We were listening, always listening for the voice. At last we hardly dared address each other, for even our own voices took on a chill of fear. And then we heard the *thump*.

It came suddenly. We had almost forgotten that they were awaiting its summons. The chill of the room suddenly increased. Dogs howled—that unearthly howl, lifted from the canine throat in long-drawn, agonizing moans. The men lifted their covers and looked at me accusingly. Something was moving beneath the floor of our house. Below, everything was sealed against the inrush of wind and cold. Many feet of snow banked the walls. There was but one entrance, the square trap in the middle of the floor.

By an almost superhuman effort I left my bunk and braced myself in the cold, the dim lamp throwing my shadow on the wall. I stood over the trap, the cold sweat trickling from my forehead. Behind me Paul and Morten peered with breath suspended.

I lifted the trap. It seemed to lift itself, to yield without weight. My whole balance was disturbed for the effort I had nerved myself to exert.

"Look!"

Both men in the bunks shrieked at once. The open trap gave out a musty draft; it was impenetrable to sight. A fog swam before my eyes, my breath halted, my legs shook. Someone besides us was in the room. Oh, how cold it became— how unnaturally cold! We shook violently. I pushed down the suspended trap and the men huddled in their bunks.

A white form came up out of the trap and dissolved when the door was back in place. It was only a mist—the colder air of the cellar condensing in the warmth of the room, for the room was certainly warmer than the dank hole below. But does cold air rise against warmer air? And the thump?

We were again in our bunks. That morning we said nothing. Already we had talked too much—too lightly, perhaps—of the relics of men scattered about us under the snow. The continual night made us secretive, morose. We could not sleep; then, of a sudden, we could not stay awake.

Everything was asleep about us; everything dead. A resistless gravity pulled down our eyelids, smothered our thoughts. When we slept, we were warm, we were secure and, in the depth of delightful dreams, we heard ravishing music and bell-like laughter. Limpid water cascaded over sunlit falls and we again knew the beauty of flowers.

But these slumbers were also interspersed with the low grumbling of men talking in their sleep, and the fire went out and the lamp burned its wick to a brittle carbon. The outside chill penetrated the room and the increasing snow mounted each day in a shroud of dull white already many fathoms deep above the house top. Even Deadman's Isle was levelled in the thickening pall and the high Sarcophagus Stone became a mere bulge on the surrounding plain. The black sides of Smedburg's Mountain, too steep to afford a hold for snow, towered in stark grandeur, a giant sounding board, against which the wailing of hungry dogs set up a constant din.

The chronometer had run its indicater down to "wind," the anemometer clock died down and the scratch of the pen on the cylinder and the metallic click of the ratchet were silent. Everything seemed prepared for our burial. The dark was thick with the hoarfrost of men who still breathe and, in a moment, voices were apparent in the gloom. I lay still, as if dead. My feet were cold, devoid of feeling. Then low words, guttural and slow, told me my companions were still alive.

"I saw it." A voice, thick and indistinct. "Below the house."

"The grave is under my bunk. I have just been down there with *her*."

"Did she touch him?"

"Yes. He's dead now."

"He's dead."

I heard no more. I drifted into oblivion. Was this also a dream?

The dogs, flattened close against the house door, moaned with pitiful insistence. An avalanche descended upon the house, shocking it to its creaking frames, and a sluicing rain, a terrific downpour of warm black water, swept through the valley, washing deep canyons in the piled-up snow. The room was heavy with damp. The warm, sweet odor of fresh rain lifted me from my bunk like a green stalk striking upward. I tottered on claylike feet, the dead nerves tingling with the shooting pains of a million needles. The impossible had happened— rain in the arctic night!

I stumbled toward the corner of the room. My numb fingers sought the shelf of the medicine chest; a bottle of whisky was stowed behind the bandages, an almost forgotten bottle. I lifted this and drank. For a while there was no taste, nothing but a bitter, nauseating trickle down my dry throat and along my spine. Then my heart seemed to awaken, my brain began to throb, I stumbled to the door and the wet dogs burst in from the storm, and great draughts of moist air filled the house. The skinny dogs jumped on me, howling incessantly. This, with the thunder of an internal tornado in my head, steadied me. The northern shores of Spitsbergen were being laved by the freak intrusion of a violent southern storm. Unholy clouds of fog rose upward from the melting ice, mists and humors upset the frozen equilibrium of the night.

I found matches and a can of oil; I lit the smudgy lamp and searched for hard tack and canned beef. My head was light as I reeled about and dragged half a sack of coal to the fire, lighting it with precious scraps of newspaper and kindling wood. I walked about and talked like a fool. The dogs were snapping at the half-frozen beef, panting and snuffing and nuzzling the cans. I kept away from the two silent forms lumped up under the blankets in their bunks. Then the half-empty bottle standing on the table looked at me accusingly. I pulled back the blanket from Paul's head and forced a thick tumbler of whisky between the reluctant teeth, spilling the stuff on the old man's matted beard. The sailor grunted. I went to Morten, forced his jaws apart and poured down a fiery shot. For an hour I fed them, drinking myself whenever the clutch of cold seized me. The room reeked of liquor; the fire roared; the dogs, giving off wet vapor, were clustered at the base of the red-hot stove, sometimes thumping their tails on the floor and barking in short, ecstatic grunts.

That night the wind veered into the north. The cold came back and the country lay beneath a frosting of translucent ice. We sat before a stew of reindeer meat, bending our heads, our eyes dimmed, our minds humble.

In a few weeks the twilight told of the returning sun. A month later three thin, yellow-faced men, with long, light-colored beards, stood on the summit of Smedburg's Mountain, gazing to the south at noon. The upper limb of the sun lifted for a moment above saw-toothed crags of ice. A purple, wind-sped cloud rode across the brilliant arc of day. Without comment we slid back down into the dimming valley of our experience and entered the small house filled with memories.

When our relief ship burst into view past the Cape de Geer in the early weeks of June, summer and daylight had long returned and the world of birds and song replaced the blackness of night.

The surgeon, in charge of commissariat, was seeking stowage for additional stores. He reported finding the remarkable skeleton of a female resting below the trap. The coffin boards, better than usual in those rude graves, lay in a heap below the bunk of Paul.

A Novice and His Dogteam

FRANK DUFRESNE

One of America's foremost nature writers and Director of the Alaska Game Commission, Frank Dufresne was a true spokesman of the Arctic. He was given his first field job by Dr. E. W. Nelson, Chief of the Department of Agriculture's Bureau of Biological Survey. One of Dufresne's frontier adventures involved learning how to handle a dogteam and sled—a combination of man and dog that was to make polar exploration possible.

EARLY in the winter of that year I suffered a misadventure which was never "fully reported" to Dr. Nelson, nor to anybody else. The incident occurred on my first solo dogteam trip into the wild Aghiapuk Valley. A veteran of dogsled travel along the lower Yukon River forty years earlier, and aware of the dangers of traveling alone, Dr. Nelson had instructed me to engage the services of an experienced musher for my winter surveys. But I had wanted to do it on my own, and this ambition was due in no small part to one of my Nome neighbors at that time, a Norwegian by the name of Roald Amundsen.

The Captain, as he was called around Nome, had covered thousands of miles by sledge, and had already become famous for his dash across the Antarctic to discover the South Pole. Now, by driving a team of sled dogs to the end of land at Point Barrow, then taking off across the Arctic Ocean, in a single-engined airplane, he hoped also to be first over the North Pole. During my practice sessions on the Nome tundra, I would often meet the distinguished, hawk-nosed Viking out hardening his muscles for the perilous journey ahead. Sometimes he would be poling along on his skis as graceful as a swooping bird. At other times he would be driving a string of especially selected, high-spirited Siberian Huskies. As they overtook and swept past my malemutes, Amundsen would raise a mitted hand in courteous salute. In his spotted reindeer parka with its white wolf ruff and his sealskin snowboots, the arrow-straight Captain—always handling his own team—cut a heroic figure. In that early winter, life held no higher ambition for me than to emulate this great man's skill on the snow.

"If Captain Amundsen can do it, so can I," I said grimly to myself, and soon came the day when with sled loaded for travel, I set out from Nome to prove it.

The winter mail trail through the Sawtooth Mountains led along the "pupmobile" railroad, now buried under the drifts. As the dogs scratched their way up the hard-packed slopes around Anvil Mountain I looked down on the frozen river pool where Uncle Charley had tried to teach me how to pan for "colors," and where he had bashed a salmon on the nose with the flat of his shovel. High up in a snowdrifted gulch, a streamer of blue smoke rose thinly out of the whiteness, and I knew that in a shack deep out of sight an old sourdough was hibernating like a bear in its den. The weather was clear, calm, and comfortably cold at thirty degrees below zero. Once over the first rise of mountains, the dogs trotted easily, heads in the air as they routed out occasional white arctic hares and foxes, unseen against the snow until they went racing away. When we stopped at a government shelter cabin that night, I was brimming with confidence at my ability to handle a dogteam, and when I cooked my first "trail" meal and then crawled into my warm sleeping bag, I felt as superior to ordinary mortals as Roald Amundsen looked. This dog-handling was a cinch!

The next day was even better. The trail to the Eskimo village of Mary's Igloo led down into a quiet river valley and through a forest of sheltering, tall willows. Hordes of ptarmigan from the surrounding, snow-heaped wastelands had assembled here for the winter. They hung like popcorn balls from every willow, the branches sagging with their combined weight as they nipped off the frozen tips on which they would be subsisting until next summer's sun again uncovered the bountiful tundra.

The vast valley was of peculiar interest to Dr. Nelson as one of the most important ptarmigan wintering areas on Seward Peninsula, and he had asked me to give him a rough count. The white grouse were subject, like the snowshoe hares, to

drastic rise and fall in populations, reaching unbelievable numbers only to die off with dramatic suddenness. For a year or
two, scarcely a bird could be seen, then slowly over the next
eight or ten years they would mount into the millions again.

This was one of their peaks of cyclic abundance. As they
clung to the bushes almost within touching distance, their
challenging cackles were almost deafening. In their enormous
numbers they had lost much of their normal awareness of man.
Only once or twice did a flock, directly in the trail, roar into
the air with thunderous clapping of wings. Trying to count
them was like trying to count snowflakes falling. My estimate
of those within near distances rose to ten thousand, then the
job got entirely out of hand before I reached Mary's Igloo. I
had no idea what kind of a guess to submit to Dr. Nelson,
and the village Eskimos weren't much help. They said that
whatever number I decided on, I'd better multiply it by all
my fingers and toes to take in that part of the valley bottom
I hadn't seen from the dog trail.

Mary's Igloo consumed hundreds of ptarmigan during such
mountains of plenty. Mostly, they gathered the birds without
firing a shot, by the aid of snares strung in the willows. Though
they were sharing the harvest with extraordinary numbers of
foxes, weasels, hawks, and owls, the toll of all predators could
not keep pace with the booming populations when the native
grouse were on the upswing of their cycle. It took something
more drastic in the way of Nature's control to prevent the
ptarmigan from devouring their willow-bud food supply. Every
nine or ten years a deadly epizootic disease scythed down the
millions until scarcely a grouse could be found on the tundra,
and then they would have to start another build-up. The
Mary's Igloo Eskimos told me they feared such a big die-off
would occur this very winter.

In a sing-songy mixture of Innuit and English, they also
told me of danger on the uninhabited stretch between their
village and the trading post at Teller on the Bering Sea: something about tides and winds on the Imuruk Basin, a saltwater
estuary at the mouth of the Aghiapuk River. I was so eager
to tackle new adventures, I didn't wait to hear more details.
The dogteam trail led out onto the frozen river, slick with
windswept ice, and I had to keep pressing down on the foot

brake to prevent the sled overrunning the loping dogs. I was fifteen miles downriver when the sled runners under my feet suddenly broke through the ice and water started spurting up. Instantly, I gee'd the lead dog toward the nearest shore and stepped off the sled to investigate this puzzling phenomena of thin ice at thirty degrees below zero.

It wasn't as bad as I feared—at least, I thought it wasn't. There was less than an inch of water below the top sheet of ice, and beneath the slight overflow was another layer which appeared to be several feet thick. I swung a camp ax to test its strength. "Heavy enough to bear a horse," I concluded, as I swung my dogteam back onto the river and went racing merrily downstream with twin roostertails squirting into the air behind me.

I was thoroughly enjoying the ride when calamity struck. The top skim of ice began undulating ahead of the dogs, the sled runners began settling, and water rose up around my mukluks as I stood on the runners at the rear of the sled, hanging onto the handlebars. There was a sloping bank some distance ahead and I swung the team toward it, cracking a blacksnake whip in the air to urge the dogs into a full-speed race for dry land. We didn't make it. Suddenly, the thinning ice collapsed under the entire team. I rode the sled runners down to the second layer of ice, strangling for breath in water up to my armpits. The dogs, burdened by their harnesses and the heavy load behind them, were paddling madly to hold their noses above the icy caldron, and it seemed to me they would all perish within seconds. My own chances looked no better. The water was paralyzingly cold, and I had been told that no human could stand more than ten minutes' exposure to it and live. Even if I could reach shore, my sodden fur garments would become an icy straitjacket.

I have learned that in such sudden peril there is no awareness of reasoning; only a blind instinct to stay alive as long as possible. This is what saved me now; this and a higher power. I floundered to the lead dog, grasped him by the collar and towed the struggling huskies to a low place on the shoreline where they could scramble out of the churning ice water. I could not get them to pull the waterlogged sled clear, but with an inherent sense of what to do for themselves, they rolled in the snow to blot the water out of their thick fur. Soon, they were all on their feet, shaking off the frozen clods, apparently none the worse for their frigid ducking. While I was still able to move, I wanted to help them more by unsnapping the towline to the sled. My hands were too stiff; my fingers already turning white and without feeling. I had to desert them. When the situation became desperate enough, they could always chew themselves free from the rawhide harnesses. They had a chance, which seemed to be more than I had.

Realizing that whatever action I took would have to be fast, I started to climb a sort of path, or game trail, leading from the river bank up into a copse of willows from which I could get a view of the surrounding wilderness. As I left them behind, the sled dogs lunged wildly into their collars. Their yowling uproars filled the air, and suddenly, unbelievably, there came an answering howl!

There was no way of knowing whether it came from a wild timber wolf, a tame sled dog, or was but an echo of my imagination. It meant only that there might still be a slim chance to live. If I could reach the bank top and look into the willows! My mukluk soles, frozen hard as glass, skidded out from under me on the steep incline. I fell with a bone-jarring thump and for a moment lay half conscious while my furs froze fast to the snow. I was aware of no pain, no discomfort, only a creeping weariness. Was this what it was like to freeze to death?

The leaden feeling passed, followed by a panic of energy. Suddenly, I was struggling with every ounce of strength, ripping myself free of the snow. On hands and knees I clawed my way up to the top of the river bank, and there I came face to face with the most beautiful sled dog I have ever seen. It was a battle-scarred malemute, and it appeared to be blind with age. Its ragged coat was rimed with frost, and as it sensed my presence, its curled bushy tail wagged a greeting; its gray muzzle pointed straight up into the sky as it poured out another long, tremulous howl.

The old dog was chained to a stake alongside a low, sod-covered igloo from the top of which curled a thin wisp of smoke. With a surge of hope, I finished crawling to the entrance to this underground hovel, and tumbled down through a skin-hung doorway onto a twig-covered floor to look up into a face that appeared to be all red whiskers and bugged-out blue eyes. For a long moment, the shock of what he had seen was too much for the surprised occupant to grasp. He hadn't seen another human for months. Now here was a total stranger dropped at his feet. Eyes fastened on me in utter disbelief, he continued to fry a skilletful of flapjacks, turning them with care. Then as the full meaning of my unannounced visit slowly became clear to him, Redbeard flipped the flapjacks onto a tin plate and shoved them toward the back of the sheet-iron camp stove. Not until then did he speak. His voice was oddly falsetto, I remember, loud like that of man with defective hearing.

"Where's ya' dogs?"

I croaked a reply. The trapper didn't hear me and had to cup an ear close while I shouted at the top of my lungs. Stone deaf, I thought, but Redbeard had heard enough to send him charging up out of the underground hovel. When he had gone, I struggled to my feet and stoked the sheet-iron camp stove with dry willows until it glowed cherry-red, then stripped down to my bare hide. Teeth chattering uncontrollably, I picked up the sodden clothes and hung them on pegs around the low wall of the igloo, wherever there was room between the cased peltries of foxes and mink and ermine. As the heat of the stove warmed me and started the blood circulating again, I began to experience the torture of frostbitten toes and fingers, ears, nose, and cheeks coming to life. I knew then that another few minutes of exposure in the thirty-degree-below-zero winds would have maimed me for life; that in an hour I would have been frozen stiff as a board—all for a mistake that only a dumb cheechako would make!

How the lone trapper accomplished it, I'll never know, but after a while there was a clamor of sled dogs outside the igloo. When Redbeard came pushing down into the dark hole he was carrying a canvas sack over his shoulder. Not only had he managed to drag the sled out of the river; he had also credited me with enough sense to have a change of clothing in a waterproof duffle bag. Without a word, he went outside again to unharness the dogs and stake them out among the willows with a dried salmon ration to chew on, after which they would dig into the snow and curl themselves up to sleep. My reindeer sleeping bag, soaked and frozen into a block of ice, was dragged in and stretched behind the stove. Then, Redbeard handed me a tin plate and calmly resumed his flapjack cooking.

His name, he yelled, was Dunc MacBain. He was the only man on the river, and who the hell was I to be pulling such a fool stunt? I told him humbly, and slowly we began shouting ourselves into a friendship which was to endure through all my years in Alaska. Trapper MacBain insisted that I share his igloo until every item of clothing and equipment was thoroughly dried out, and while we hunkered shoulder to shoulder in the confines of his "beaver house" home, he explained why I had broken through the ice. There had been a gale from Bering Sea, washing salt water across the anchored ice and pushing a wind-tide far up the Aghiapuk River. When I came along, the first spurts of water around my sled runners should have been enough to warn me that the ice would become weaker, the overflow deeper, as I traveled downstream to meet the sea.

Redbearded Dunc didn't let me make the same mistake twice. When he figured it was safe for me to travel again, he snowshoed a trail through the willows upstream to a narrow place, led the way over to the other side by swinging his ax to test the new ice, and put me on the overland dogteam trail to Teller on the coast. From this trading post the winter mail route led eighty-five miles south to Nome, and there shouldn't have been any further trouble or delays. But when I came to the government shelter cabin at Cape Douglas, I ran into what I thought was a sort of polar cyclone, a seething wall of horizontally driven snow which seemed to rip the breath from my lungs, and into which I could not see the length of the dogsled. Frostbitten and unsure of myself, I retreated to the empty shelter cabin to wait for better weather.

I was still there the next evening when two dogteams from Nome bucked through howling gale, and a pair of fur-clad figures stomped the snow off their fur mukluks and pushed into the cabin. One was Ralph Lomen, a prominent merchant and reindeer owner in Nome. The other was his good friend

Roald Amundsen. They were on their way to Teller—where several years later Captain Amundsen was to land down in the dirigible *Norge* after flying nonstop across the North Pole from Spitzbergen, Norway, with the Italian Commander Nobile.

Just before sacktime, the Captain stood beside his sleeping bag doing his daily calisthenics; stripped down to his flaming red long johns, acquiline nose ruddy of hue, resplendent as a scarlet ibis flapping wings at the edge of its nest. After he had finished his gymnastics, I asked him about the blinding gale through which he and Lomen had come that day. He peered at me curiously. It was nothing, he replied after a while, just a narrow snow belt blowing down out of Tishou Pass, as it did practically every day all winter. Only half a mile wide, and beyond it clear as a bell all the way into Nome.

The great explorer added that what a dogmusher really had to watch out for along the coast were the overflowed river mouths. His wise blue eyes had been studying my face, all purpled and bruised like an overripe plum from freezing, and now I saw a twinkle of crows' feet forming at their corners. Plainly, he wanted to know what had happened to me. But I wasn't about to do any explaining, neither to Captain Amundsen nor to Dr. Nelson.

THE LURE OF THE NORTH
POLE

circa 320 B.C.:	The Greek, Pytheas, is rumored to have been the first arctic explorer. He was supposed to have discovered a place called Ultima Thule. The nights of Thule, like the arctic nights, lasted only a couple of hours. Ultima Thule was Norway or perhaps Iceland or Greenland.
circa A.D. 870:	St. Brendan, a famous Irish monk, explorer and superb storyteller may have entered the Arctic on roughly this date. It is clear that in the ninth century Irish monks did establish themselves in Iceland.
A.D. 900:	The Norse began their exploration of northern islands, Greenland being one of them. For nearly 500 years the Norse had some connections with Greenland.
1492:	We do not think of Columbus' first voyage as one of the important dates of arctic exploration but the main purpose of his trip was to find a new route from Europe to the Orient —a search for what was to become the Northwest Passage that would eventually open up all of the arctic area.
1577:	Sir Martin Frobisher was sent by Queen Elizabeth to seek the Northwest Passage. He discovered Frobisher Bay.
1587:	The Englishman, John Davis, discovered Davis Strait.

1594–96:   Willem Barents and Jacob van Heemskerck, of Holland, sought the Northwest Passage. On his first voyage in 1594, Barents penetrated the Kara Sea. In 1596, this crew was the first to winter in the Arctic. Barents died of exposure the following spring at the age of thirty-seven.

1607–10:   Henry Hudson, an Englishman, first sailed to Greenland's east coast, then north to Spitzbergen. On a later voyage, 1610, his crew mutinied and he was set adrift in the ice.

1616:   William Baffin and Robert Bylot of England discovered Baffin Bay.

1728:   Vitus Bering, a Danish captain in the service of Russia, made the greatest explorations of the eighteenth century. Not only did he prove Asia and America were separated by Bering Strait, but he traveled 500 miles across Russia, discovered arctic islands and, on his last voyage, established Russia's claim to Alaska.

1771:   Samuel Hearne, English explorer of the Hudson's Bay Company, went overland in the Arctic from Prince of Wales Fort in Churchill on Hudson's Bay to the Coppermine River.

1778:   James Cook, British explorer, sailed through Bering Strait to Icy Cape, Alaska and North Cape, Siberia.

1789:   Sir Alexander Mackenzie, English explorer in the employ of the Northwest Company, went to the mouth of the Mackenzie River.

1806:   William Scoresby of England went north of Spitzbergen.

1818:   Sir John Ross, the British arctic explorer, not only led a continued search for the Northwest Passage but also conducted one of the first scientific ventures in the Arctic. His orders read: "Although the first and most important object of this voyage is to discover a passage from Davis Strait along the northern coast of America and through Bering Strait, in specific it is hoped at the same time that it may likewise be the means of improving the geography and hydrography of the arctic regions of which so little is hitherto known and contribute to the advance of science and natural knowledge."

His expedition was to study, too, the evaluation and estimation of the magnetic needle; to take temperature readings of both air and sea; to study the strength of the tides and the velocity of currents; to take samplings of the ocean bottom. On August 20, Ross discovered the so-called Crocker Mountains, which turned out to be a mirage.

1819: Sir William Parry, the British arctic explorer, almost penetrated the Northwest Passage.

1819–45: In the same year, Sir John Franklin of England began his arctic explorations. Franklin's most famous voyage was his final one in 1845 when his two ships, *Erebus* and *Terror*, were last seen entering Lancaster Sound. Attempts to locate his lost party were many.

1820–23: The Russian, Baron Ferdinand von Wrangel, completed the survey of the Siberian arctic coast.

1850–57: The explorations of Elisha Kent Kane, one of the first American pioneers of the arctic region, and the first to popularize the Arctic. He was one of the first explorers to study the Eskimos and follow their eating habits and their techniques of hunting.

1879:	Lieutenant Commander George Washington DeLong, American explorer, was fitted out in the steamer, *Jeannette,* to explore the Arctic, a trip sponsored by James Gordon Bennett, Jr., the New York newspaperman. It was a complete disaster; the ship was trapped by ice and crushed. DeLong and eleven others died of starvation; twelve crew members were rescued.
1882:	Lieutenant A. W. Greely, of the American Signal Service, was sent to the Arctic to establish a geographic station. His ship, too, was crushed in the ice.
1887–88:	Fridtjof Nansen, of Norway, crossed the Greenland icecap.
1891–92:	Robert E. Peary of America explored the coast of Greenland.
1893:	Peary tried for the North Pole.
1893–96:	Nansen and his ship, the *Fram,* drifted from New Siberian Islands to Spitzbergen. He also tried to reach the Pole. He failed but did succeed in reaching Franz Josef Land.
1896:	Salomon A. Andrée, of Sweden, tried to reach the North Pole by balloon. He failed.
1900:	Peary reached the northern limit of Greenland.
1903–06:	The Norwegian explorer, Roald Amundsen, first sailed the Northwest Passage.
April 6, 1909:	Peary reached the Pole, 90° North. In his party at the Pole were a Negro, Matthew Henson, and four Eskimos.
1914:	Donald McMillan of America tried to find Crocker Land.
1915–17:	The Canadian explorer, Vilhjalmur Stefansson, discovered many Arctic islands including Borden, Brock, and Lougheed islands.

1918–20: Roald Amundsen sailed through the Northeast Passage.

1925: Amundsen and Lincoln Ellsworth, of the United States, attempted to fly to the North Pole.

1926: Richard E. Byrd and Floyd Bennett of America flew over the North Pole on May 9.

1926: Amundsen, Ellsworth and Umberto Nobile, of Italy, flew from Spitzbergen over the North Pole in the dirigible, *Norge*.

1928: Nobile crossed the North Pole in the airship, *Italia*, May 24. He crashed the following day and Roald Amundsen was lost while trying to rescue him by plane.

1958: August 3, the *Nautilus*, under Commander William R. Anderson, was the first ship to cross the North Pole beneath the Arctic Icecap.

1959: In March, the ship, *Skate*, broke through the North Pole. This was the first time any ship had been on the surface at 90° North.

To date: Many scientific expeditions studying archeological remains, navigation, weather, water chemistry, geomagnetism, ice formation and prediction, oceanography, marine biology, and communications.

Arctic Mutiny

ABECUK PRICKETT

Henry Hudson was one of the major Arctic explorers—and one of the first to die there abandoned by his own men. This is the story of the mutiny that occurred on Hudson's ship Discovery *in 1610. The trouble started off Iceland when Hudson took the side of Henry Greene, a ne'er-do-well protégé of his in an argument with the ship's surgeon. A great explorer, Hudson was a poor judge of men, as were many explorers of the North and South Polar regions. He overestimated how far he could push his men, and he planned to continue his explorations long after his crew had decided to sail for home.*

The following story by Abecuk Prickett, an observer for the organizers of the expedition, is the only surviving record of the mutiny in which Hudson; his young son, John; Thomas Woodhouse, a mathematician; Philip Staffe, the ship's carpenter; and a group of sick sailors were set adrift to die in the ice. They had no provisions of any kind, but were given one musket and one iron kettle. They were never seen again.

WE BEGAN our voyage for the Northwest Passage, the seventeenth of April, 1610. Thwart of Shepey, our master sent Master Colbert back to the owners with his letter. The next day we weighed from hence and stood for Harwich, and came thither the eighth and twentieth of April. From Harwich we set sail the first of May, along the coast to the north, till we came to the isles of Orkney, from thence to the isles of Faro, and from thence to Iceland: on which we fell in a fog, hearing the rut of the sea ashore, but saw not the land whereupon our master came to an anchor. Here we were embayed in the southeast part of the land. We weighed and stood along the coast, on the west side toward the north: but one day being calm, we fell a-fishing, and caught good store of fish, as cod, and ling and butt, with some other sorts that we knew not. The next day we had a good gale of wind at southwest, and raised the isles of Westmonie, where the King of Denmark hath a fortress, by which we passed to raise the Snow Hill foot, a mountain so called on the northwest part of the land. But in our course we saw that famous hill, Mount Hecla, which cast out much fire, a sign of foul weather to come in short time. We left Iceland astern of us, and met a main of ice, which did hang on the north part of Iceland, and stretched down to the west, which when our master saw, he stood back for Iceland to find a harbor, which we did on the northwest part, called Derefer, where we killed a good store of fowl. From hence we put to sea again, but neither wind nor weather serving, our master stood back for this harbor again, but could not reach it, but fell with another to the south of that, called by our Englishmen Lousie Bay: where on the shore we found a hot bath, and here all our Englishmen bathed themselves: the water was so hot that it would scald a fowl.

From hence, the first of June, we put to sea for Greenland, but to the west we saw land as we thought, for which we bear the best part of a day, but it proved but a foggy bank. So we gave it over and made for Froneland, which we raised the fourth of June. Upon the coast thereof hung a good store of ice, so that our master could not attain to the shore by any means. The land in this part is very mountainous, and full of round hills, like to sugar loaves, covered with snow. We turned the land on the south side, as near as the ice would suffer us. Our course for the most part was between the west and northwest, till we raised the Desolations, which is a great island in the west part of Greenland. On this coast we saw store of whales, and at one time three of them came close by us, so as we could hardly shun them: then two passing very near, and the third going under our ship, we received no harm by them, praised be God.

From the Desolations, our master made his way northwest, the wind being against him, who else would have gone more to the north: but in this course we saw the first great island or mountain of ice, whereof after we saw store. About the latter end of June, we raised land to the north of us, which our master took to be that island which Master Davis setteth down in his chart. On the west side of his strait, our master would have gone to the north of it, but the wind would not suffer him: so we fell to the south of it, into a great rippling or overfall of current, the which setteth to the west. Into the current we went, and made our way to the north of the west, till we met with ice which hung on this island. Wherefore our master casting about, cleared himself of this ice, and stood to the south, and then to the west, through store of floating ice, and upon the ice store of seals. We gained a clear sea, and continued our course till we met ice; first, with great islands, and then with store of the smaller sort. Between them we made our course northwest, till we met with ice again. But, in this our going between the ice, we saw one of the great islands of ice overturn, which was a good warning to us, not to come near them nor within their reach. Into the ice we put ahead, as between two lands. The next day we had a storm, and the wind brought the ice so fast upon us, that in the end we were driven to put her into the chiefest of the ice, and there to let her lie. Some of our men this day fell sick, I will not say it was for fear, although I saw small sign of other grief.

The storm ceasing, we stood out of the ice, where we saw any clear sea to go to: which was sometime more and sometime less. Our course was as the ice did lie, sometime to the north, then to the northwest, and then to the west and to the southwest: but still enclosed with ice. Which when our master saw, he made his course to the south, thinking to clear himself of the ice that way: but the more he strove the worse he was, and the more enclosed, till we could go no further. Here our master was in despair, and (as he told me after) he thought he should never have got out of this ice, but there have perished. Therefore he brought forth his card, and showed all the company, that he was entered above a hundred leagues further than ever any English was: and left it to their choice, whether they would proceed any further; yea, or nay. Whereupon some were of one mind and some of another, some wishing themselves at home and some not caring where, so they were out of the ice: but there were some who then spake words, which were remembered a great while after.

There was one who told the master, that if he had an hundred pounds, he would give four-score and ten to be at home: but the carpenter made answer, that if he had a hun-

dred, he would not give ten upon such condition, but would think
it to be as good money as ever he had any, and to bring it
as well home, by the leave of God. After many words to no
purpose, to work we must on all hands, to get ourselves out
and to clear our ship. After much labor and time spent, we
gained room to turn our ship in, and so by little and little,
to get clear in the sea a league or so off, our course being
north and northwest.

In the end we raised land to the southwest, high land
and covered with snow. Our master named this land, Desire
Provokes. Lying here, we heard the noise of a great overfall
of a tide, that came out of the land: for now we might see
well that we had been embayed before, and time had made
us know, being so well acquainted with the ice, that when
night, or fog or foul weather took us, we would seek out the
broadest island of ice and there come to anchor, and run,
and sport, and fill water that stood on the ice in ponds, both
sweet and good. But after we had brought this land to bear
south of us, we had the tide and the current to open the ice,
as being carried first one way and then another: but in bays
they lay as in a pond without moving. In this bay where we
were thus troubled with ice, we saw many of those mountains
of ice aground, in six or seven score fathom water. In this our
course we saw a bear upon a piece of ice by itself, to the
which our men gave chase with their boat; but before they
came nigh her, the tide had carried the ice and the bear on it,
and joined it with the other ice; so they lost their labor, and
came aboard again.

We continued our course to the northwest, and raised land
to the north of our course, toward which we made, and coming
nigh it, there hung on the easternmost point many islands of
floating ice, and a bear on one of them, which from one to
another came toward us, till she was ready to come aboard.
But when she saw us look at her, she cast her head between
her hind legs, and then dived under the ice: and so from one
piece to another, till she was out of our reach. We stood
along by the land on the south side ahead of us; we met with
ice that hung on a point of land that lay to the south, more
than this that we came up by: which when our master saw,
he stood in for the shore. At the west end of this island (for

so it is) we found a harbor, and came in (at a full sea) over a rock, which had two fathoms and a half on it, and was so much bare at a low water. But by the great mercy of God, we came to an anchor clear of it: and close by it our master named them the Isles of God's Mercy. This is a harbor for need, but there must be care had how they came in. Here our master sent me, and others with me, to discover to the north and northwest: and in going from one place to another, we sprung a covey of partridges which were young: at the which Thomas Woodhouse shot, but killed only the old one.

This island is a most barren place, having nothing on it but plashes of water and riven rocks, as it were subject to earthquakes. To the north there is a great bay or sea (for I know not what it will prove), where I saw a great island of ice aground, between the two lands which with the spring tide was set afloat, and carried into this bay or sea to the northwestward, but came not back again, nor within sight. Here we took in some drift wood that we found ashore.

From hence we stood to the southwest, to double the land to the west of us, through much floating ice: in the end we found a clear sea, and continued therein, till we raised land to the northwest. Then our master made his course more to the south than before, but it was not long ere we met with ice which lay ahead of us. Our master would have doubled this ice to the north, but could not; and in the end put into it down to the southwest through much ice, and then to the south, where we embayed again. Our master strove to get the shore, but could not, for the great store of ice that was on the coast. From out of this bay we stood to the north, and were soon out of the ice: then down to the southwest, and so to the west, where we were enclosed (to our sight) with land and ice. For we had land from the south to the northwest on one side, and from the east to the west on the other; but the land that was to the north of us and lay by east and west was but an island. On we went till we could go no further for ice: so we made our ship fast to the ice which the tide brought upon us, but when the ebb came, the ice did open, and made way; so as in seven or eight hours we were clear from the ice, till we came to weather; but only some of the great islands, that were carried along with us to the northwest.

Having a clear sea, our master stood to the west along by the south shore, and raised three capes or headlands lying one above another. The middlemost is an island, and maketh a bay or harbor, which (I take) will prove a good one. Our master named them Prince Henry's Cape or Foreland. When we had laid this we raised another, which was the extreme point of the land looking toward the north: upon it are two hills, but one (above the rest) like a haycock, which our master named King James's Cape. To the north of this lie certain islands, which our master named Queen Anne's Cape or Foreland. We followed the north shore still. Beyond the King's Cape there is a sound or bay, that hath some islands in it: and this is not to be forgotten, if need be. Beyond this lieth some broken land, close to the main, but what it is I know not, because we passed by it in the night.

We stood to the north to double this land, and after to the west again, till we fell with land that stretched from the main, like a shower from the south to the north, and from the north to the west, and then down to the south again. Being short of this land a storm took us, the wind at west: we stood to the north and raised land, which when our master saw he stood to the south again, for he was loath at any time that we should see the north shore. The storm continuing, and coming to the south shore again, our master found himself shot to the west a great way, which made him muse, considering his leeward way. To the southwest of this land, on the main, there is a high hill, which our master named Mount Charles. To the north and beyond this lieth an island, that to the east had a fair head, and beyond it to the west other broken land, which maketh a bay within, and a good road may be found there for ships. Our master named the first Cape Salisbury.

When we had left this to the northeast, we fell into a rippling or overfall of a current, which at the first we took to be a shoal: but the lead being cast, we had no ground. On we passed, still in sight of the south shore, till we raised land lying from the main some two leagues. Our master took this to be a part of the main of the north land; but it is an island, the north side stretching out to the west more than the south. This island had a fair head to the east, and very high

land, which our master named Deepes Cape: and the land
on the south side, now falling away to the south, makes another cape or headland, which our master named Worsenhams Cape. When we were nigh the North or Island Cape,
our master sent the boat ashore, with myself (who had the
charge) and the carpenter, and divers others, to discover to
the west and northwest, and to the southwest; but we had
further to it than we thought, for the land is very high, and
we were overtaken with a storm of rain, thunder, and lightning.
But to it we came on the northeast side, and up we got from
one rock to another, till we came to the highest of that part.
Here we found some plain ground, and saw some deer; at first,
four or five, and after, a dozen or sixteen in a herd, but could
not come nigh them with a musket shot.

Thus, going from one place to another, we saw to the west
of us a high hill above all the rest, it being nigh us; but it
proved further off when we made account; for, when we
came to it, the land was steep on the east and northeast parts
that we could not get unto it. To the southwest we saw that
we might, and toward that part we went along by the side
of a great pond of water, which lieth under the east side of
this hill: and there runneth out of it a stream of water as
much as would drive an overshot mill; which falleth down
from an high cliff into the sea on the south side. In this place
great store of fowl breed, and there is the best grass that I
had seen since we came from England. Here we found sorrel,
and that which we call scurvy grass in great abundance.
Passing along we saw some round hill of stone, like to grass
cocks, which at the first I took to be the work of some
Christian. We passed by them, till we came to the south side
of the hill; we went into them and there found more; and
being nigh them I turned off the uppermost stone, and found
them hollow within and full of fowls hanged by their necks.
Then Greene and I went to fetch the boat to the south side,
while Robert Bylot and he got down a valley to the sea side,
where we took them in.

Our master (in this time) came in between the two lands,
and shot off some pieces to call us aboard; for it was a fog.
We came aboard and told him what we had seen, and persuaded him to stay a day or two in this place, telling him

1. An Eskimo mother and child.

2. Eskimos drying fish.

3. An Eskimo making a sled with frozen fish wrapped in seal-skin for the runners and caribou antler pieces tied on with sealskin lines as cross slats.

4. A herd of caribou.

5. Stefansson proves his prowess as a hunter.

6. The arctic tundra.

7. The arctic ptarmigan in spring.

8. Drawings of wooly mammoths were made by stone age man on the walls of caves.

9. A large walrus looks at the land of ghosts.

10. This is the way Frank Dufresne learned to travel.

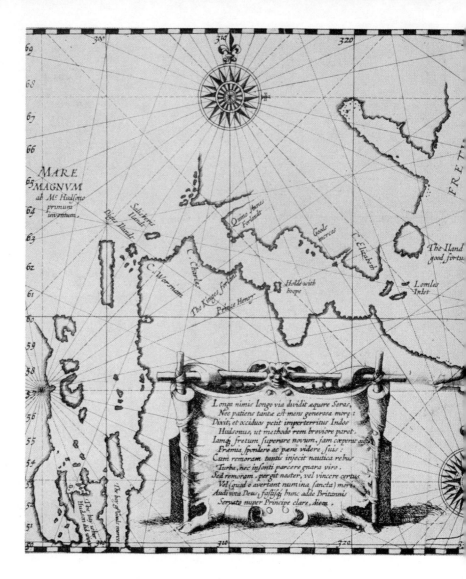

MARE
MAGNVM
ab M.ʳ Hudſono
primum
inventum.

Saluberis
Iland.

Digſer Iland.

C. Charles

C. Worſnam

Qune Anes
Forlande

Good
merices

C. Elizabeth

FRETI

The Iland
good fortu.

Lomles
Inlet

The Kinges fortant
Holde with
hoope
Prince Henry

The bay where
Hudſon did wint.

The bay of Gods mercie

Longa nimis longo via dividit æquore Seras,
Nec patiens tantæ eſt mens generoſa moræ :
Dixit, et occiduos petit imperterritus Indos
Hudſonus, ut methodo rem breviore paret.
Iamq́; fretum ſuperare novum, iam cœpirit auſtis
Prœmia ſpondere ac pæne videre ſuas :
Cum remoram tantis injecit nautica rebus
Turba, nec inſonti parcere gnara viro.
Sed remoram, pergit naſter, vel vincere certus
Vel (quod e avertant numina ſancta) mori.
Audi vota Deus, faſtiſq́; hunc adde Britannis
Servato nuper Principe clare, diem.

11. A chart of Henry Hudson's discovery of the Northwest Passage by Hessel Gerritz.

12. A view of the Arctic Sea from the mouth of the Copper Mine River, midnight, July 1821. From Sir John Franklin's *Narrative of a Journey to the Shores of the Polar Sea, 1819-1822.*

13. Some of Sir John Franklin's officers.
Top left to right: Mr. Couch (mate), Lieutenant Fairholme, C. H. Osmer (purser), Mr. Des Voeux (mate).
Bottom: Captain Crozier, Lieutenant Graham Gore, Commander Fitzjames, J. Stanley (surgeon).

what refreshing might there be had: but by no means would
he stay, who was not pleased with the motion. So we left the
fowl, and lost our way down to the southwest, before they
went in sight of the land which now bears to the east from
us, being the same mainland that we had all this while followed. Now we had lost the sight of it, because it falleth
away to the east after some five and twenty or thirty leagues.
Now we came to the shallow water, wherewith we were not
acquainted since we came from Iceland; now we came into
broken ground and rocks, through which we passed down to
the south. In this our course we had a storm, and the water
did shoal apace. Our master came to an anchor in fifteen
fathoms water.

We weighed and stood to the southeast, because the land
in this place did lie so. When we came to the point of the
west land (for we now had land on both sides of us), we
came to an anchor. Our master sent the boat ashore to see
what that land was, and whether there were any way through.
They soon returned, and showed that beyond the point of
land to the south there was a large sea. This land on the west
side was a very narrow point. We weighed from hence and
stood in for this sea between the two lands, which (in this
place) is not two leagues broad down to the south, for a great
way in sight of the east shore. In the end we lost sight thereof,
and saw it not till we came to the bottom of the bay, into
six or seven fathoms water. Hence we stood up to the north
by the west shore, till we came to an island, where we took
in water and ballast.

From hence we passed toward the north: but some two or
three days after (reasoning concerning our coming into this
bay and going out) our master took occasion to revive old
matters, and to displace Robert Juet from being his mate,
and the boatswain from his place, for the words spoken in
the first great bay of ice. Then he made Robert Bylot his
mate, and William Wilson our boatswain. Up to the north we
stood till we raised land, then down to the south, and up to
the north, then down again to the south, and on Michaelmas
Day came in and went out of certain lands, which our master
sets down by the name of Michaelmas Bay, because we came
in and went out on that day. From hence we stood to the

north, and came into shoal water; and the weather being
thick and foul, we came to an anchor in seven or eight
fathoms water, and there lay eight days, in all which time
we could not get one hour to weigh our anchor. But the eighth
day, the wind beginning to cease, our master would have the
anchor up, against the mind of all who knew what belonged
thereunto. Well, to it we went, and when we had brought it to
a peak, a sea took her, and cast us all off from the capstan
and hurt divers of us. Here we lost our anchor, and if the
carpenter had not been [quick?], we had lost our cable too;
but he (fearing such a matter) was ready with his ax, and
so cut it.

From hence we stood to the south and to the southwest,
through a clear sea of divers sounding, and came to a sea of
two colors, one black and the other white, sixteen or seventeen
fathom water, between which we went four or five leagues.
But the night coming, we took in our topsails, and stood
afore the wind with our mainsail and foresail, and came into
five or six fathoms, and saw no land, for it was dark. Then
we stood to the east and had deep water again, then to the
south and southwest, and so came to our westermost bay of
all, and came to an anchor nearest to the north shore. Out
went our boat to the land that was next us; when they came
near it our boat could not float to the shore it was so shallow:
yet ashore they got. Here our men saw the footing of a man
and a duck in the snowy rocks, and wood good store, whereof
they took some and returned aboard. Being at anchor in this
place, we saw a ledge of rocks to the south of us, some league
of length; it lay north and south, covered at a full sea; for a
strong tide setteth in here. At midnight we weighed, and
stood to go out as we came in; and had not gone long, but
the carpenter came and told the master, that if he kept that
course he would be upon the rocks: the master conceived
that he was past them, when presently we ran on them, and
there stuck fast twelve hours; but (by the mercy of God) we
got off unhurt, though not unscarred.

We stood up to the east and raised three hills, lying north
and south: we went to the furthermost, and left it to the north
of us, and so into a bay, where we came to an anchor. Here
our master sent out our boat, with myself and the carpenter

to seek a place to winter in; and it was time, for the nights were long and cold, and the earth covered with snow. Having spent three months in a labyrinth without end, being now the last of October, we went down to the east, to the bottom of the bay; but returned without speeding of that we went for. The next day we went to the south and the southwest, and found a place, whereunto we brought our ship, and sailed her aground: and this was the first of November. By the tenth thereof we were frozen in: but now we were in, it behoved us to have care of what we had; for that we were sure of, but what we had not was uncertain.

We were victualed for six months in good proportion, and of that which was good: if our master would have had more, he might have had it at home and in other places. Here we were now, and therefore it behooved us so to spend, that we might have (when time came) to bring us to the capes where the fowl bred, for that was all the hope we had to bring us home. Wherefore our master took order, first for the spending of that we had, and then to increase it, by propounding a reward to them that killed either beast, fish, or fowl, as in his journal you have seen. About the middle of this month of November, died John Williams, our gunner: God pardon the master's uncharitable dealing with this man. Now for that I am come to speak of him, out of whose ashes (as it were) that unhappy deed grew which brought a scandal upon all that are returned home, and upon the action itself, the multitude (like the dog) running after the stone, but not at the caster: therefore, not to wrong the living nor slander the dead, I will (by the leave of God) deliver the truth as near as I can.

You shall understand that our master kept (in his house at London) a young man, named Henry Greene, born in Kent, of worshipful parents, but by his lewd life and conversation he had lost the good will of all his friends, and had spent all that he had. This man our master would have to sea with him, because he could write well: our master gave him meat, and drink, and lodging, and by means of one Master Venson, with much ado got four pounds of his mother to buy him clothes, wherewith Master Venson would not trust him, but saw it laid out himself. This Henry Greene was not set down in the owner's book, nor any wages made for him. He came first aboard at Gravesend, and at Harwich should have gone into the field, with one Wilkinson. At Iceland, the surgeon and he fell out in Dutch, and he beat him ashore in English, which set all the company in a rage; so that we had much ado to get the surgeon aboard. I told the master of it, but he bade me let it alone, for (said he) the surgeon had a tongue that would wrong the best friend he had. But Robert Juet (the master's mate) would needs burn his finger in the embers, and told the carpenter a long tale (when he was drunk) that our master had brought in Greene to crack his credit that should displease him: which words came to the master's ears, who when he understood it, would have gone back to Iceland, when he was forty leagues from thence, to have sent home his mate Robert Juet in a fisherman. But, being otherwise persuaded, all was well. So Henry Greene stood upright, and very inward with the master, and was a serviceable man every way for manhood: but for religion, he would say, he was clean paper whereon he might write what he would. Now, when our gunner was dead, and (as the order is in such cases) if the company stand in need of anything that belonged to the man deceased, then is it brought to the main mast, and there sold to them that will give most for the same. This gunner had a gray cloth gown, which Greene prayed the master to friend him so much as to let him have it, paying for it as another would give: the master sayeth he should, and thereupon he answered some, that sought to have it, that Greene should have it, and none else, and so it rested.

Now out of season and time the master calleth the carpenter to go in hand with a house on shore, which at the beginning our master would not hear, when it might have been done. The carpenter told him, that the snow and frost were such, as he neither could nor would go in hand with such work. Which when our master heard, he ferreted him out of his cabin to strike him, calling him by many foul names, and threatening to hang him. The carpenter told him that he knew what belonged to his place better than himself, and that he was no house carpenter. So this passed, and the house was (after) made with much labor, but to no end. The next day after the master and the carpenter fell out, the carpenter took his piece and Henry Greene with him, for it was an order that none should go out alone, but one with a piece, and another with a pike. This did move the master so much the more against Henry Greene, that Robert Bylot his mate must have the gown, and had it delivered unto him; which when Henry Greene saw, he challenged the master's promise: but the master did so rail on Greene, with so many words of disgrace, telling him that all his friends would not trust him with twenty shillings, and therefore why should he. As for wages he had none, nor none should have, if he did not please him well. Yet the master had promised him to make his wages as good as any man's in the ship; and to have him one of the prince's guard when we came home. But you shall see how the devil out of this so wrought with Greene, that he did the master what mischief he could in seeking to discredit him, and to thrust him and many other honest men out of the ship in the end. To speak of all our trouble in this time of winter (which was so cold, as it lamed the most of our company, and myself do yet feel it) would be too tedious.

But I must not forget to show how mercifully God dealt with us in this time; for the space of three months we had such store of fowl of one kind (which were partridges as white as milk) that we killed above a hundred dozen, besides others of sundry sorts: for all was fish that came to the net. The spring coming, this fowl left us, yet they were with us all the extreme cold. Then in their places came divers sort of other fowl, as swan, geese, duck, and teal, but hard to come by. Our master hoped they would have bred in those broken grounds, but they do not; but came from the south, and flew to the north, further than we were this voyage; yet if they be taken short with the wind at north, or northwest, or northeast, then they fall and stay till the wind serve them, and then fly to the north. Now in time these fowls are gone, and few or none to be seen. Then we went into the woods, hills, and valleys, for all things that had any show of substance in them, how vile soever: the moss of the ground, than the which I take the powder of a post to be much better, and the frog (in his engendering time as loathsome as a toad) was not spared. But amongst the divers sorts of buds, it pleased God that Thomas Woodhouse brought home a bud of a tree full of a turpentine substance. Of this our surgeon made a decoction to drink, and applied the buds hot to them that were troubled with ache in any part of their bodies; and for my part I confess, I received great and present ease of my pain.

About this time, when the ice began to break out of the bays, there came a savage to our ship, as it were to see and to be seen, being the first that we had seen in all this time, whom our master treated well, and made much of him, promising unto himself great matters by his means, and therefore would have all the knives and hatchets (which any man had) to his private use, but received none but from John King the carpenter, and myself. To this savage our master gave a knife, a looking glass, and buttons, who received them thankfully, and made signs that after he had slept he would come again, which he did. When he came he brought with him a sled, which he drew after him, and upon it two deers' skins and two beaver skins. He had a scrip [sack] under his arm, out of which he drew those things which the master had given him. He took the knife and laid it upon one of the beaver skins, and his glasses and buttons upon the other, and so gave them to the master, who received them; and the savage took those things which the master had given him, and put them up into his scrip again. Then the master showed him a hatchet, for which he would have given the master one of his deer skins, but our master would have them both, and so he had, although not willingly. After many signs of people to the north and to the south, and that after so many sleeps he would come again, he went his way, but never came more.

Now the ice begin out of the sounds, so that our boat might go from one place unto another, a company of men were appointed by the master to go a-fishing with our net; their names were as followeth: William Wilson, Henry Greene, Michael Perce, John Thomas, Andrew Moter, Bennet Mathewes, and Arnold Lodlo. These men, the first day they went, caught five hundred fish, as big as good herrings, and some trouts, which put us all in some hope to have our wants supplied, and our commons amended; but these were the most that ever they got in one day, for many days they got not a quarter so many. In this time of their fishing, Henry Greene and William Wilson, with some others, plotted to take the net and the shallop, which the carpenter had now set up, and so to shift for themselves. But the shallop being ready, our master would go in it himself to the south and southwest, to see if he could meet with the people; for to that end was it set up, and (that way) we might see the woods set on fire by them. So the master took the seine and the shallop, and so much victual as would serve for eight or nine days, and to the south he went. They that remained aboard were to take in water, wood, and ballast, and to have all things in a readiness against he came back. But he set no time of his return, for he was persuaded, if he could meet with the people, he should have flesh of them, and that good store: but he returned worse than he went forth. For he could by no means meet with the people, although they were near them, yet they would set the woods on fire in his sight.

Being returned, he fitted all things for his return, and first, delivered all the bread out of the bread room (which came to a pound apiece for every man's share) and delivered also a bill of return, willing them to have that to show, if it pleased God that they came home: and he wept when he gave it unto them. But to help us in this poor estate with some relief, the boat and seine went to work on Friday morning, and stayed till Sunday noon, at which time they came aboard, and brought fourscore small fish, a poor relief for so many hungry bellies. Then we weighed and stood out of our wintering place, and came to an anchor without, in the mouth of the bay: from whence we weighed and came to an anchor without in the sea, where our bread being gone, that store of cheese we had was to stop a gap, whereof there were five, whereat the company grudged, because they made account of nine. But those that were left were equally divided by the master, although he had counsel to the contrary: for there were some who, having it, would make haste to be rid thereof, because they could not govern it. I knew when Henry Greene gave half his bread, which he had for fourteen days, to one to keep, and prayed him not to let him have any until the next Monday, but before Wednesday at night he never left till he had it again, having eaten up his first week's bread before. So Wilson the boatswain hath eaten (in one day) his fortnight's bread, and hath been two or three days sick for his labor. The cause that moved the master to deliver all the cheese, was because they were not all of one goodness, and therefore they should see that they had no wrong done them: but every man should have alike the best and the worst together, which was three pounds and a half for seven days.

The wind serving, we weighed and stood to the northwest, and on Monday at night (the eighteenth day of June) we fell into the ice, and the next day, the wind being at west, we lay there till Sunday in sight of land. Now being here, the master told Nicholas Simmes that there would be a breaking up of chests and a search for bread, and willed him, if he had any, to bring it to him, which he did, and delivered to the master thirty cakes in a bag. This deed of the master (if it be true) hath made me marvel what should be the reason that he did not stop the breach in the beginning, but let it grow to that height, as that it overthrew himself and many other honest men: but "there are many devices in the heares of man, but the counsel of the Lord shall stand."

Being thus in the ice on Saturday, the one and twentieth of June, at night, Wilson the boatswain, and Henry Greene, came to me lying (in my cabin) lame, and told me that they and the rest of their associates would shift the company, and turn the master and all the sick men into the shallop, and let them shift for themselves. For there was not fourteen days' victual left for all the company, at that poor allowance they were at, and that there they lay, the master not caring to go one way or other, and that they had not eaten anything these three days, and therefore were resolute, either to mend or end, and what they had begun they would go through with it, or die. When I heard this, I told them I marveled to hear so much from them, considering that they were married men, and had wives and children, and that for their sakes they should not commit so foul a thing in the sight of God and man as that would be; for why should they banish themselves from their native country? Henry Greene bade me hold my peace, for he knew the worst, which was to be hanged when he came home, and therefore of the two he would rather be hanged at home than starved abroad; and for the good will they bare me, they would have me stay in the ship. I gave them thanks, and told them that I came into her, not to forsake her, yet not to hurt myself and others by any such deed. Henry Greene told me then, that I must take my fortune in the shallop. If there be no remedy (said I) the will of God be done.

Away went Henry Greene in a rage, swearing to cut his throat that went about to disturb them, and left Wilson by me, with whom I had some talk, but to no good, for he was so persuaded that there was no remedy now but to go on while it was hot, lest their party should fail them, and the mischief they had intended to others should light on themselves. Henry Greene came again, and demanded of him what I said. Wilson answered: He is in his old song, still patient. Then I spake to Henry Greene to stay three days, in which time I would so deal with the master that all should be well. So I dealt with him to forbear but two days, nay twelve hours; there is no way then (say they) but out of hand. Then I told them, that if they would stay till Monday, I would join with them to share all the victuals in the ship, and would justify it when I came home; but this would not serve their turns. Wherefore I told them, it was some worse matter they had in hand than they made show of, and that it was blood and revenge he sought, or else he would not at such a time of night undertake such a deed. Henry Greene (with that) taketh my Bible which lay before me, and swore that he would do no man harm, and what he did was for the good of the voyage, and for nothing else; and that all the rest should do the like. The like did Wilson swear.

Henry Greene went his way, and presently came Juet who, because he was an ancient man, I hoped to have found some reason in him; but he was worse than Henry Green, for he swore plainly that he would justify this deed when he came home. After him came John Thomas and Michael Perce as birds of one feather; but because they are not living, I will let them go, as then I did. Then came Moter and Bennet, of whom I demanded if they were well advised what they had taken in hand. They answered, they were, and therefore came to take their oath.

Now, because I am much condemned for this oath, as one of them that plotted with them, and that by an oath I should bind them together to perform what they had begun, I thought good here to set down to the view of all, how well their oath and deeds agreed, and thus it was: "You shall swear truth to God, your prince and country you shall do nothing, but to the glory of God and the good of the action in hand, and harm to no man." This was the oath, without adding or diminishing. I looked for more of these companions (although these were too many) but there came no more. It was dark, and they in a readiness to put this deed of darkness in execution. I called to Henry Greene and Wilson, and prayed them not to go in hand with it in the dark, but to stay till the morning. Now, every man (I hope) would go to his rest, but wickedness sleepeth not: for Henry Greene keepeth the master company all night (and gave me bread, which his cabinmate gave him) and others are as watchful as he. Then I asked Henry Greene, whom he would put out with the master? he said, the carpenter John King, and the sick men. I said they should not do well to part with the carpenter, what need soever they should have. Why the carpenter was in no more regard amongst them was, first, for that he and John King were condemned for wrong done in the victual. But the chiefest cause was for that the master loved him and made him his mate, upon his return out of our wintering place, thereby displacing Robert Bylot, whereat they did grudge, because he could neither write nor read. And therefore (said they) the master and his ignorant mate would carry the ship whither the master pleased, the master forbidding any man to keep account or reckoning, having taken from all men whatsoever served for that purpose. Well, I obtained of Henry Greene and Wilson that the carpenter should stay, by whose means I hoped (after they had satisfied themselves) that the master and the poor man might be taken into the ship again. Or, I hoped, that some one or other would give some notice, either to the carpenter John King or the master; for so it might have come to pass by some of them that were the most forward.

Now, it shall not be amiss to show how we were lodged, and to begin in the cook room; there lay Bennet and the cooper lame; without the cook room, on the steerboard side, lay Thomas Woodhouse sick; next to him lay Sydrack Funer lame; then the surgeon, and John Hudson with him; next to them lay Wilson the boatswain, and then Arnold Lodlo next to him: in the gun room lay Robert Juet and John Thomas; on the larboard side lay Michael Bute and Adria Moore, who had never been well since we lost our anchor; next to them lay Michael Perce and Andrew Moter. Next to them, without the gun room, lay John King, and with him Robert Bylot, next to them myself, and next to me Francis Clements. In the midship, between the capstan and the pumps, lay Henry Greene and Nicholas Simmes. This night John King was late up, and they thought he had been with the master, but he was with the carpenter, who lay on the poop, and coming down from him was met by his cabinmate, as it were by chance, and so they came to their cabin together. It was not long ere it was day; then came Bennet for water for the kettle; he rose and went into the hold. When he was in they shut the hatch on him (but who kept it down I know not); up upon the deck went Bennet.

In the meantime, Henry Greene and another went to the carpenter, and held him with a talk till the master came out of his cabin (which he soon did); then came John Thomas and Bennet before him, while Wilson bound his arms behind him. He asked them what they meant. They told him he should know when he was in the shallop. Now Juet, while this was a-doing, came to John King into the hold, who was provided for him, for he had got a sword of his own, and kept him at bay, and might have killed him, but others came to help him; and so he came up to the master. The master called to the carpenter and told him that he was bound, but I heard no answer he made. Now Arnold Lodlo and Michael Bute railed at them, and told them their knavery would show itself. Then was the shallop haled up to the ship side, and the poor, sick, and lame men were called upon to get them out of their cabins into the shallop. The master called to me, who came out of my cabin as well as I could, to the hatchway to speak with him; where, on my knees, I besought them, for the love of God, to remember themselves, and to do as they would be done unto. They bade me keep myself well, and get me into my cabin; not suffering the master to speak with me. But when I came into my cabin again, he called to me at the horn which gave light into my cabin, and told me that Juet would overthrow us all; nay (said I) it is that villain Henry Greene, and I spoke it not softly.

Now was the carpenter at liberty, who asked them if they would be hanged when they came home; and as for himself, he said, he would not stay in the ship unless they would force him. They bade him go then, for they would not stay him. I will (said he) so I may have my chest with me, and all that is in it; they said he should, and presently they put it into the shallop. Then he came down to me to take his leave of me, who persuaded him to stay, which if he did, he might so work that all should be well; he said he did not think but they would be glad to take them in again. For he was so persuaded by the master that there was not one in all the ship that could tell how to carry her home; but (saith he) if we must part (which we will not willingly do, for they would follow the ship) he prayed me, if we came to the Capes before them, that I would leave some token that we had been there, near to the place where the fowls bred, and he would do the like for us. And so (with tears) we parted. Now were the sick men driven out of their cabins into the shallop; but John Thomas was Francis Clements' friend, and Bennet was the Coopers, so as there were words between them and Henry Greene, one saying that they should go, and the other swearing that they should not go, but such as were in the shallop should return. When Henry Greene heard that, he was compelled to give place, and to put out Arnold Lodlo and Michael Bute, which with much ado they did.

In the meantime, there were some of them that plied their work as if the ship had been entered by force and they had free leave to pillage, breaking up chests and rifling all places. One of them came by me, who asked me what they should do. I answered, he should make an end of what he had begun; for I saw him do nothing but shark up and down. Now were all the poor men in the shallop, whose names are as follows: Henry Hudson, John Hudson, Arnold Lodlo, Sidrack Faner, Phillip Staffe, Thomas Woodhouse or Wydhouse, Adam Moore, Henry King, Michael Bute. The carpenter got of them a piece, and powder, and shot, and some pikes, an iron pot, with some meal, and other things. They stood out of the ice, the shallop being fast to the stern of the ship, and so (when they were nigh out, for I cannot say they were clean out) they cut her head fast from the stern of our ship, then out with their topsails, and toward the east they stood in a clear sea. In the end they took in their topsails, righted their helm, and lay under their foresail till they had ransacked and searched all places in the ship. In the hold they found one of the vessels of meal whole, and the other half spent, for we had but two; we found also two firkins of butter, some twenty-seven pieces of pork, half a bushel of peas; but in the master's cabin we found two hundred of biscuit cakes, a peck of meal, of beer to the quantity of a butt, one with another. Now it was said that the shallop was come within sight, they let fall the mainsail, and out with their topsails, and flew as from an enemy.

Then I prayed them yet to remember themselves; but William Wilson (more than the rest) would hear of no such matter. Coming nigh the east shore they cast about, and stood to the west and came to an island, and anchored in sixteen or seventeen fathom water. So they sent the boat and the net ashore to see if they could have a draught; but could not for rocks and great stones. Michael Perse killed two fowl, and here they found good store of that weed which we called cockle grass in our wintering place, whereof they gathered store, and came aboard again. Here we lay that night and the best part of the next day, in all which time we saw not the shallop, or ever after. Now Henry Greene came to me and told me, that it was the company's will that I should come up into the master's cabin and take charge thereof. I told him it was more fit for Robert Juet; he said he should not come in it, nor meddle with the master's card or journals. So up I came, and Henry Greene gave me the key of the master's chest, and told me then that he had laid the master's best things together, which he would use himself when time did serve; the bread was also delivered to me by tale [by count].

The wind serving, we stood to the northeast, and this was Robert Bylot's course, contrary to Robert Juet, who would have gone to the northwest. We had the eastern shore still in sight, and (in the night) had a stout gale of wind, and stood afore it till we met with ice, into the which we ran from thin to thick, till we could go no further for ice, which lay so thick ahead of us (and the wind brought it after us astern) that we could not stir backward nor forward; but so lay embayed fourteen days in worse ice than ever we met to deal withal, for we had been where there was greater store, but it was not so broad upon the water as this; for this floating ice contained miles and half miles in compass, where we had a deep sea, and a tide of flood and ebb, which set northwest and southeast. Here Robert Juet would have gone to the northwest, but Robert Bylot was confident to go through to the northeast, which he did. At last, being clear of this ice, he continued his course in sight of the eastern shore till he raised four islands, which lay north and south; but we passed them six or seven leagues, the wind took us so short. Then we stood back to them again, and came to an anchor between two of the most northernmost. We sent the boat ashore, to see if there were anything there to be had, but found nothing but cockle grass, whereof they gathered store, and so returned aboard. Before we came to this place, I might well see that I was kept in the ship against Henry Greene's mind, because I did not favor their proceedings better than I did. Then he began (very subtly) to draw me to take upon me to search for those things which himself had stolen, and accused me of a matter no less than treason amongst us, that I had deceived the company of thirty cakes of bread. Now they began to talk amongst themselves, that England was no safe place for them, and Henry Greene swore the ship should not come into any place (but keep the sea still) till he had the king's majesty's hand and seal to show for his safety. They had many devices in their heads, but Henry Greene in the end was their captain, and so called of them.

From these islands we stood to the northeast and the

eastern land still in sight: we raised those islands, that our master called Rumnies Islands. Between these islands and the shallow ground, to the east of them, our master went down into the first great bay. We kept the east shore still in our sight, and coming thwart of the low land, we ran on a rock that lay under water, and struck but once; for if she had, we might have been made inhabitants of that place; but God sent us soon off without any harm that we saw. We continued our course and raised land ahead of us, which stretched out to the north, which when they saw, they said plainly, that Robert Bylot by his northerly course had left the capes to the south, and that they were best to seek down to the south in time for relief before all was gone; for we had small store left. But Robert Bylot would follow the land to the north, saying that he hoped in God to find somewhat to relieve us that way as soon as to the south. I told them that this land was the main of Worsenhams Cape, and that the shallow rocky ground was the same that the master went down by when he went into the great bay. Robert Juet and all said it was not possible, unless the master had brought the ship overland, and willed them to look into the master's card and their course how well they did agree. We stood to the east and left the mainland to the north, by many small islands into a narrow gut between two lands, and there came to an anchor. The boat went ashore on the north side, where we found the great horn, but nothing else. The next day we went to the south side, but found nothing there save cockle grass, of which we gathered. This grass was a great relief unto us, for without it we should hardly have got to the capes for want of victual. The wind serving, we stood out, but before we could get clean out, the wind came to the west, so that we were constrained to anchor on the north side.

The next day, we weighed and doubled the point of the North Land, which is high land, and so continued to the capes, lying north and south, some five-and-twenty or thirty leagues. To the north we stood to see a store of those fowls that breed in the Capes, and to kill some without shot, and to fetch them with our boat. We raised the Capes with joy and bare for them, and came to the islands that lie in the mouth of the strait; but bearing in between the Rocky Isles, we ran on a rock that lay under water, and there stuck fast eight or nine hours. It was ebbing water when we thus came on, so the flood set us afloat, God guiding both wind and sea, that it was calm and fair weather: the ebb came from the east, and the flood from the west. When we were afloat we stood more near to the east shore, and there anchored.

The next day, being the seven and twentieth of July, we sent the boat to fetch some fowl, and the ship should way and stand as near as they could, for the wind was against us. They had a great way to row, and by that means they could not reach to the place where the fowl bred; but found good store of gulls, yet hard to come by, on the rocks and cliffs; but with their pieces they killed some thirty, and toward night returned. Now we had brought our ship more near to the mouth of the straits, and there came to an anchor in eighteen or twenty fathom water, upon a rifle or shelf of ground; which after they had weighed their anchor, and stood more near to the place where the fowl bred, they could not find it again, nor no place like it: but were fain to turn to and fro in the mouth of the strait, and be in danger of rocks, because they could not find ground to let fall an anchor in, the water was so deep.

The eight and twentieth day, the boat went to Digges Cape for fowl, and made directly for the place where the fowl bred, and being near, they saw seven boats come about the eastern point toward them. When the savages saw our boat, they drew themselves together, and drew their lesser boats into their bigger: and when they had done, they came rowing to our boat, and made signs to the west, but they made ready for all assays. The savages came to them, and by signs grew familiar one with another, so as our men took one of theirs into our boat, and they took one of ours into their boat. Then they carried our man to a cove where their tents stood toward the west of the place, where the fowl bred: so they carried him into their tents, where he remained till our men returned with theirs. Our boat went to the place where the fowl bred, and were desirous to know how the savages killed their fowl. He showed them the manner how, which was thus: they take a long pole with a snare at the end, which they put about the fowl's neck, and so pluck them down. When our men knew that they had a better way of their own, they showed him the use of our pieces, which at one shot would kill seven or eight. To be short, our boat returned to their cove for our man and to deliver theirs. When they came they made great joy, with dancing, and leaping, and stroking of their breasts: they offered divers things to our men, but they only took some morses' teeth, which they gave them for a knife and two glass buttons; and so receiving our man they came aboard, much rejoicing at this chance, as if they had met with the most simple and kind people of the world.

And Henry Greene (more than the rest) was so confident that (by no means) we should take care to stand on our guard: God blinding him so, that where he made reckoning to receive great matters from these people, he received more than he looked for, and that suddenly, by being made a good example for all men: that make no conscience of doing evil, and that we take heed of the savage people, how simple soever they seem to be.

The next day, the nine and twentieth of July, they made haste to be ashore, and because the ship rid too far off, they weighed and stood as near to the place where the fowl bred as they could; and because I was lame, I was to go in the boat, to carry such things as I had in the cabin, of everything somewhat; and so, with more haste then good speed (and not without swearing) away we went, Henry Greene, William Wilson, John Thomas, Michael Perse, Andrew Moter, and myself. When we came near the shore, the people were on the hills dancing and leaping. To the cove we came, where they had drawn up their boats; we brought our boat to the east side of the cove, close to the rocks. Ashore they went, and made fast the boat to a great stone on the shore; the people came, and every one had somewhat in his hand to barter; but Henry Greene swore they should have nothing till he had venison, for they had so promised him by signs.

Now when we came, they made signs to their dogs (whereof there were many like mongrels, as big as hounds), and pointed to their mountain and to the sun, clapping their hands. Then

Henry Greene, John Thomas, and William Wilson stood hard by the boathead, Michael Perse and Andrew Moter were got up upon the rock a-gathering of sorrel; not one of them had any weapon about him, not so much as a stick, save Henry Greene only, who had a piece of a pike in his hand; nor saw I anything that they had wherewith to hurt us. Henry Greene and William Wilson had looking glasses, and Jew's trumps, and bells, which they were showing the people. The savages standing round about them, one of them came into the boat's head to me to show me a bottle; I made signs to him to get him ashore, but he made as though he had not understood me, whereupon I stood up and pointed him ashore. In the meantime another stole behind me to the stern of the boat, and when I saw him ashore that was in the head of the boat I sat down again, but suddenly I saw the leg and foot of a man by me. Wherefore I cast up my head, and saw the savage with his knife in his hand, who stroke at my breast over my head. I cast up my right arm to save my breast, he wounded my arm, and struck me into the body under my right pap. He struck a second blow, which I met with my left hand, and then he struck me into the right thigh, and had like to have cut off my little finger of the left hand. Now I had got hold of the string of the knife, and had wound it about my left hand, he striving with both his hands to make an end of that he had begun: I found him but weak in the grip (God enabling me), and getting hold of the sleeve of his left arm, so bare him from me. His left side lay bare to me, which when I saw, I put his sleeve off his left arm into my left hand, holding the string of the knife fast in the same hand; and having got my right hand at liberty, I sought for somewhat wherewith to strike him (not remembering my dagger at my side), but looking down I saw it, and therewith struck him into the body and the throat.

While I was thus assaulted in the boat, our men were set upon on the shore. John Thomas and William Wilson had their bowels cut, and Michael Perse and Henry Greene, being mortally wounded, came tumbling into the boat together. When Andrew Moter saw this medley, he came running down the rocks, and leaped into the sea, and so swam to the boat hanging on the stern thereof, till Michael Perse took him in, who manfully made good the head of the boat against the savages, that pressed sore upon us. Now Michael Perse had got a hatchet, wherewith I saw him strike one of them, that he lay sprawling in the sea. Henry Greene crieth *Coragio*, and layeth about him with his truncheon. I cried to them to clear the boat, and Andrew Moter cried to be taken in. The savages betook them to their bows and arrows, which they sent amongst us, wherewith Henry Greene was slain outright, and Michael Perse received many wounds, and so did the rest. Michael Perse cleareth the boat, and puts it from the shore, and helpeth Andrew Moter in; but in turning of the boat I received a cruel wound in my back with an arrow. Michael Perse and Andrew Moter rowed the boat away, which, when the savages saw, they ran to their boats, and I feared they would have launched them to have followed us, but they did not, and our ship was in the middle of the channel and could not see us.

Now, when they had rowed a good way for the shore, Michael Perse fainted, and could row no more. Then was Andrew Moter driven to stand in the boathead, and waft to the ship, which at the first saw us not, and when they did they could not tell what to make of us, but in the end they stood for us, and so took us up. Henry Greene was thrown out of the boat into the sea, and the rest were had aboard, the savage being yet alive, yet without sense. But they died all there that day, William Wilson swearing and cursing in most fearful manner. Michael Perse lived two days after, and then died. Thus you have heard the tragical end of Henry Greene and his mates, whom they called captain, these four being the only lusty men in all the ship.

The poor number that was left were to ply our ship to and fro in the mouth of the strait, for there was no place to anchor in near hand. Besides, they were to go in the boat to kill fowl to bring us home, which they did, although with danger to us all. For if the wind blew, there was an high sea, and the eddies of the tides would carry the ship so near the rocks as it feared our master, for so I will now call him. After they had killed some two hundred fowl, with great labor, on the south cape, we stood to the east, but when we were six or seven leagues from the capes, the wind came up at east. Then we stood back to the capes again, and killed an hundred fowl more. After this the wind came to the west, so we were driven to go away, and then our master stood (for the most) along by the north shore, till he fell into broken ground about the Queen's Foreland, and there anchored. From thence we went to God's Mercies, and from thence to Rose Islands, which lay in the mouth of our strait, not seeing the land till we were ready to run our bowsprit against the rocks in a fog. But it cleared a little, and then we might see ourselves enclosed with rocky islands, and could find no ground to anchor in. There our master lay a-try [lay to] all night, and the next day, the fog continuing, they sought for ground to anchor in, and found some in an hundred and odd fathoms of water. The next day we weighed and stood to the east, but before we came here we had put ourselves to hard allowance, as half a fowl a day with the pottage, for yet we had some meal left and nothing else. Then they began to make trial of all whatsoever. We had flayed our fowl, for they will not pull, and Robert Juet was the first that made use of the skins by burning of the feathers; so they became a great dish of meat, and as for the garbage, it was not thrown away.

After we were clear of these islands, which lie out with two points, one to the southeast and the other to the north, making a bay to the sight as if there were no way through, we continued our course east-southeast and south and by east, to raise the Desolations, from thence to shape our course for Ireland. Thus we continued divers days; but the wind coming against us made us to alter our course, and by the means of Robert Juet, who persuaded the company that they should find great relief in Newfoundland if our countrymen were there, and if they were gone before we came, yet should we find great store of bread and fish left ashore by them; but how true, I give God thanks we did not try. Yet we stood to the southwest and to the west almost to fifty-seven degrees, when (by the will of God) the wind came up at southwest. Then the master asked me if he should take the benefit of this wind, and shape his course for Ireland. I said it was best to go where we knew corn grew, and not to seek it where it was cast away and not to be found. Toward Ireland now we stood, with prosperous winds for many days together. Then was all our meal spent, and our fowl resty [rancid] and dry; but (being no remedy) we were content with the salt broth for dinner and the half fowl for supper. Now went our candles to wrack, and Bennet, our cook, made a mess of meat of the bones of the fowl, frying them with candle grease till they were crisp, and, with vinegar put to them, made a good dish of meat. Our vinegar was shared, and to every man a pound of candles delivered for a week, as a great dainty. Now Robert Juet (by his reckoning) saith we were within sixty or seventy leagues of Ireland, when we had two hundred thither. And sure our course was so much the longer through our evil steerage, for our men became so weak that they could not stand at the helm, but were fain to sit.

Then Robert Juet died for mere want, and all our men were in despair, and said we were past Ireland, and our last fowl were in the steep tub. So our men cared not which end went forward, insomuch as our master was driven to look to their labor as well as his own; for some of them would sit and see the foresail or mainsail fly up to the tops, the sheets being either flown or broken, and would not help it themselves nor call to others for help, which much grieved the master. Now in this extremity it pleased God to give us sight of land, not far from the place our master said he would fall withal, which was the Bay of Galloway, and we fell to the west of the Derses, and so stood along by the coast to the southwest. In the end there was a joyful cry, a sail, a sail, toward which they stood. Then they saw more, but to the nearest we stood, and called to him; his bark was of Fowy, and was at anchor a-fishing. He came to us, and brought us into Bere Haven. Here we stayed a few days, and dealt with the Irish to supply our wants, but found no relief, for in this place there was neither bread, drink, nor money to be had amongst them. Wherefore they advised us to deal with our countrymen who were there a-fishing, which we did, but found them so cold in kindness that they would do nothing without present money, whereof we had none in the ship. In the end we procured one John Waymouth, master of the barque that brought us into this harbor, to furnish

us with money, which he did, and received our best cable
and anchor in pawn for the same. With this money our
master, with the help of John Waymouth, bought bread, beer,
and beef.

Now, as we were beholden to Waymouth for his money,
so were we to one Captain Taylor for making of our contracts
with Waymouth, by whose means he took a bill for our
cable and anchor and for the men's wages, who would not
go with us unless Waymouth would pass his word for the
same; for they made show that they were not willing to go
with us for any wages. Whereupon Captain Taylor swore he
would press them, and then, if they would not go, he would
hang them.

In conclusion, we agreed for three pound ten shillings a
man to bring our ship to Plymouth or Dartmouth, and to
give the pilot five pound; but if the wind did not serve,
but that they were driven to put into Bristol, they were to
have four pound ten shillings a man, and the pilot six pound.
Omitting therefore further circumstances, from Bere Haven we
came to Plymouth, and so to an anchor before the castle;
and from Plymouth, with fair wind and weather without stop
or stay, we came to the Downs, from thence to Gravesend,
where most of our men went ashore, and from thence came
on this side Erith, and there stopped: where our master Robert
Bylot came aboard, and so had me up to London with him.

Nightmare at Fort Enterprise

SIR JOHN FRANKLIN

The logistics of supplies constantly haunted polar explorations, and no journey was more fraught with hunger and exhaustion than British explorer Sir John Franklin's journey to the shores of the Polar Sea and the return to winter quarters in 1821.

This land party consisted of a sailor, Hepburn, two midshipmen, Back and Hood, Franklin's friend Richardson, whose report of the return journey follows, Franklin himself, and some Canadian Voyageurs. They reached the Arctic Ocean successfully—but the return was a nightmare. The nearly starved party had to split up in order to reach a source of supplies quickly, but they discovered that winter quarters, Fort Enterprise, was desolate and the Indians who were to furnish food were absent.

In 1825, Franklin returned to the Arctic, charted 1200 miles of new coastline and then retired from exploration. Twenty years later, when he was fifty-nine, Franklin headed an expedition which was lost. His disappearance created one of the great arctic mysteries. What had happened to the lost ships? In ensuing years many explorers attempted to find Franklin, and his indefatigable widow never gave up hope. Authorities now agree that Sir John died on June 11, 1847, by which time twenty-four others were dead. The rest made a tragic march that left their bones scattered on the ice.

Franklin never quite learned the secrets of living or traveling in polar areas. He never tried the Eskimo kayak but used clumsy boats that had to be dragged over the ice; he overloaded his sledges; his sailors carried heavy equipment, from telescopes to iron pots, strapped to their bodies. The story of his early journey shows the pitiful lack of information about polar living in the first part of the nineteenth century.

AT LENGTH we reached Fort Enterprise, and to our infinite dissapointment and grief found it a perfectly desolate habitation. There was no deposit of provision, no trace of the Indians, no letter from Mr. Wentzel to point out where the Indians might be found. It would be impossible to describe our sensations after entering this miserable abode, and discovering how we had been neglected: the whole party shed tears, not so much for our own fate, as for that of our friends in the rear, whose lives depended entirely on our sending immediate relief from this place.

I found a note, however, from Mr. Back, stating that he had reached the house two days before and was going in search of the Indians, at a part where St. Germain deemed it probable they might be found. If he was unsuccessful, he purposed walking to Fort Providence, and sending succor from thence: but he doubted whether either he or his party could perform the journey to that place in their present debilitated state. It was evident that any supply that could be sent from Fort Providence would be long in reaching us, neither could it be sufficient to enable us to afford any assistance to our companions behind, and that the only relief for them must be procured from the Indians. I resolved, therefore, on going also in search of them; but my companions were absolutely incapable of proceeding, and I thought by halting two or three days they might gather a little strength, whilst the delay would afford us the chance of learning whether Mr. Back had seen the Indians.

We now looked round for the means of subsistence, and were gratified to find several deerskins, which had been thrown away during our former residence. The bones were gathered from the heap of ashes; these with the skins, and the addition of tripe-de-roche, we considered would support us tolerably well for a time. As to the house, the parchment being torn from the windows, the apartment we selected for our abode was exposed to all the rigor of the season. We endeavored to exclude the wind as much as possible, by placing loose boards against the apertures. The temperature was now between fifteen and twenty degrees below zero. We procured fuel by pulling up the flooring of the other rooms, and water for cooking, by melting the snow. Whilst we were seated round the fire, singeing the deerskin for supper, we were rejoiced by the unexpected entrance of Augustus. He had followed quite a different course from ours, and the circumstance of his having found his way through a part of the country he had never been in before must be considered a remarkable proof of sagacity. The unusual earliness of this winter became manifest to us from the state of things at this spot. Last year at the same season, and still later, there had been very little snow on the ground, and we were surrounded by vast herds of reindeer; now there were but few recent tracks of these animals, and the snow was upward of two feet deep. Winter River was then open, now it was frozen two feet thick.

When I arose the following morning, my body and limbs were so swollen that I was unable to walk more than a few yards. Adam was in a still worse condition, being absolutely incapable of rising without assistance. My other companions happily experienced this inconvenience in a less degree, and went to collect bones, and some tripe-de-roche which supplied us with two meals. The bones were quite acrid, and the soup extracted from them excoriated the mouth if taken alone, but it was somewhat milder when boiled with tripe-de-roche, and we even thought the mixture palatable, with the addition of salt, of which a cask had been fortunately left here in the spring. Augustus today set two fishing lines below the rapid. On his way thither he saw two deer, but had not the strength to follow them.

On October thirteenth, the wind blew violently from southeast, and the snow drifted so much that the party were confined to the house. In the afternoon of the following day Belanger arrived with a note from Mr. Back, stating that he had seen no trace of the Indians, and desiring further instructions as to the course he should pursue. Belanger's situation, however, required our first care, as he came in almost speechless, and covered with ice, having fallen into a rapid, and, for the third time since we left the coast, narrowly escaped drowning. He did not recover sufficiently to answer our questions, until we had rubbed him for some time, changed his dress, and given him some warm soup. My companions nursed him with the greatest kindness, and the desire of restoring him to health seemed to absorb all regard for their own situation. I witnessed with peculiar pleasure this conduct, so different from that which they had recently pursued, when every tender feeling was suspended by the desire of self-preservation. They now no longer betrayed impatience or despondency, but were composed and cheerful, and had entirely given up the practice of swearing, to which the Canadian voyagers are so lamentably addicted. Our conversation naturally turned upon the prospect of getting relief, and upon the means which were best adapted for obtaining it. The absence of all traces of Indians on Winter River, convinced me that they were at this time on the way to Fort Providence, and that by proceeding toward that post we should overtake them, as they move slowly when they have their families with them. This route also offered us the prospect of killing deer, in the vicinity of Reindeer Lake, in which neighborhood, our men in their journey to and fro last winter, had always found them abundant. Upon these grounds I determined on taking the route to Fort Providence as soon as possible, and wrote to Mr. Back, desiring him to join me at Reindeer Lake, and detailing the occurrences since we parted, that our friends might receive relief, in case of any accident happening to me.

Belanger did not recover sufficient strength to leave us before the eighteenth. His answers as to the exact part of Round-Rock Lake in which he had left Mr. Back, were very unsatisfactory; and we could only collect that it was at a considerable distance, and that he was still going on with the intention of halting at the place where Akaitcho was encamped last summer, about thirty miles off. This distance appeared so great, that I told Belanger it was very unsafe for him to attempt it alone, and that he would be several days in accomplishing it. He stated, however, that as the track was beaten, he should experience little fatigue and seemed so confident, that I suffered him to depart with a supply of singed hide. Next day I received information which explained why he was so unwilling to acquaint us with the situation of Mr. Back's party. He dreaded that I should resolve upon joining it, when our numbers would be so great as to consume at once everything St. Germain might kill, if by accident he should be successful in hunting. He even endeavored to entice away our other hunter, Adam, and proposed to him to carry off the only kettle we had, and without which we could not have subsisted two days. Adam's inability to move, however, precluded him from agreeing to the proposal, but he could assign no reason for not acquainting me with it previous to Belanger's departure. I was at first inclined to consider the whole matter as a fiction of Adam's, but he persisted in his story without wavering; and Belanger, when we met again, confessed that every part of it was true. It is painful to have to record a fact so derogatory to human nature, but I have deemed it proper to mention it, to show the difficulties we had to contend with, and the effect which distress had in warping the feelings and understanding of the most diligent and obedient of our party; for such Belanger had been always esteemed up to this time.

In making arrangements for our departure, Adam disclosed to me, for the first time, that he was affected with edematous swellings in some parts of the body, to such a degree as to preclude the slightest attempt at marching; and upon my expressing my surprise at his having hitherto concealed from me the extent of his malady, among other explanations, the details of the preceding story came out. It now became necessary to abandon the original intention of proceeding with the whole party toward Fort Providence, and Peltier and Samandré having volunteered to remain with Adam, I determined on setting out with Benoit and Augustus, intending to send them relief by the first party of Indians we should meet. My clothes were so much torn as to be quite inadequate to screen me from the wind, and Peltier and Samandré, fearing that I might suffer on the journey in consequence, kindly exchanged with me parts of their dress, desiring me to send them skins in return by the Indians. Having patched up three pairs of snowshoes, and singed a quantity of skin for the journey, we started on the morning of the twentieth. Previous to my departure, I packed up the journals of the officers, the charts, and some other documents, together with a letter addressed to the Under Secretary of State, detailing the occurrences of the Expedition up to this period, which package was given in charge to Peltier and Samandré with directions that it should be brought away by the Indians who might come to them. I also instructed them to send succor immediately on its arrival to our companions in the rear, which they solemnly promised to do, and I left a letter for my friends, Richardson and Hood, to be sent at the same time. I thought it necessary to admonish Peltier, Samandré, and Adam, to eat two meals every day, in order to keep up their strength, which they

promised me they would do. No language that I can use
could adequately describe the parting scene. I shall only say
there was far more calmness and resignation to the Divine
will evinced by every one than could have been expected.
We were all cheered by the hope that the Indians would
be found by the one party, and relief sent to the other.
Those who remained entreated us to make all the haste we
could, and expressed their hope of seeing the Indians in ten
or twelve days.

At first starting we were so feeble as scarcely to be able
to move forward, and the descent of the bank of the river
through the deep snow was a severe labor. When we came
upon the ice, where the snow was less deep, we got on better,
but after walking six hours we had only gained four miles,
and were then compelled by fatigue to encamp on the borders of Round-Rock Lake. Augustus tried for fish here, but
without success, so that our fare was skin and tea. Composing
ourselves to rest, we lay close to each other for warmth.
We found the night bitterly cold, and the wind pierced through
our famished frames.

The next morning was mild and pleasant for traveling, and
we set out after breakfast. We had not, however, gone many
yards before I had the misfortune to break my snowshoes
by falling between two rocks. This accident prevented me
from keeping pace with Benoit and Augustus, and in the
attempt, I became quite exhausted. Feeling convinced that
their being delayed on my account might prove of fatal consequence to the rest, I resolved on returning to the house,
and letting them proceed alone in search of the Indians. I
therefore halted them only whilst I wrote a note to Mr.
Back, stating the reason of my return, and desiring he would
send meat from Reindeer Lake by these men, if St. Germain
should kill any animals there. If Benoit should miss Mr. Back,
I directed him to proceed to Fort Providence, and furnished
him with a letter to the gentleman in charge of it, requesting
that immediate supplies might be sent to us.

On my return to the house I found Samandré very dispirited,
and too weak, as he said, to render any assistance to Peltier;
upon whom the whole labor of getting wood and collecting
the means of subsistence would have devolved. Conscious, too,

that his strength would have been unequal to these tasks, they had determined upon taking only one meal each day; so that I felt my going back particularly fortunate, as I hoped to stimulate Samandré to exertion, and at any rate could contribute some help to Peltier. I undertook the office of cooking, and insisted they should eat twice a day whenever food could be procured; but as I was too weak to pound the bones, Peltier agreed to do that in addition to his more fatiguing task of getting wood. We had a violent snowstorm all the next day, and this gloomy weather increased the depression of spirits under which Adam and Samandré were laboring. Neither of them would quit their beds, and they scarcely ceased from shedding tears all day; in vain did Peltier and myself endeavor to cheer them. We had even to use much entreaty before they would take the meals we had prepared for them. Our situation was indeed distressing, but in comparison with that of our friends in the rear, we thought it happy. Their condition gave us unceasing solicitude, and was the principal subject of our conversation.

Though the weather was stormy on the twenty-sixth, Samandré assisted me to gather tripe-de-roche. Adam, who was very ill and could not now be prevailed upon to eat this weed, subsisted principally on bones, though he also partook of the soup. The tripe-de-roche had hitherto afforded us our chief support, and we naturally felt great uneasiness at the prospect of being deprived of it, by its being so frozen as to render it impossible for us to gather it.

We perceived our strength decline every day, and every exertion began to be irksome; when we were once seated the greatest effort was necessary in order to rise, and we had frequently to lift each other from our seats; but even in this pitiable condition we conversed cheerfully, being sanguine as to the speedy arrival of the Indians. We calculated indeed that if they should be near the situation where they had remained last winter, our men would have reached them by this day. Having expended all the wood which we could procure from our present dwelling, without danger of its fall, Peltier began this day to pull down the partitions of the adjoining houses. Though these were only distant about twenty yards, yet the increase of labor in carrying the wood fatigued him so much, that by the evening he was exhausted. On the next day his weakness was such, especially in the arms, of which he chiefly complained, that he with difficulty lifted the hatchet; still he persevered, whilst Samandré and I assisted him in bringing in the wood, but our united strength could only collect sufficient to replenish the fire four times in the course of the day. As the insides of our mouths had become sore from eating the bone soup, we relinquished the use of it, and now boiled the skin, which mode of dressing we found more palatable than frying it, as we had hitherto done.

On the twenty-ninth, Peltier felt his pains more severe, and could only cut a few pieces of wood. Samandré, who was still almost as weak, relieved him a little time, and I aided them in carrying in the wood. We endeavored to pick some tripe-de-roche, but in vain, as it was entirely frozen. In turning up the snow, in searching for bones, I found several pieces of bark, which proved a valuable acquisition, as we were almost destitute of dry wood proper for kindling the fire. We saw a herd of reindeer sporting on the river, about half a mile from the house; they remained there a long time, but none of the party felt themselves strong enough to go after them, nor was there one of us who could have fired a gun without resting it.

Whilst we were seated round the fire this evening, discoursing about the anticipated relief, the conversation was suddenly interrupted by Peltier's exclaiming with joy, "Ah! le monde!" imagining that he heard the Indians in the other room; immediately afterward, to his bitter disappointment, Dr. Richardson and Hepburn entered, each carrying his bundle. Peltier, however, soon recovered himself enough to express his delight at their safe arrival, and his regret that their companions were not with them. When I saw them alone my own mind was instantly filled with apprehensions respecting my friend Hood, and our other companions, which were immediately confirmed by the doctor's melancholy communication, that Mr. Hood and Michel were dead. Perrault and Fontano had neither reached the tent, nor been heard of by them. This intelligence produced a melancholy despondency in the minds of my party, and on that account the particulars were deferred until another opportunity. We were all shocked at beholding

the emaciated countenances of the doctor and Hepburn, as
they strongly evidenced their extremely debilitated state. The
alteration in our appearance was equally distressing to them,
for since the swellings had subsided, we were little more
than skin and bone. The doctor particularly remarked the
sepulchral tone of our voices, which he requested us to make
more cheerful if possible, unconscious that his own partook
of the same key.

Hepburn having shot a partridge, which was brought to
the house, the doctor tore out the feathers, and having held
it to the fire a few minutes divided it into six portions. I
and my three companions ravenously devoured our shares, as
it was the first morsel of flesh any of us had tasted for
thirty-one days, unless, indeed, the small gristly particles which
we found occasionally adhering to the pounded bones may
be termed flesh. Our spirits were revived by this small supply,
and the doctor endeavored to raise them still higher by the
prospect of Hepburn's being able to kill a deer next day,
as they had seen, and even fired at several near the house.
He endeavored, too, to rouse us into some attention to the
comfort of our apartment, and particularly to roll up, in the
day, our blankets which (expressly for the convenience of
Adam and Samandré), we had been in the habit of leaving
by the fire where we lay on them. The doctor having brought
his prayer book and testament, some prayers and psalms, and
portions of scripture, appropriate to our situation, were read,
and we retired to bed.

Next morning the doctor and Hepburn went out early in
search of deer; but though they saw several herds and fired
some shots, they were not so fortunate as to kill any, being
too weak to hold their guns steadily. The cold compelled the
former to return soon, but Hepburn persisted until late in
the evening.

My occupation was to search for skins under the snow,
it being now our object immediately to get all that we could,
but I had not strength to drag in more than two of those
which were within twenty yards of the house until the doctor
came and assisted me. We made up our stock to twenty-six,
but several of them were putrid and scarcely eatable even
by men suffering the extremity of famine. Peltier and Samandré

continued very weak and dispirited and they were unable to cut firewood. Hepburn had in consequence that laborious task to perform after he came back. The doctor having scarified the swelled parts of Adam's body, a large quantity of water flowed out, and he obtained some ease, but still kept his bed.

After our usual supper of singed skin and bone soup, Dr. Richardson acquainted me with the afflicting circumstances attending the death of Mr. Hood and Michel, and detailed the occurrences subsequent to my departure from them, which I shall give from his Journal, in his own words; but I must here be permitted to express the heartfelt sorrow with which I was overwhelmed at the loss of so many companions; especially of my friend Mr. Hood, to whose zealous and able co-operation I had been indebted for so much invaluable assistance during the Expedition, whilst the excellent qualities of his heart engaged my warmest regard. His scientific observations, together with his maps and drawings, evince a variety of talent, which, had his life been spared, must have rendered him a distinguished ornament to his profession, and which will cause his death to be felt as a loss to the service.

DR. RICHARDSON'S NARRATIVE

After Captain Franklin had bidden us farewell, we remained seated by the fireside as long as the willows the men had cut for us before they departed, lasted. We had no tripe-de-roche that day, but drank an infusion of the country tea plant, which was grateful from its warmth, although it afforded no sustenance. We then retired to bed, where we remained all the next day, as the weather was stormy, and the snowdrift so heavy, as to destroy every prospect of success in our endeavors to light a fire with the green and frozen willows, which were our only fuel. Through the extreme kindness and forethought of a lady, the party, previous to leaving London, had been furnished with a small collection of religious books, of which we still retained two or three of the most portable, and they proved of incalculable benefit to us. We read portions of them to each other as we lay in bed, in addition to the morning and evening service, and found that they inspired us on each perusal with so strong a sense of the omnipresence of a beneficent God, that our situation, even in these wilds, appeared no longer destitute; and we conversed, not only with calmness, but with cheerfulness, detailing with unrestrained confidence the past events of our lives, and dwelling with hope on our future prospects. Had my poor friend been spared to revisit his native land, I should look back to this period with unalloyed delight.

On the morning of the ninth, the weather, although still cold, was clear, and I went out in quest of tripe-de-roche, leaving Hepburn to cut willows for a fire, and Mr. Hood in bed. I had no success, as yesterday's snowdrift was so frozen on the surface of the rocks that I could not collect any of the weed; but on my return to the tent, I found that Michel, the Iroquois, had come with a note from Mr. Franklin which stated that this man and Jean Baptiste Belanger being unable to proceed were about to return to us, and that a mile beyond our present encampment there was a clump of pine trees, to which he recommended us to remove the tent. Michel informed us that he quitted Mr. Franklin's party yesterday morning, but that having missed his way, he had passed the night on the snow a mile or two to the northward of us. Belanger, he said, being impatient, left the fire about two hours earlier, and, as he had not arrived, he supposed must have gone astray. It will be seen that we had more than sufficient reason to doubt the truth of this story.

Michel now produced a hare and a partridge which he had killed in the morning. This unexpected supply of provision was received by us with a deep sense of gratitude to the Almighty for His goodness, and we looked upon Michel as the instrument He had chosen to preserve all our lives. He complained of cold, and Mr. Hood offered to share his buffalo robe with him at night: I gave him one of two shirts which I wore, whilst Hepburn in the warmth of his heart, exclaimed, "How I shall love this man if I find that he does not tell lies like the others." Our meals being finished, we arranged that the greatest part of the things should be carried to the pines the next day; and after reading the evening service, retired to bed full of hope.

Early in the morning Hepburn, Michel, and myself, carried

the ammunition, and most of the other heavy articles to the pines. Michel was our guide and it did not occur to us at the time that his conducting us perfectly straight was incompatible with his story of having mistaken his road in coming to us. He now informed us that he had, on his way to the tent, left on the hill above the pines a gun and forty-eight balls, which Perrault had given to him when with the rest of Mr. Franklin's party, he took leave of him. It was later shown in Mr. Franklin's journal, that Perrault carried his gun and ammunition with him when they parted from Michel and Belanger. After we had made a fire, and drunk a little of the country tea, Hepburn and I returned to the tent, where we arrived in the evening, much exhausted with our journey. Michel preferred sleeping where he was, and requested us to leave him the hatchet, which we did, after he had promised to come early in the morning to assist us in carrying the tent and bedding. Mr. Hood remained in bed all day. Seeing nothing of Belanger today, we gave him up for lost.

On the eleventh, after waiting until late in the morning for Michel, who did not come, Hepburn and I loaded ourselves with the bedding, and, accompanied by Mr. Hood, set out for the pines. Mr. Hood was much affected with dimness of sight, giddiness, and other symptoms of extreme debility, which caused us to move very slowly, and to make frequent halts.

On arriving at the pines, we were much alarmed to find that Michel was absent. We feared that he had lost his way in coming to us in the morning, although it was not easy to conjecture how that could have happened, as our footsteps of yesterday were very distinct. Hepburn went back for the tent, and returned with it after dusk, completely worn out with the fatigue of the day. Michel, too, arrived at the same time, and relieved our anxiety on his account. He reported that he had been in chase of some deer which passed near his sleeping place in the morning, and although he did not come up with them, yet that he found a wolf which had been killed by the stroke of a deer's horn, and had brought a part of it. We implicitly believed this story then, but afterwards became convinced from the circumstances, the detail of which may be spared, that it must have been a portion of the body of

Belanger or Perrault. A question of moment here presents itself; namely, whether he actually murdered these men, or either of them, or whether he found the bodies in the snow. Captain Franklin, who is the best able to judge of this matter from knowing their situation when he parted from them, suggested the former idea, and that both Belanger and Perrault had been sacrificed. When Perrault turned back, Captain Franklin watched him until he reached a small group of willows, which was immediately adjoining to the fire, and concealed it from view, and at this time the smoke of fresh fuel was distinctly visible. Captain Franklin conjectures that Michel, having already destroyed Belanger, completed his crime by Perrault's death, in order to screen himself from detection. Although this opinion is founded only on circumstances, and is unsupported by direct evidence, it has been judged proper to mention it, especially as the subsequent conduct of the man showed that he was capable of committing such a deed. The circumstances are very strong. It is not easy to assign any other adequate motive for his concealing from us that Perrault had turned back; while his request overnight that we should leave him the hatchet, and his cumbering himself with it when he went out in the morning, unlike a hunter who makes use only of his knife when he kills a deer, seem to indicate that he took it for the purpose of cutting up something that he knew to be frozen. These opinions, however, are the result of subsequent consideration. We passed this night in the open air.

On the following morning, the tent was pitched; Michel went out early, refused my offer to accompany him, and remained out the whole day. He would not sleep in the tent at night, but chose to lie at the fireside.

On the thirteenth there was a heavy gale of wind, and we passed the day by the fire. Next day, about two P.M., the gale abating, Michel set out, as he said, to hunt, but returned unexpectedly in a very short time. This conduct surprised us, and his contradictory and evasive answers to our questions excited some suspicions, but they did not turn toward the truth.

During the fifteenth, Michel expressed much regret that he had stayed behind Mr. Franklin's party, and declared that he would set out for the house at once if he knew the way.

We endeavored to soothe him, and to raise his hopes of the Indians speedily coming to our relief, but without success. He refused to assist us in cutting wood, but about noon, after much solicitation, he set out to hunt. Hepburn gathered a kettleful of tripe-de-roche, but froze his fingers. Both Hepburn and I fatigued ourselves much in pursuing a flock of partridges from one part to another of the group of willows, in which the hut was situated, but we were too weak to be able to approach them with sufficient caution. In the evening Michel returned, having met with no success.

Next day he refused either to hunt or cut wood, spoke in a very surly manner, and threatened to leave us. Under these circumstances, Mr. Hood and I deemed it better to promise if he would hunt diligently for four days, that then we would give Hepburn a letter for Mr. Franklin, a compass, inform him what course to pursue, and let them proceed together to the fort. The non-arrival of the Indians to our relief now led us to fear that some incident had happened to Mr. Franklin, and we placed no confidence in the exertions of the Canadians that accompanied him, but we had the fullest confidence in Hepburn's returning the moment he could obtain assistance.

On the seventeenth I went to conduct Michel to where Vaillant's blanket was left, and after walking about three miles, pointed out the hills to him at a distance, and returned to the hut, having gathered a bagful of tripe-de-roche on the way. It was easier to gather this weed on a march than at the tent, for the exercise of walking produced a glow of heat, which enabled us to withstand for a time the cold to which we were exposed in scraping the frozen surface of the rocks. On the contrary, when we left the fire to collect it in the neighborhood of the hut, we became chilled at once, and were obliged to return very quickly.

Michel proposed to remain out all night, and to hunt next day on his way back. He returned in the afternoon of the eighteenth, having found the blanket, together with a bag containing two pistols, and some other things which had been left beside it. We had some tripe-de-roche in the evening, but Mr. Hood from the constant griping it produced, was unable to eat more than one or two spoonfuls. He was now so weak as to be scarcely able to sit up at the fireside, and complained that the least breeze of wind seemed to blow through his frame. He also suffered much from cold during the night. We lay close to each other, but the heat of the body was no longer sufficient to thaw the frozen rime formed by our breaths on the blankets that covered him.

At this period we avoided as much as possible conversing upon the hopelessness of our situation, and generally endeavored to lead the conversation toward our future prospects in life. The fact is, that with the decay of our strength, our minds decayed, and we were no longer able to bear the contemplation of the horrors that surrounded us. Each of us, if I may be allowed to judge from my own case, excused himself from so doing by a desire of not shocking the feelings of others, for we were sensible of one another's weakness of intellect though blind to our own. Yet we were calm and resigned to our fate, not a murmur escaped us, and we were punctual and fervent in our addresses to the Supreme Being.

On the nineteenth Michel refused to hunt, or even to assist in carrying a log of wood to the fire, which was too heavy for Hepburn's strength and mine. Mr. Hood endeavored to point out to him the necessity and duty of exertion, and the cruelty of his quitting us without leaving something for our support; but the discourse, far from producing any beneficial effect, seemed only to excite his anger, and amongst other expressions, he made use of the following remarkable one: "It is no use hunting, there are no animals, you had better kill and eat me." At length, however, he went out, but returned very soon, with a report that he had seen three deer, which he was unable to follow from having wet his foot in a small stream of water thinly covered with ice, and being consequently obliged to come to the fire. The day was rather mild, and Hepburn and I gathered a large kettleful of tripe-de-roche; Michel slept in the tent this night.

In the morning of the twentieth we again urged Michel to go a-hunting that he might if possible leave us some provision, tomorrow being the day appointed for his quitting us; but he showed great unwillingness to go out, and lingered about the fire, under the pretence of cleaning his gun. After we had read the morning service I went about noon to gather some tripe-de-roche, leaving Mr. Hood sitting before the tent at the fireside arguing with Michel; Hepburn was employed cutting down a tree at a short distance from the tent, being desirous of accumulating a quantity of firewood before he left us. A short time after I went out, I heard the report of a gun, and about ten minutes afterward Hepburn called to me in a voice of great alarm, to come directly. When I arrived, I found poor Hood lying lifeless at the fireside, a ball having apparently entered his forehead. I was at first horror-struck with the idea that in a fit of despondency he had hurried himself into the presence of his Almighty Judge by an act of his own hand; but the conduct of Michel soon gave rise to other thoughts, and excited suspicions which were confirmed, when upon examining the body, I discovered that the shot had entered the back part of the head, and passed out at the forehead and that the muzzle of the gun had been applied so close as to set fire to the nightcap behind. The gun, which was of the longest kind supplied to the Indians, could not have been placed in a position to inflict such a wound, except by a second person. Upon inquiring of Michel how it happened, he replied that Mr. Hood had sent him into the tent for the short gun, and that during his absence the long gun had gone off, he did not know whether by accident or not. He held the short gun in his hand at the time he was speaking to me. Hepburn afterward informed me that previous to the report of the gun Mr. Hood and Michel were speaking to each other in an elevated angry tone; that Mr. Hood being seated at the fireside, was hid from him by intervening willows, but that on hearing the report he looked up and saw Michel rising up from before the tent door, or just behind where Mr. Hood was seated, and then going into the tent. Thinking that the gun had been discharged for the purpose of cleaning it, he did not go to the fire at first; and when Michel called to him that Mr. Hood was dead, a considerable time had elapsed. Although I dared not openly to evince any suspicion that I thought Michel guilty of the deed, yet he repeatedly protested that he was incapable of committing such an act, kept constantly on his guard, and carefully avoided leaving Hepburn and me together. He was evidently afraid of permitting us to converse in private, and whenever Hepburn spoke, he inquired if he accused him of the murder. It is to be remarked that he understood English very imperfectly, yet sufficiently to render it unsafe for us to speak on the subject in his presence. We removed the body into a clump of willows behind the tent, and, returning to the fire, read the funeral service in addition to the evening prayers. The loss of a young officer of such distinguished and varied talents and application may be felt and duly appreciated by the eminent characters under whose command he had served; but the calmness with which he contemplated the probable termination of a life of uncommon promise, and the patience and fortitude with which he sustained, I may venture to say, unparalleled bodily sufferings, can only be known to the companions of his distresses. Owing to the effect that the tripe-de-roche invariably had, when he ventured to taste it, he undoubtedly suffered more than any of the survivors of the party. *Bickersteth's Scripture Help* was lying open beside the body, as if it had fallen from his hand, and it is probable that he was reading it at the instant of his death. We passed the night in the tent together without rest, every one being on his guard. Next day, having determined on going to the fort, we began to patch and prepare our clothes for the journey. We singed the hair off a part of the buffalo robe that belonged to Mr. Hood, and boiled and ate it. Michel tried to persuade me to go to the woods on the Copper-Mine River, and hunt for deer instead of going to the fort. In the afternoon a flock of partridges coming near the tent, he killed several which he shared with us.

Thick, snowy weather and a head wind prevented us from starting the following day, but on the morning of the twenty-third we set out, carrying with us the remainder of the singed robe. Hepburn and Michel had each a gun, and I carried a small pistol which Hepburn had loaded for me. In the course of the march, Michel alarmed us much by his gestures and conduct, was constantly muttering to himself, expressed an unwillingness to go to the fort, and tried to persuade me to go to the southward to the woods, where he said he could maintain himself all the winter by killing deer. In consequence of this behavior and the expression of his countenance, I requested him to leave us and to go to the southward by himself. This proposal increased his ill-nature, he threw out some obscure hints of freeing himself from all restraint on the morrow; and I overheard his muttering threats against Hepburn, whom he openly accused of having told stories against him. He also, for the first time, assumed such a tone of superiority in addressing me, as evinced that he considered us to be completely in his power, and he gave vent to several expressions of hatred toward the white people, or as he termed us in the idiom of the voyageurs, the French, some of whom, he said, had killed and eaten his uncle and two of his relations. In short, taking every circumstance of his conduct into consideration, I came to the conclusion that he would attempt to destroy us on the first opportunity that offered, and that he had hitherto abstained from doing so from his ignorance of his way to the fort, but that he would never suffer us to go thither in company with him. In the course of the day, he had several times remarked that we were pursuing the same course that Mr. Franklin was doing when he left him, and that by keeping toward the setting sun he could find his way himself. Hepburn and I were not in a condition to resist even an open attack, nor could we by any device escape from him. Our united strength was far inferior to his, and, besides his gun, he was armed with two pistols, an Indian bayonet and a knife. In the afternoon, coming to a rock on which there was some tripe-de-roche, he halted, and said he would gather it whilst we went on, and that he would soon overtake us. Hepburn and I were now left together for the first time since Mr. Hood's death, and he acquainted me with several material circumstances which he had observed of Michel's behavior, and which confirmed me in the opinion that there was no safety for us except in his death, and he offered to be the instrument of it. I determined, however, as I was thoroughly convinced of the necessity of such a dreadful act, to take the whole responsibility upon myself; and immediately upon Michel's coming up, I put an end to his life by shooting him through the head with a pistol. Had my own life alone been threatened, I would not have purchased it by such a measure; but I considered myself as entrusted also with the protection of Hepburn's, a man who, by his humane attentions and devotedness, had so endeared himself to me, that I felt more anxiety for his safety than for my own. Michel had gathered no tripe-de-roche, and it was evident to us that he had halted for the purpose of putting his gun in order, with the intention of attacking us, perhaps, whilst we were in the act of encamping.

I have dwelt in the preceding part of the narrative upon many circumstances of Michel's conduct, not for the purpose of aggravating his crime, but to put the reader in possession of the reasons that influenced me in depriving a fellow creature of life. Up to the period of his return to the tent, his conduct had been good and respectful to the officers, and in a conversation between Captain Franklin, Mr. Hood, and myself at Obstruction Rapid, it had been proposed to give him a reward upon our arrival at a post. His principles, however, unsupported by a belief in the divine truths of Christianity, were unable to withstand the pressure of severe distress. His countrymen, the Iroquois, are generally Christians, but he was totally uninstructed and ignorant of the duties inculcated by Christianity; and from his long residence in the Indian country, seems to have imbibed, or retained, the rules of conduct which the southern Indians prescribe to themselves.

On the two following days we had mild but thick snowy weather, and as the view was too limited to enable us to preserve a straight course, we remained encamped amongst a few willows and dwarf pines, about five miles from the tent. We found a species of *cornicularia*, a kind of lichen, that was good to eat when moistened and toasted over the fire; and we had a good many pieces of singed buffalo hide remaining.

On the twenty-sixth, the weather being clear and extremely cold, we resumed our march which was very painful from the depth of the snow, particularly on the margins of the small lakes that lay in our route. We frequently sunk under the load of our blankets, and were obliged to assist each other in getting up. After walking about three miles and a half, however, we were cheered by the sight of a large herd of reindeer, and Hepburn went in pursuit of them; but his hand being unsteady through weakness he missed. He was so exhausted by this fruitless attempt that we were obliged to encamp upon the spot, although it was a very unfavorable one.

Next day, we had fine and clear, but cold, weather. We set out early, and, in crossing a hill, found a considerable quantity of tripe-de-roche. About noon we fell upon Little Marten Lake, having walked about two miles. The sight of a place that we knew inspired us with fresh vigor, and there being comparatively little snow on the ice, we advanced at a pace to which we had lately been unaccustomed. In the afternoon we crossed a recent track of a wolverene, which, from a parallel mark in the snow, appeared to have been dragging something. Hepburn traced it, and upon the borders of the lake found the spine of a deer that it had dropped. It was clean picked, and at least one season old; but we extracted the spinal marrow from it, which, even in its frozen state, was so acrid as to excoriate the lips. We encamped within sight of the Dog-Rib Rock, and from the coldness of the night and the want of fuel, rested very ill.

On the twenty-eighth we rose at daybreak, but from the want of the small fire that we usually made in the mornings to warm our fingers, a very long time was spent in making up our bundles. This task fell to Hepburn's share, as I suffered so much from the cold as to be unable to take my hands out of my mittens. We kept a straight course for the Dog-Rib Rock, but, owing to the depth of the snow in the valleys we had to cross, did not reach it until late in the afternoon. We would have encamped, but did not like to pass a second night without fire; and though scarcely able to drag our limbs after us, we pushed on to a clump of pines, about a mile to the southward of the rock, and arrived at them in the dusk of the evening. During the last few hundred yards of our march, our track lay over some large stones, amongst which I fell down upward of twenty times, and became at length so exhausted that I was unable to stand. If Hepburn had not exerted himself far beyond his strength, and speedily made the encampment and kindled a fire, I must have perished on the spot. This night we had plenty of dry wood.

On the twenty-ninth we had clear and fine weather. We set out at sunrise, and hurried on in our anxiety to reach the house, but our progress was much impeded by the great depth of the snow in the valleys. Although every spot of ground over which we traveled today had been repeatedly trodden by us, yet we got bewildered in a small lake. We took it for Marten Lake, which was three times its size, and fancied that we saw the rapids and the grounds about the fort, although they were still far distant. Our disappointment when this illusion was dispelled by our reaching the end of the lake, so operated on our feeble minds as to exhaust our strength, and we decided upon encamping; but upon ascending a small eminence to look for a clump of wood, we caught a glimpse of the Big Stone, a well-known rock upon the summit of a hill opposite to the fort, and determined upon proceeding. In the evening we saw several large herds of reindeer, but Hepburn, who used to be considered a good marksman, was now unable to hold the gun straight, and although he got near them, all his efforts proved fruitless. In passing through a small clump of pines, we saw a flock of partridges, and he succeeded in killing one after firing several shots. We came in sight of the fort at dusk, and it is impossible to describe our sensations, when on attaining the eminence that overlooks it, we beheld the smoke issuing from one of the chimneys. From not having met with any footsteps in the snow, as we drew nigh our once cheerful residence, we had been agitated by many melancholy forebodings. Upon entering the now desolate building, we had the satisfaction of embracing Captain Franklin, but no words can convey an idea of the filth and wretchedness that met our eyes on looking around. Our own misery had stolen upon us by degrees, and we were accustomed to the contemplation of each other's emaciated figures, but the ghastly countenances, dilated eyeballs, and sepulchral voices of Captain Franklin and those with him were more than we could at first bear.

Conclusion of Dr. Richardson's Narrative.

First Lessons from the Eskimos

ELISHA KENT KANE

Elisha Kent Kane was crippled by a rheumatic heart when he was only eighteen years old. He became a doctor so that he might care for himself and others. Kane was fascinated by the secrets of the Far North, and from 1850 to 1857, he investigated and then wrote about the Arctic in a fashion that opened a window upon that frozen world.

He served on the first Grinnell Expedition of 1850, sponsored by the United States Government, the purpose of which was to find the lost expedition of Sir John Franklin.

In 1853, Kane returned to the Arctic on the second Grinnell Expedition. He and his adjutant, Dr. Morton, spent more than two years studying techniques of living in the Arctic. Their findings were later used by Peary in his dash to the Pole, as well as by all those who attempted to travel extensively in the Arctic. Kane learned the secrets of igloo making and how to hunt seal, walrus, and even polar bear. These are his observations as they appeared over a hundred years ago—a picture of the Arctic that influenced many explorers and scientists.

My RESOLVE was to practice on the lessons we had learned from the Eskimos. I had studied them carefully, and determined that their form of habitations and their peculiarities of diet, without their unthrift and filth, were the safest and best to which the necessity of our circumstances invited us.

My journal tells how these resolves were carried out:

"September 6, Wednesday—We are at it, all hands, sick and well, each man according to his measure, working at our winter's home. We are none of us in condition to brave the frost, and our fuel is nearly out. I have determined to borrow a lesson from our Eskimo neighbors, and am turning the brig into an igloo.

"The sledge is to bring us moss and turf from wherever the men can scrape it. This is an excellent non-conductor;

and when we get the quarter-deck well padded with it, we shall have a nearly coldproof covering. Down below we will enclose a space some eighteen feet square, and pack it from floor to ceiling with inner walls of the same material. The floor itself we are calking carefully with plaster of Paris and common paste, and will cover it when we have done with Manilla oakum a couple of inches deep, and a canvas carpet. The entrance is to be from the hold, by a low moss-lined tunnel, the *tossut* of the native huts, with as many doors and curtains to close it up as our ingenuity can devise. This is to be our apartment of all uses—not a very large one; but we are only ten to stow away, and the closer the warmer.

"September 9, Saturday—All hands but the carpenter and Morton are out 'mossing.' This mossing, though it has a very May-day sound, is a frightfully wintry operation. The mixed turf of willows, heaths, grasses, and moss is frozen solid. We cannot cut it out from the beds of the snow-streams any longer, and are obliged to seek for it on the ledges of the rocks, quarrying it with crowbars and carrying it to the ship like so much stone. I would escape this labor if I could, for our party have all of them more or less scurvy in their systems, and the thermometer is often below zero. But there is no help for it. I have some eight sledgeloads more to collect before our little home can be called windproof: and then, if we only have snow enough to bank up against the brig's sides, I shall have no fear either for height or uniformity of temperature.

"September 10, Sunday—'The work goes bravely on.' We have got moss enough for our roof, and something to spare for below. Tomorrow we begin to strip off the outer-deck planking of the brig, and to stack it for firewood. It is cold work, hatches open and no fires going; but we saved time enough for our Sunday's exercises, though we forego its rest.

"It is twelve months today since I returned from the weary foot tramp that determined me to try the winter search. Things have changed since then, and the prospect ahead is less cheery. But I close my pilgrim experience of the year with devout gratitude for the blessings it has registered, and an earnest faith in the support it pledges for the times to come.

"September 11, Monday—Our stock of game is down to a mere mouthful—six long-tailed ducks not larger than a partridge, and three ptarmigan. The rabbits have not yet come to us, and the foxes seem tired of touching our trap baits.

"I determined last Saturday to try a novel expedient for catching seal. Not more than ten miles to seaward the icebergs keep up a rude stream of broken ice and water, and the seals resort there in scanty numbers to breathe. I drove out with my dogs, taking Hans along; but we found the spot so hemmed in by loose and fragile ice that there was no approaching it. The thermometer was eight degrees, and a light breeze increased my difficulties.

"*Deo volente,* I will be more lucky tomorrow. I am going to take my long Kentucky rifle, the kayak, an Eskimo harpoon with its attached line and bladder, *naligeit* and *awahtok,* and a pair of large snowshoes to boot. My plan this time is to kneel where the ice is unsafe, resting my weight on the broad surface of the snowshoes, Hans following astride of his kayak, as a sort of life-preserver in case of breaking in. If I am fortunate enough to stalk within gun range, Hans will take to the water and secure the game before it sinks. We will be gone for some days probably, tenting it in the open air; but our sick men—that is to say, all of us—are languishing for fresh meat."

I started with Hans and five dogs, all we could muster from our disabled pack, and reached the "Pinnacly Berg" in a single hour's run. But where was the water? Where were the seal? The floes had closed, and the crushed ice was all that told of our intended hunting ground.

Ascending a berg, however, we could see to the north and west the dark cloud stratus which betokens water. It ran through our old battleground, the "Bergy Belt"—the labyrinth of our wanderings after the frozen party of last winter. I had not been over it since, and the feeling it gave me was any thing but joyous.

But in a couple of hours we emerged upon a plain unlimited to the eye and smooth as a billiard table. Feathers of young frosting gave a plushlike nap to its surface, and toward the horizon dark columns of frost-smoke pointed clearly to the open water. This ice was firm enough: our experience satisfied us that it was not a very recent freezing. We pushed on without hesitation, cheering ourselves with the expectation of coming every minute to the seals. We passed a second ice growth: it was not so strong as the one we had just come over, but still safe for a party like ours. On we went, at a brisker gallop, maybe for another mile, when Hans sang out, at the top of his voice, "Pusey! puseymut! seal, seal!" At the same instant the dogs bounded forward, and, as I looked up, I saw crowds of gray netsik, the rough or hispid seal of the whalers, disporting in an open sea of water.

I had hardly welcomed the spectacle when I saw that we had passed upon a new belt of ice that was obviously unsafe. To the right and left and front was one great expanse of snow-flowered ice. The nearest solid floe was a mere lump, which stood like an island in the white level. To turn was impossible: we had to keep up our gait. We urged on the dogs with whip and voice, the ice rolling like leather beneath the sledge runners: it was more than a mile to the lump of solid ice. Fear gave to the poor beasts their utmost speed, and our voices were soon hushed to silence.

The suspense, unrelieved by action or effort, was intolerable: we knew that there was no remedy but to reach the floe, and that every thing depended upon our dogs, and our dogs alone. A moment's check would plunge the whole concern into the rapid tideway: no presence of mind or resource bodily or mental could avail us. The seals—for we were now near enough to see their expressive faces—were looking at us with that strange curiosity which seems to be their characteristic expression: we must have passed some fifty of them, breast-high out of water, mocking us by their self-complacency.

This desperate race against fate could not last: the rolling of the tough salt-water ice terrified our dogs; and when within fifty paces from the floe, they paused. The left-hand runner went through: our leader "Toodlamick" followed, and in one second the entire left of the sledge was submerged. My first thought was to liberate the dogs. I leaned forward to cut poor Tood's traces, and the next minute was swimming in a little circle of pasty ice and water alongside him. Hans, dear good fellow, drew near to help me, uttering piteous expressions in broken English; but I ordered him to throw himself on his belly, with his hands and legs extended, and to make for the island by cogging himself forward with his jackknife. In the meantime—a mere instant—I was floundering about with sledge, dogs, and lines, in a confused puddle around me.

I succeeded in cutting poor Tood's lines and letting him scramble to the ice, for the poor fellow was drowning me with his piteous caresses, and made my way for the sledge; but I found that it would not buoy me, and that I had no resource but to try the circumference of the hole. Around this I paddled faithfully, the miserable ice always yielding when my hopes of a lodgement were greatest. During this process I enlarged my circle of operations to a very uncomfortable diameter, and was beginning to feel weaker after every effort. Hans meanwhile had reached the firm ice, and was on his knees, like a good Moravian, praying incoherently in English and Eskimo; at every fresh crushing-in of the ice he would ejaculate "God!" and when I recommenced my paddling, he recommenced his prayers.

I was nearly gone. My knife had been lost in cutting out the dogs; and a spare one which I carried in my trousers pocket was so enveloped in the wet skins that I could not reach it. I owed my extrication at last to a newly broken team dog, who was still fast to the sledge and in struggling carried one of the runners chock against the edge of the circle. All my previous attempts to use the sledge as a bridge had failed, for it broke through, to the much greater injury of the ice. I felt that it was a last chance. I threw myself on my back, so as to lessen as much as possible my weight, and placed the nape of my neck against the rim or edge of the ice; then with caution slowly bent my leg, and, placing the ball of my moccasined foot against the sledge, I pressed steadily against the runner, listening to the half-yielding crunch of the ice beneath.

Presently I felt that my head was pillowed by the ice, and that my wet fur jumper was sliding up the surface. Next came my shoulders; they were fairly on. One more decided push, and I was launched up on the ice and safe. I reached the ice floe, and was frictioned by Hans with frightful zeal. We saved all the dogs; but the sledge, kayak, tent, guns, snowshoes, and every thing besides, were left behind. The thermometer at eight degrees will keep them frozen fast in the sledge till we can come and cut them out.

On reaching the ship, after a twelve-mile trot, I found so

much of comfort and warm welcome that I forgot my failure. The fire was lit up, and one of our few birds slaughtered forthwith. It is with real gratitude that I look back upon my escape, and bless the great presiding Goodness for the very many resources which remain to us.

"September 14, Thursday—Tiger, our best remaining dog, the partner of poor Bruiser, was seized with a fit, ominously resembling the last winter's curse. In the delirium which followed his seizure, he ran into the water and drowned himself, like a sailor with the horrors. The other dogs are all doing well."

I have not yet described one of the most exciting incidents of Eskimo life. Morton was full of the one—the walrus hunt he witnessed; and his account of it when he came back was so graphic that I should be glad to escape from the egotism of personal narrative by giving it in his own words. Let me first, however, endeavor to describe the animal.

The head of the walrus has not the characteristic oval of the seal: on the contrary, the frontal bone is so covered as to present a steep descent to the eyes and a square, blocked-out aspect to the upper face. The muzzle is less protruding than the seal's, and the cheeks and lips are completely masked by the heavy quill-like bristles. Add to this the tusks as a garniture to the lower face; and you have for the walrus a grim, ferocious aspect peculiarly his own. I have seen him with tusks nearly thirty inches long; his body not less than eighteen feet. When of this size he certainly reminds you of the elephant more than any other living monster.

The resemblance of the walrus to man has been greatly overrated. The notion occurs in our systematic treatises, accompanied with the suggestion that this animal may have represented the merman and mermaid. The square, blocked-out head which I have noticed, effectually destroys the resemblance to humanity when distant, and the colossal size does the same when near. Some of the seals deserve the distinction much more: the size of the head, the regularity of the facial oval, the droop of the shoulders, even the movements of this animal, whether singly or in a group, remind you strikingly of man.

The party which Morton attended upon their walrus hunt had three sledges. One was to be taken to a cache in the neighborhood; the other two dragged at a quick run toward the open water, about ten miles off to the southwest. They had but nine dogs to these two sledges, one man only riding, the others running by turns. As they neared the new ice, and where the black wastes of mingled cloud and water betokened the open sea, they would from time to time remove their hoods and listen intently for the animal's voice.

After a while Myouk the Eskimo became convinced, from signs or sounds, or both—for they were inappreciable by Morton—that the walrus were waiting for him in a small space of recently open water that was glazed over with a few days' growth of ice; and, moving gently on, they soon heard the characteristic bellow of a bull awuk. The walrus, like some of the higher order of beings to which he has been compared, is fond of his own music, and will lie for hours listening to himself. His vocalization is something between the mooing of a cow and the deepest baying of a mastiff: very round and full, with its barks or detached notes repeated rather quickly seven to nine times in succession.

The party now formed in single file, following in each other's steps; and, guided by an admirable knowledge of ice topography, wound behind hummocks and ridges in a serpentine approach toward a group of pondlike discolorations, recently frozen ice spots, but surrounded by firmer and older ice.

When within half a mile of these, the line broke, and each man crawled toward a separate pool; Morton on his hands and knees following Myouk. In a few minutes the walrus were in sight. They were five in number, rising at intervals through the ice in a body, and breaking it up with an explosive puff that might have been heard for miles. Two large grim-looking males were conspicuous as the leaders of the group.

Now for the marvel of the craft. When the walrus is above water, the hunter is flat and motionless; as he begins to sink, alert and ready for a spring. The animal's head is hardly below the waterline before every man is in a rapid run; and again, as if by instinct, before the beast returns, all are motionless behind protecting knolls of ice. They seem to know beforehand not only the time he will be absent, but the very spot at which he will reappear. In this way, hiding and advancing by turns, Myouk, with Morton at his heels, has reached a plate of thin ice, hardly strong enough to bear them, at the very brink of the water pool the walrus are curvetting in.

Myouk, till now phlegmatic, seems to waken with excitement. His coil of walrus hide, a well-trimmed line of many fathoms' length, is lying at his side. He fixes one end of it in an iron barb, and fastens this loosely by a socket upon a shaft of bone: the other end is already looped, or, as sailors would say, "doubled in a bight." It is the work of a moment. He has grasped the harpoon: the water is in motion. Puffing with pent-up respiration, the walrus is within a couple of fathoms, close before him. Myouk rises slowly; his right arm thrown back, the left flat at his side. The walrus looks about him, shaking the water from his crest: Myouk throws up his left arm; and the animal, rising breast-high, fixes one look before he plunges. It has cost him all that curiosity can cost: the harpoon is buried under his left flipper.

Though the awuk is down in a moment, Myouk is running at desperate speed from the scene of his victory, paying off his coil freely, but clutching the end by its loop. He seizes as he runs a small stick of bone, rudely pointed with iron, and by a sudden movement drives it into the ice: to this he secures his line, pressing it down close to the ice surface with his feet.

Now comes the struggle. The hole is dashed in mad commotion with the struggles of the wounded beast; the line is drawn tight at one moment, the next relaxed: the hunter has not left his station. There is a crash of the ice; and rearing up through it are two walruses, not many yards from where he stands. One of them, the male, is excited and seemingly terrified: the other, the female, collected and vengeful. Down they go again, after one grim survey of the field; and on the instant Myouk has changed his position, carrying his coil with him and fixing it anew.

He has hardly fixed it before the pair have again risen, breaking up an area of ten feet diameter about the very spot he left. As they sink once more he again changes his place. And so the conflict goes on between address and force, till the victim, half exhausted, receives a second wound, and is played like a trout by the angler's reel.

The instinct of attack which characterizes the walrus is interesting to the naturalist, as it is characteristic also of the land animals, the pachyderms, with which he is classed. When wounded, he rises high out of the water, plunges heavily against the ice, and strives to raise himself with his foreflippers upon its surface. As it breaks under his weight, his countenance assumes a still more vindictive expression, his bark changes to a roar, and the foam pours out from his jaws till it froths his beard.

Even when not excited, he manages his tusks bravely. They are so strong that he uses them to grapple the rocks with, and climbs steeps of ice and land which would be inaccessible to him without their aid. He ascends in this way rocky islands that are sixty and a hundred feet above the level of the sea; and I have myself seen him in these elevated positions basking with his young in the cool sunshine of August and September.

He can strike a fearful blow; but prefers charging with his tusks in a soldierly manner. I do not doubt the old stories of the Spitzbergen fisheries and Cherie Island, where the walrus put to flight the crowds of European boats. Awuk is the lion of the Danish Eskimos, and they always speak of him with the highest respect.

I have heard of umiaks being detained for days at a time at the crossings of straits and passages which he infested. Governor Flaischer told me that, in 1830, a brown walrus, which, according to the Eskimos, is the fiercest, after being lanced and maimed near Upernavik, routed his numerous assailants, and drove them in fear to seek for help from the settlement. His movements were so violent as to jerk out the harpoons that were stuck into him. The governor slew him with great difficulty after several rifle shots and lance wounds from his whaleboat.

On another occasion, a young and adventurous Innuit plunged his nalegeit into a brown walrus; but, startled by the savage demeanor of the beast, called for help before using the lance. The older men in vain cautioned him to desist. "It is a brown walrus," said they: *"Aúvek-Kaiok!"* "Hold back!" Finding the caution disregarded, his only brother rowed forward and plunged the second harpoon. Almost in an instant the animal charged upon the kayaker, ripping him up, as the description went, after the fashion of his sylvan brother, the wild boar. The story was told to me with much animation; how the brother remaining rescued the corpse of the brother dead; and how, as they hauled it up on the ice floes, the ferocious beast plunged in foaming circles, seeking fresh victims in that part of the sea which was discolored by his blood.

Some idea may be formed of the ferocity of the walrus, from the fact that the battle which Morton witnessed, not without sharing some of its danger, lasted four hours; during which the animal rushed continually at the Eskimos as they approached, tearing off great tables of ice with his tusks, and showing no indications of fear whatever. He received upward of seventy lance wounds—Morton counted over sixty; and even then he remained hooked by his tusks to the margin of the ice, unable or unwilling to retire. His female fought in the same manner, but fled on receiving a lance wound.

The Eskimos seemed to be fully aware of the danger of venturing too near; for at the first onset of the walrus, they jumped back far enough to be clear of the broken ice. Morton described the last three hours as wearing, on both sides, the aspect of an unbroken and seemingly doubtful combat.

The method of landing the beast upon the ice, too, showed a great deal of clever contrivance. They made two pair of incisions in the neck, where the hide is very thick, about six inches apart and parallel to each other, so as to form a couple of bands. A line of cut hide, about a quarter of an inch in diameter, was passed under one of these bands and carried up on the ice to a firm stick well secured in the floe, where it went through a loop, and was then taken back to the animal, made to pass under the second band, and led off to the Eskimos. This formed a sort of "double purchase," the blubber so lubricating the cord as to admit of a free movement. By this contrivance the beast, weighing some seven hundred pounds, was hauled up and butchered at leisure.

The two sledges now journeyed homeward, carrying the more valued parts of their prize. The intestines and a large share of the carcass were buried up in the cavities of a berg: Lucullus himself could not have dreamed of a grander ice-house.

As they doubled the little island which stood in front of

their settlement, the women ran down the rocks to meet them. A long hail carried the good news; and, as the party alighted on the beach, knives were quickly at work, the allotment of the meat being determined by well-understood hunter laws. The Eskimos, however gluttonously they may eat, evidently bear hunger with as little difficulty as excess. None of the morning party had breakfasted; yet it was after ten o'clock at night before they sat down to dinner. "Sit down to dinner!" This is the only expression of our own gastrology which is applicable to an Eskimo feast. They truly sit down, man, woman, and child, knife in hand, squatting cross-legged around a formidable joint—say forty pounds—and, without waiting for the tardy coction of the lamp, falling to like college commoners after grace. I have seen many such feeds. Hans's account, however, of the glutton festival at Etah is too characteristic to be omitted.

"Why, Cappen Ken, sir, even the children ate all night: You know the little two year old that Awiu carried in her hood— the one that bit you, when you tickled it?—yes. Well, Cappen Ken, sir, that baby cut for herself, with a knife made out of an iron hoop and so heavy that it could barely lift it, and cut and ate, and ate and cut, as long as I looked at it."

"Well, Hans, try now and think; for I want an accurate answer: how much as to weight or quantity would you say that child ate?" Hans is an exact and truthful man: he pondered a little and said that he could not answer my question. "But I know this, sir, that it ate a *sipak*"—the Eskimo name for the lump which is cut off close to the lips—"as large as its own head; and three hours afterward, when I went to bed, it was cutting off another lump and eating still." A sipak, like the Dutch governor's foot, is, however, a varying unit of weight.

Bay-ice, ice of recent formation, so called because forming most readily in bays and sheltered spots.

Berg, (see Iceberg.)

Beset, so enclosed by floating ice as to be unable to navigate.

Bight, an indentation.

Blasting, breaking the ice by gunpowder introduced in canisters.

Blink, (see Ice-blink.)

Bore, to force through loose or recent ice by sails or steam.

Brash, ice broken up into small fragments.

Calf, detached masses from berg or glacier, rising suddenly to the surface.

Crow's nest, a look-out place attached to the top-gallant-masthead.

Dock, an opening in the ice, artificial or natural, offering protection.

Drift ice, detached ice in motion.

Field-ice, an extensive surface of floating ice.

Fiord, an abrupt opening in the coast-line, admitting the sea.

Fire-hole, a well dug in the ice as a safeguard in case of fire.

Floe, a detached portion of a field.

Glacier, a mass of ice derived from the atmosphere, sometimes abutting upon the sea.

Hummocks, ridges of broken ice formed by collision of fields.

Ice-anchor, a hook or grapnel adapted to take hold upon ice.

Ice-belt, a continued margin of ice, which in high northern latitudes adheres to the coast above the ordinary level of the sea.

Iceberg, a large floating mass of ice detached from a glacier.

Ice-blink, a peculiar appearance of the atmosphere over distant ice.

Ice-chisel, a long chisel for cutting holes in ice.

Ice-face, the abutting face of the ice-belt.

Ice-foot, the Danish name for the limited ice-belt of the more southern coast.

Ice-hook, a small ice-anchor.

Ice-raft, ice, whether field, floe, or detached belt, transporting foreign matter.

Ice-table, a flat surface of ice.

Land-ice, floes or fields adhering to the coast or included between headlands.

Lane or *lead,* a navigable opening in the ice.

Nip, the condition of a vessel pressed upon by the ice on both sides.
Old ice, ice of more than a season's growth.
Pack, a large area of floating ices driven together more or less closely.
Polynia, a Russian term for an open-water space.
Rue-raddy, a shoulder-belt to drag by.
Tide-hole, a well sunk in the ice for the purpose of observing tides.
Tracking, towing along a margin of ice.
Water-sky, a peculiar appearance of the sky over open water.
Young ice, ice formed before the setting in of winter; recent ice.

Three Years of Arctic Service

ADOLPHUS W. GREELY

By 1880, interest in the scientific secrets of the polar regions was steadily growing. An International Polar Commission was established, and Adolphus Greely, a young American Lieutenant in the United States Army, commanded the Lady Franklin Bay Expedition in 1881. However, scientists did not yet have the skill necessary to acquire satisfactory specimens of plants, and Greely's notes have pathetic references to the lack of botanists, oceanography specialists and other scientific personnel. His expedition was stranded and was not rescued until 1884. Greely's account of daily living in the Arctic is not only poignant, but proved of great value to the explorers who were to follow him.

MAY OPENED dismally, with a snowstorm. Brainard continued indefatigably his work of catching shrimps, of which he brought in no less than four hundred and fifty pounds from April 8 to April 30. On May 3, however, our last bread was gone, and but nine days' meat remained, even at the small ration then issued. Every one favored, for once, a reduction to the minimum. Our hunters kept the field daily but saw little game. On the third, Long visited Rice Strait and killed a seal, which, drifting toward him, sank within ten feet of him.

In the early days of May, I was very ill and expected hourly to pass away. When I was in the worst condition, Whisler was detected by Bender and Henry with bacon from the storehouse. The three men were outside, and Whisler claimed that the door was forced by the others, and he, passing by, saw the food, and was too ravenous to resist. Bender and Henry said that Whisler forced the door, and they detected him. I was too sick to do much in the matter. The entire party expressed themselves in the harshest manner, and Whisler, pleading guilty to having been unable to resist the temptation to take the food, announced himself ready to pay any penalty. Henry, who was on parole, joined in the cry.

"May 6—A violent storm commenced at three o'clock this morning, and gradually abated, dying away at noon. Dr. Pavy made trouble today by false statements on three different points, as regards his reports made daily to me in French, and an acrid discussion followed. I ordered him four times to drop the matter, and finally told him were he not the doctor I would kill him. As a consequence, Private Bender attempted to defend the doctor, and, despite repeated orders, would not be quiet. A mutiny seemed imminent and I would have killed him could I have got Long's gun. Things have come to such a point that my orders, by these two men, are considered as binding or not at their pleasure. I fear for the future."

This entry is given as it was written by me at the time. I was then suffering greatly from the only serious illness of my three years' absence, and I doubt not now but that my mental condition was irritable, and perhaps unsound; but, looking back at the affair, I cannot think otherwise than that my decision was just and proper under the circumstances. When reiterated orders given by a commanding officer of a party in such extremities are not obeyed, it is evident that all bonds of discipline are at an end, and that threats and force to ensure obedience are fully justifiable.

"May 7—A high wind all night. Spent nearly all day in getting my personal effects in order, so as to ensure their preservation in case of my death. I have pinned to most of the few little articles which I have, a paper setting forth that they are my property, and what has been their history. Others of the party are engaged in a similar manner, although they are all in good spirits. The storm being too violent for hunting, Frederick and Long cut out a part of the boat and covered the aperture with canvas."

"May 9—Frederick was back from hunting at 1 A.M. He reports having seen a school of twelve white whales and many seals, but unfortunately all of them were in open water. I wrote out wills today for Whisler and Salor. The party appear generally stronger. Israel's extra allowance of four ounces of meat stops tomorrow."

"May 10—An exceedingly cold morning, the temperature

standing at zero (−17.8° C.) at 1 A.M., at which time Frederick returned from a nine hours' hunt. He saw four seals and a white whale. The channel is entirely clear of ice, as indeed it has been for several days. It is positive that there is no party at Littleton Island, or we should have seen some one here from there by boat ere this. Long was out all day, but saw no seals. The ice was very rotten and dangerous, and he broke through in several places. The party somewhat improved in condition."

"May 11—The temperature at 2 A.M., when Frederick returned from hunting, was −4° (−20° C.), an extremely low one for this time of the year. Frederick succeeded in killing an oosuk seal in a water pool, but unfortunately he sank instead of floating into the fast ice. The temperature at noon in the sun was 37° (2.8° C.). The party are in much better spirits than for some time. It seems strange that it should be so, as we have, after tomorrow, but two or perhaps two and a half days' rations."

"May 12—Frederick back about 1 A.M., having seen only a seal and a (burgomaster?) gull. Long out all day, but saw no game. Consulting with Brainard today, I decided that it would be best to divide the last of our regular rations, which will last until noon of the fifteenth, with a small quantity of tallow for the afternoon stew of that day. I thought it best to pursue this course and remove one source of uneasiness, as it was barely possible that one or two of the worst men of the party might break in and appropriate the remaining food, hoping thus to save themselves at the expense of the others."

"May 14—Brainard got shrimps and kelp as usual. Discovered today that about five ounces of Elison's bacon has been taken by some unknown person. A couple of days since an ounce of Long's lunch was stolen. Extremity is demoralizing some of the party, but I have urged on them that we should die like men, and not as brutes. Elison's spirits are wonderfully high. He now lives on the same ration as the rest of us. He thanked me most touchingly for the consideration he thinks I have shown him, which is only the poor fellow's due. Dr. Pavy says that he will outlive all of us."

"May 15—Long suffered so much from weakness that he was compelled to return early from hunting. The party are all very weak, but continue in good spirits. The sea kelp and shrimps form our only food from today, until we are driven to eating the sealskins."

"May 17—Ordered Bierderbick to divide up all the remaining lard which had been saved for medicinal purposes. He divided it as accurately as possible, each person getting about three ounces. Dr. Pavy, however, objected both to disposition and division."

"May 18—Very stormy last night and this morning. I heard a raven croaking this morning and called Long, who succeeded in killing him. Gave Long the liver, and concluded to use the bird for shrimp bait, thinking we could obtain more from him that way than in eating. A violent storm kept everybody in the hut today except Brainard, who went for shrimps. Ellis very weak today. Bender treated him brutally, so that even Henry rebuked him. I reprimanded Bender sharply for his lack of feeling, although he is probably somewhat insane and not entirely responsible."

Ralston says: "Tried a feed on saxifrage (*Saxifraga oppositifolia*); it is beginning to show green on the ends. I am going to keep up hope as long as I am able to walk, although my feet are in horrible condition. We are only praying for one small seal. A few snow buntings now seen every day. Psalms and prayers read by the commanding officer."

"May 19—Frederick going out to get ice to cook breakfast this morning returned immediately, reporting that as he emerged from the passageway he saw a bear within a few yards of the house. Long and Frederick dressed for the hunt, and started after the bear, but returned about 10.30 A.M., having been unable even to get a shot at him. Their weakened condition was such that the bear easily outstripped them. Our agony of hope and fear while the hunters were absent cannot be adequately expressed by language. The last alcohol issued today, except a few ounces for medical purposes which the doctor will prescribe. Israel and Whisler have quite broken down, and the whole party is in lower spirits than ever before. Private Ellis died at 10.15 A.M." Ellis was a strong, active man, capable at times of great endurance.

"May 20—Ellis buried at noon today; the first death from starvation in six weeks. The day was too stormy for hunting,

THREE YEARS OF ARCTIC SERVICE 181

but Brainard managed to obtain shrimps as usual. The party are decidedly weaker. In order to give Israel the last chance, and on Dr. Pavy's recommendation, four ounces of the raven was given him today, that being our only meat."

"May 21—A saxifrage seen in blossom. We are now mixing saxifrage in our stews; fully nineteen-twentieths of it is the dead plant, with but the faintest tinge of green at the ends. My appetite and health continue good. It is evident that I shall die, as have the others, of lack of food, which induces dropsy of the heart. Lieutenant Kislingbury and Ralston are very weak. Dr. Pavy is working wonderfully hard getting ice for water, and, strange to say, is making a collection of stones covered with lichens. His strength and energy lately are quite surprising; I am glad to write something good of him."

Later I learned from Sergeant Israel that Dr. Pavy had persuaded him to copy a certificate written by the doctor as to his professional services, and that during my absence from the hut it had been circulated for signatures. The writing of the certificate was followed that evening by a recommendation from Dr. Pavy to give Israel our last meat.

"May 22—It is now eight days since the last regular food was issued. It is astonishing to me how the party holds out. I have been obliged to feed Ralston for a couple of days past. About 2 P.M. he succeeded in eating a part of his dinner, but the rest he could not force down. When tea came, about 3.30 P.M., I asked him if he wanted it, and he said yes. I raised him up, but he became unconscious in my arms, and was unable to drink it. The strength of the party has been devoted today to pitching the wall tent some three hundred yards southeast of the present hut, on a level, gravelly spot in the sun's rays. The doctor says that the party will all die in a few days without we succeed in moving from this wretched hut. The melting snow rains down such a quantity of water upon us that we are saturated to the skin and are in a wretched condition."

"May 23—Ralston died about 1 A.M. Israel left the bag before his death, but I remained until driven out about 5 A.M., chilled through by contact with the dead. I read the burial service over him, and ordered him to be buried in the ice-foot northwest of the camp, if the party were unable to haul him to the hill. The weakest of the party moved to the tent upon the hill this afternoon. Whisler managed to get up the hill alone; he became weaker, however, in the afternoon, and is unconscious this evening. Israel was able to walk half way, but the strongest had to haul him the rest of the distance. I succeeded in getting to the tent with great difficulty, carrying the afghan in which I have been sleeping, using it as an inner bag.

"The barometer was broken in removing it to the hill—a great misfortune, as I had hoped to continue the observations until the last man died. We have made these observations regularly, with few or no breaks, until the present month, when the rapidly diminishing strength of the party compelled a discontinuance of certain of them. Long hunting today saw a gull (long-tailed skua). Brainard got only ten pounds of shrimps; less by far than we are eating. It is a sad state of affairs, and the end must be near."

Ralston was an excellent observer and an efficient man in the field, with whom I never found a shadow of fault until his last days at Sabine.

"May 24—The tent is much more comfortable. The temperature reached 39° (3.9° C.) inside it this morning. Whisler unconscious this morning, and died about noon. I read the service over him, and he was left outside near the tent, where he had died, for the present. Ralston buried this morning on the hill, I believe. The last issue of rum was made today, and a gill or so remains for medical purposes. Israel is exceedingly weak; he realizes that his end is near and is reconciled. Frederick and Long worked hard to complete the change of camp. For dinner we had a handful of saxifrage, two or three spoonfuls of shrimps, and a pint and a half of tea. Schneider was guilty of abusive language to Whisler yesterday when he was dying; the second case of this kind. I gave him a severe reprimand, and asked him whether he had any humanity or not. Dr. Pavy, Brainard, Long, Henry, Salor, and Frederick, the strongest of the party, are yet quartered in the remains of the old hut; taking their meals, however, with us at the tent. We have not enough canvas to cover them all here, as we were unable to get out the

tent flies, which were frozen to the ground in the hut. Frederick
and Schneider are trying to construct an addition to the tent
out of blankets and old canvas, so that we may all sleep
under the same shelter. The sick men complain of Schneider's
unfairness in dividing the food, which is undoubtedly true.
Frederick, ordered to watch him, reports that he is unfairly
dividing our wretched shrimps, giving equal soup but keeping
too great a portion of shrimps, and I ordered him relieved
as cook. It is wretched. Of the party, at present seven are
helpless. Brainard is breaking himself down getting our shrimps.
A violent storm again last night, which is not very bad this
morning, but still no hunting is possible."

Whisler was a man of fine physique, who had always labored
his best to advance the interests of the expedition.

"May 26—The storm was so bad this morning that Brainard
could not go shrimping, but this afternoon he got eight pounds.
Owing to his failure to obtain shrimps, we had a stew last
night and this morning of the sealskin thongs which have
been used in lashing together the sledge and for similar purposes. How we live I do not know, unless it is because we are
determined to. We all passed an exceedingly wretched night.
The stronger of the party succeeded in burying Whisler very
early this morning. Israel is now in an exceedingly weak
condition, and unable even to sit up in his bag. I am compelled
to raise him and feed him, which is a tremendous drain on
my physical strength. He talks much of his home and younger
days, and seems thoroughly reconciled to go. I gave him a
spoonful of rum this morning; he begged for it so exceedingly
hard. It was perhaps not fair to the rest to have given it to
him, as it was evident it could not benefit him, as he was
so near his end. However it was a great comfort and relief
to him, and I did by him as I should like to have been
done by in such a time. Nobody objected to my action openly,
as Israel has always been a great favorite. Long hunting
today; saw a flock of king ducks, and succeeded in killing
three dovekies, which fell into the water beyond reach. It is
a comfort to us that some game has appeared, and that there
is a possible chance."

"May 27—Long killed a dovekie, which he could not get.
Israel died very easily about three o'clock this morning. I

gave him yesterday evening the last food he ate. A very unpleasant scene occurred today. Dr. Pavy in the afternoon took
all the remaining iron from the medicine chest. I ordered
him to return it there, he having been accused to me by
Steward Bierderbick, Sergeant Elison, and others of taking
large quantities of Dover's powders, and he has lately failed
to issue iron to the party as he promised. There was a violent
scene, and Lieutenant Kislingbury, as usual, thought Dr. Pavy
right. Lieutenant Kislingbury interfered more than I thought
proper, and I ordered him to cease criticizing."

Sergeant Israel was a young man of some fortune, a graduate
of Ann Arbor University, a promising astronomer, with a future
before him. His death affected me seriously, as his cheerful and
hopeful words during the long months he was my bag companion
did much to hold up my hands and relieve my overtaxed
brain. He had always endeared himself to all by his kindness,
consideration, and unvarying equanimity, and was often called
at Sabine our Benjamin. His services were very valuable in
our scientific work, and despite his weak physique he had
sought field service. In reading the burial service, I was mindful
of him and his people, and omitted every portion which could
be distasteful to his coreligionists.

"May 28—Long shot two dovekies today, but got only one
of them. I divided it between him and Brainard, the men
who are feeding us at present. Long saw king and eider
ducks, but they were not near enough for a shot, being too
shy. The men this evening are in very good spirits: however
they all believe and say that we have no chance of surviving."

"May 29—Brainard returned exhausted and half frozen from
his shrimping trip, and was obliged to sleep outside the tent
in the storm, as Dr. Pavy and Salor, who are in Brainard's
bag, crowded him out, refusing to make room for him inside.
Brainard took the matter very quietly, although in his weak
condition he suffered greatly from cold and exposure."

"May 31—A violent southerly storm set in at midnight, and
lasted twenty-four hours, keeping everybody in their bags. The
wind must have reached a velocity of fifty miles per hour
at times, and averaged at least thirty miles per hour for six
or seven consecutive hours. These long stretches without food
or water are very exhausting to us."

Brainard, commenting on the conflicting feelings at first engendered by the sight of his comrades' graves passed daily, says: "But later my own wretched circumstances served to counteract these feelings, and I can pass and repass the place without emotion and almost with indifference."

"May 30—Snowing this morning. Succeeded in getting some food warmed, it being the only food or drink for twenty-eight hours. Brainard got very few shrimps today. He saw, however, some geese. A great deal of conversation took place regarding Decoration Day, and what was being done in the world from which we are cut off."

In these days thought was an effort, save when I was irritated by some unpleasant occurrence, or important event, into unusual energy, and writing a great labor; so that the contents of my journal became at times exceedingly meager.

Adrift on the Polar Seas

FRIDTJOF NANSEN

Competition, indeed, even jealousy, often existed among arctic heroes. Adolphus Greely publicly stated his distrust of Fridtjof Nansen, the Norwegian scientist and adventurer who was attempting to prove his theory of polar drift. Nansen thought that ice in the Arctic Ocean drifted from Siberia across the Pole and melted around Greenland. If a ship allowed itself to be frozen into the water at the right spot, would it not be carried over the Pole, Nansen wondered. "Incredible," hooted Greely. But Nansen built the right kind of ship and proved his theory. He called the ship Fram *—the Norwegian word for* forward. *The following is his account of day-to-day living in the Arctic.*

IT REALLY looked as if we were now frozen in for good, and I did not expect to get the *Fram* out of the ice till we were on the other side of the Pole, nearing the Atlantic Ocean. Autumn was already well advanced; the sun stood lower in the heavens day by day, and the temperature sank steadily. The long night of winter was approaching—that dreaded night. There was nothing to be done except prepare ourselves for it, and by degrees we converted our ship, as well as we could, into comfortable winter quarters; while at the same time we took every precaution to assure her against the destructive influences of cold, drift-ice, and the other forces of nature to which it was prophesied that we must succumb. The rudder was hauled up, so that it might not be destroyed by the pressure of the ice. We had intended to do the same with the screw; but as it, with its iron case, would certainly help to strengthen the stern, and especially the rudder-stock, we let it remain in its place. We had a good deal of work with the engine, too; each separate part was taken out, oiled, and laid away for the winter; slide-valves, pistons, shafts, were examined and thoroughly cleaned. All this was done with the very greatest care. Amundsen looked after that engine as if it had been his own child; late and early he was down tending it lovingly; and we used to tease him about it, to see the defiant look come into his eyes and hear him say: "It's all very well for you to talk, but there's not such another engine in the world, and it would be a sin and a shame not to take good care of it." Assuredly he left nothing undone. I don't suppose a day passed, winter or summer, all these three years, that he did not go down and caress it, and do something or other for it.

We cleared up in the hold to make room for a joiner's workshop down there; our mechanical workshop we had in the engine room. The smithy was at first on deck, and afterwards on the ice; tinsmith's work was done chiefly in the chart room; shoemaker's and sailmaker's, and various odd sorts of work, in the saloon. And all these occupations were carried on with interest and activity during the rest of the expedition. There was nothing, from the most delicate instruments down to wooden shoes and ax handles, that could not be made on board the *Fram*. When we were found to be short of sounding-line, a grand rope walk was constructed on the ice. It proved to be a very profitable undertaking, and was well patronized.

Presently we began putting up the windmill which was to drive the dynamo and produce the electric light. While the ship was going, the dynamo was driven by the engine, but for a long time past we had had to be contented with petroleum lamps in our dark cabins. The windmill was erected on the port side of the foredeck, between the main hatch and the rail. It took several weeks to get this important appliance into working order.

We had also brought with us a "horse mill" for driving the dynamo. I had thought that it might be of service in giving us exercise whenever there was no other physical work for us. But this time never came, and so the "horse mill" was never used. There was always something to occupy us; and it was not difficult to find work for each man that gave him sufficient exercise, and so much distraction that the time did not seem to him unbearably long.

There was the care of the ship and rigging, the inspection of sails, ropes, etc.; there were provisions of all kinds to be got out from the cases down in the hold, and handed over to the cook; there was ice—good, pure, fresh-water ice— to be found and carried to the galley to be melted for cooking, drinking, and washing water. Then, as already mentioned, there was always something doing in the various workshops. Now "Smith Lars" had to straighten the long-boat davits, which had been twisted by the waves in the Kara Sea; now it was a hook, a knife, a bear trap, or something else to be forged. The tinsmith, again "Smith Lars," had to solder to- gether a great tin pail for the ice-melting in the galley. The mechanician, Amundsen, would have an order for some instru- ment or other—perhaps a new current gauge. The watchmaker, Mogstad, would have a thermograph to examine and clean, or a new spring to put into a watch. The sailmaker might have an order for a quantity of dog harness. Then each man had to be his own shoemaker—make himself canvas boots with thick, warm, wooden soles, according to Sverdrup's newest pattern. Presently there would come an order to mechanician Amundsen for a supply of new zinc music sheets for the organ—these being a brand new invention of the leader of the expedition. The electrician would have to examine and clean the accumulator batteries, which were in danger of freezing. When at last the windmill was ready, it had to be attended to, turned according to the wind, etc. And when the wind was too strong some one had to climb up and reef the mill sails, which was not a pleasant occupation in this winter cold, and involved much breathing on fingers and rubbing of the tip of the nose.

It happened now and then, too, that the ship required to be pumped. This became less and less necessary as the water froze round her and in the interstices in her sides. The pumps, therefore, were not touched from December, 1893, till July, 1895. The only noticeable leakage during that time was in the engine room, but it was nothing of any consequence: just a few buckets of ice that had to be hewn away every month from the bottom of the ship and hoisted up.

To these varied employments was presently added, as the most important of all, the taking of scientific observations, which gave many of us constant occupation. Those that involved the greatest labor were, of course, the meteorological observations, which were taken every four hours day and night; indeed, for a considerable part of the time, every two hours. They kept one man, sometimes two, at work all day. It was Hansen who had the principal charge of this department, and his regular assistant until March, 1895, was Johansen, whose place was then taken by Nordahl. The night observations were taken by whoever was on watch. About every second day, when the weather was clear, Hansen and his assistant took the astronomical observation which ascertained our position. This was certainly the work which was followed with most interest by all the members of the expedition; and it was not uncommon to see Hansen's cabin, while he was making his calculations, besieged with idle spectators, waiting to hear the result—whether we had drifted north or south since the last observation, and how far. The state of feeling on board very much depended on these results.

Hansen had also at stated periods to take observations to determine the magnetic constant in this unknown region. These were carried on at first in a tent, specially constructed for the purpose, which was soon erected on the ice; but later we built him a large snow hut, as being both more suitable and more comfortable.

For the ship's doctor there was less occupation. He looked long and vainly for patients, and at last had to give it up and in despair take to doctoring the dogs. Once a month he, too, had to make his scientific observations, which consisted in the weighing of each man, and the counting of blood corpuscles, and estimating the amount of blood pigment, in order to ascertain the number of red blood corpuscles and the quantity of red coloring matter (hemoglobin) in the blood of each. This was also work that was watched with anxious interest, as every man thought he could tell from the result obtained how long it would be before scurvy overtook him.

Among our scientific pursuits may also be mentioned the determining of the temperature of the water and of its

degree of saltness at varying depths; the collection and examination of such animals as are to be found in these northern
seas; the ascertaining of the amount of electricity in the air;
the observation of the formation of the ice, its growth and
thickness, and of the temperature of the different layers of
ice; the investigation of the currents in the water under it,
etc. I had the main charge of this department. There remains
to be mentioned the regular observation of the aurora borealis,
which we had a splendid opportunity of studying. After I
had gone on with it for some time, Blessing undertook this
part of my duties; and when I left the ship I made over
to him all the other observations that were under my charge.
Not an inconsiderable item of our scientific work were the
soundings and dredgings. At the greater depths, it was such
an undertaking that everyone had to assist; and, from the
way we were obliged to do it later, one sounding sometimes
gave occupation for several days.

One day differed very little from another on board, and
the description of one is, in every particular of any importance,
a description of all.

We all turned out at eight, and breakfasted on hard bread
(both rye and wheat), cheese (Dutch-clove cheese, Cheddar,
Gruyère, and Mysost, or goat's-whey cheese, prepared from
dry powder), corned beef or corned mutton, luncheon ham
or Chicago tinned tongue or bacon, cod caviare, anchovy roe;
also oatmeal biscuits or English ship biscuits—with orange
marmalade or Frame Food jelly. Three times a week we had
fresh-baked bread as well, and often cake of some kind. As
for our beverages, we began by having coffee and chocolate
day about; but afterward had coffee only two days a week,
tea two, and chocolate three.

After breakfast some men went to attend to the dogs—give
them their food, which consisted of half a stockfish or a
couple of dog biscuits each, let them loose, or do whatever
else there was to do for them. The others went all to their
different tasks. Each took his turn of a week in the galley—
helping the cook to wash up, lay the table, and wait. The
cook himself had to arrange his bill of fare for dinner immediately after breakfast, and to set about his preparations
at once. Some of us would take a turn on the floe to get

some fresh air, and to examine the state of the ice, its pressure, etc. At one o'clock all were assembled for dinner, which generally consisted of three courses—soup, meat, and dessert; or, soup, fish, and meat; or, fish, meat, and dessert; or sometimes only fish and meat. With the meat we always had potatoes, and either green vegetables or macaroni. I think we were all agreed that the fare was good; it would hardly have been better at home; for some of us it would perhaps have been worse. And we looked like fatted pigs; one or two even began to cultivate a double chin and a corporation. As a rule, stories and jokes circulated at table along with the bock beer.

After dinner the smokers of our company would march off, well fed and contented, into the galley, which was smoking room as well as kitchen, tobacco being tobooed in the cabins except on festive occasions. Out there they had a good smoke and chat; many a story was told, and not seldom some warm dispute arose. Afterward came, for most of us, a short siesta. Then each went to his work again until we were summoned to supper at six o'clock, when the regulation day's work was done. Supper was almost the same as breakfast, except that tea was always the beverage. Afterward there was again smoking in the galley, while the saloon was transformed into a silent reading room. Good use was made of the valuable library presented to the expedition by generous publishers and other friends. If the kind donors could have seen us away up there, sitting round the table at night with heads buried in books or collections of illustrations, and could have understood how invaluable these companions were to us, they would have felt rewarded by the knowledge that they had conferred a real boon—that they had materially assisted in making the *Fram* the little oasis that it was in this vast ice desert. About half-past seven or eight cards or other games were brought out, and we played well on into the night, seated in groups round the saloon table. One or other of us might go to the organ, and, with the assistance of the crank handle, perform some of our beautiful pieces, or Johansen would bring out the accordion and play many a fine tune. His crowning efforts were "Oh Susanna!" and "Napoleon's March Across the Alps in an Open Boat." About midnight

we turned in, and then the night watch was set. Each man
went on for an hour. Their most trying work on watch seems
to have been writing their diaries and looking out, when the
dogs barked, for any signs of bears at hand. Besides this,
every two hours or four hours the watch had to go aloft or onto
the ice to take the meteorological observations.

I believe I may safely say that on the whole the time
passed pleasantly and imperceptibly, and that we throve in
virtue of the regular habits imposed upon us.

My notes from day to day will give the best idea of our
life, in all its monotony. They are not great events that are
here recorded, but in their very bareness they give a true
picture. Such, and no other, was our life. I shall give some
quotations direct from my diary:

"Tuesday, September 26. Beautiful weather. The sun stands
much lower now; it was 9° above the horizon at midday.
Winter is rapidly approaching; there are 14½° of frost this
evening, but we do not feel it cold. Today's observations
unfortunately show no particular drift northward; according
to them we are still in 78°50′ north latitude. I wandered
about over the floe toward evening. Nothing more wonderfully
beautiful can exist than the Arctic night. It is dreamland,
painted in the imagination's most delicate tints; it is color
etherealized. One shade melts into the other, so that you
cannot tell where one ends and the other begins, and yet
they are all there. No forms—it is all faint, dreamy color music,
a far-away, long-drawn-out melody on muted strings. Is not
all life's beauty high, and delicate, and pure like this night?
Give it brighter colors, and it is no longer so beautiful. The
sky is like an enormous cupola, blue at the zenith, shading
down into green, and then into lilac and violet at the edges.
Over the ice fields there are cold violet-blue shadows, with
lighter pink tints where a ridge here and there catches the
last reflection of the vanished day. Up in the blue of the
cupola shine the stars, speaking peace, as they always do,
those unchanging friends. In the south stands a large red-yellow
moon, encircled by a yellow ring and light golden clouds
floating on the blue background. Presently the aurora borealis
shakes over the vault of heaven its veil of glittering silver—
changing now to yellow, now to green, now to red. It spreads,

it contracts again, in restless change; next it breaks into waving, many-folded bands of shining silver, over which shoot billows of glittering rays, and then the glory vanishes. Presently it shimmers in tongues of flame over the very zenith, and then again it shoots a bright ray right up from the horizon, until the whole melts away in the moonlight, and it is as though one heard the sigh of a departing spirit. Here and there are left a few waving streamers of light, vague as a foreboding— they are the dust from the aurora's glittering cloak. But now it is growing again; new lightnings shoot up, and the endless game begins afresh. And all the time this utter stillness, impressive as the symphony of infinitude. I have never been able to grasp the fact that this earth will some day be spent and desolate and empty. To what end, in that case, all this beauty, with not a creature to rejoice in it? Now I begin to divine it. *This* is the coming earth—here are beauty and death. But to what purpose? Ah, what is the purpose of all these spheres? Read the answer, if you can, in the starry blue firmament.

"Wednesday, September 27. Gray weather and strong wind from the south-southwest. Nordahl, who is cook today, had to haul up some salt meat which, rolled in a sack, had been steeping for two days in the sea. As soon as he got hold of it he called out, horrified, that it was crawling with animals. He let go the sack and jumped away from it, the animals scattering round in every direction. They proved to be sand-hoppers, or *Amphipoda*, which had eaten their way into the meat. There were pints of them, both inside and outside of the sack. A pleasant discovery; there will be no need to starve when such food is to be had by hanging a sack in the water.

"Bentzen is the wag of the party; he is always playing some practical joke. Just now one of the men came rushing up and stood respectfully waiting for me to speak to him. It was Bentzen that had told him I wanted him. It won't be long before he has thought of some new trick.

"Thursday, September 28. Snowfall with wind. Today the dogs' hour of release has come. Until now their life on board has been really a melancholy one. They have been tied up ever since we left Khabarova. The stormy seas have broken

over them, and they have been rolled here and there in the
water on the deck; they have half hanged themselves in their
leashes, howling miserably; they have had the hose played
over them every time the deck was washed; they have been
seasick; in bad as in good weather they have had to lie on
the spot hard fate had chained them to, without more exercise
than going backward and forward the length of their chains.
It is thus you are treated, you splendid animals, who are to
be our stay in the hour of need! When that time comes, you
will, for a while at least, have the place of honor. When they
were let loose, there was a perfect storm of jubilation. They
rolled in the snow, washed and rubbed themselves, and rushed
about the ice in wild joy, barking loudly. Our floe, a short
time ago so lonesome and forlorn, was quite a cheerful sight
with this sudden population; the silence of ages was broken."

It was our intention after this to tie up the dogs on the
ice.

"Friday, September 29. Dr. Blessing's birthday, in honor
of which we of course had a fête, our first great one on
board. There was a double occasion for it. Our midday
observation showed us to be in latitude 79°5′ north; so we
had passed one more degree. We had no fewer than five
courses at dinner, and a more than usually elaborate concert
during the meal. Here follows a copy of the printed menu:

'FRAM'

MENU. SEPTEMBER 29, 1893

Soupe à la julienne avec des macaroni-dumplings.
Potage de poison (sic) avec des pommes de terre.
Pudding de Nordahl.
Glacé du Greenland.
De la table bière de la Ringnæes.
Marmalade intacte.

MUSIC À DINÉ (sic)

1. Valse Myosotic.
2. Menuette de Don Juan de Mozart.
3. Les Troubadours.
4. College Hornpipe.
5. Die letzte Rose de Martha.
6. Ein flotter Studio Marsch de Phil. Farbach.

7. Valse de Lagune de Strauss.
8. Le Chanson du Nord (Du gamla, du friska . . .).
9. Hoch Habsburg Marsch de Kral.
10. Josse Karads Polska.
11. Vårt Land, vårt Land.
12. Le Chanson de Chaseuse.
13. Les Roses, Valse de Métra.
14. Fischers Hornpipe.
15. Traum-Valse de Millocher.
16. Hemlandssång. 'A le misérable.'
17. Diamanten und Perlen.
18. Marsch de 'Det lustiga Kriget.'
19. Valse de 'Det lustige Kriget.'
20. Prière du Freischütz.

I hope my readers will admit that this was quite a fine entertainment to be given in latitude 79° north; but of such we had many on board the *Fram* at still higher latitudes.

"Coffee and sweets were served after dinner; and after a better supper than usual, came strawberry and lemon ice (*alias* granitta) and limejuice toddy, without alcohol. The health of the hero of the day was first proposed 'in a few well-chosen words'; and then we drank a bumper to the seventy-ninth degree, which we were sure was only the first of many degrees to be conquered in the same way.

"Saturday, September 30. I am not satisfied that the *Fram's* present position is a good one for the winter. The great floe on the port side to which we are moored sends out an ugly projection about amidships, which might give her a bad squeeze in case of the ice packing. We therefore began today to warp her backward into better ice. It is by no means quick work. The comparatively open channel around us is now covered with tolerably thick ice, which has to be hewn and broken in pieces with axes, ice staves, and walrus spears. Then the capstan is manned, and we heave her through the broken floe foot by foot. The temperature this evening is −12.6° C. A wonderful sunset.

"Sunday, October 1. Wind from the W.S.W. and weather mild. We are taking a day of rest, which means eating, sleeping, smoking, and reading.

"Monday, October 2. Warped the ship farther astern, until we found a good berth for her out in the middle of the newly frozen pool. On the port side we have our big floe, with the dogs' camp—thirty-five black dogs tied up on the white ice. This floe turns a low, and by no means threatening, edge toward us. We have good low ice on the starboard too; and between the ship and the floes we have on both sides the newly frozen surface ice, which has, in the process of warping, also got packed in under the ship's bottom, so that she lies in a good bed.

"As Sverdrup, Juell, and I were sitting in the chart room in the afternoon, splicing rope for the sounding line, Peter [Henriksen] rushed in shouting, 'A bear! a bear!' I snatched up my rifle and tore out. 'Where is it?' 'There, near the tent, on the starboard side; it came right up to it, and had almost got hold of them!'

"And there it was, big and yellow, snuffing away at the tent gear. Hansen, Blessing, and Johansen were running at the top of their speed toward the ship. Onto the ice I jumped, and off I went, broke through, stumbled, fell, and up again. The bear in the meantime had done sniffing, and had probably determined that an iron spade, an ice staff, an ax, some tent pegs, and a canvas tent were too indigestible food even for a bear's stomach. Anyhow, it was following with mighty strides in the track of the fugitives. It caught sight of me and stopped, astonished, as if it were thinking, 'What sort of insect can *that* be?' I went on to within easy range; it stood still, looking hard at me. At last it turned its head a little, and I gave it a ball in the neck. Without moving a limb, it sank slowly to the ice. I now let loose some of the dogs, to accustom them to this sort of sport, but they showed a lamentable want of interest in it; and 'Kvik,' on whom all our hope in the matter of bear hunting rested, bristled up and approached the dead animal very slowly and carefully, with her tail between her legs—a sorry spectacle.

"I must now give the story of the others who made the bear's acquaintance first. Hansen had today begun to set up his observatory tent a little ahead of the ship, on the starboard bow. In the afternoon he got Blessing and Johansen to help him. While they were hard at work, they caught sight of the bear not far from them, just off the bow of the *Fram*.

"'Hush! Keep quiet, in case we frighten him,' says Hansen.

"'Yes, yes!' And they crouch together and look at him.
"'I think I'd better try to slip on board and announce him,'
says Blessing.
"'I think you should,' says Hansen.

"And off steals Blessing on tiptoe, so as not to frighten
the bear. By this time Bruin has seen and scented them,
and comes jogging along, following his nose, toward them.

"Hansen now began to get over his fear of startling him.
The bear caught sight of Blessing slinking off to the ship
and set after him. Blessing also was now much less concerned
than he had been as to the bear's nerves. He stopped, uncertain
what to do; but a moment's reflection brought him to the
conclusion that it was pleasanter to be three than one just
then, and he went back to the others faster than he had
gone from them. The bear followed at a good rate. Hansen
did not like the look of things, and thought the time had
come to try a dodge he had seen recommended in a book. He
raised himself to his full height, flung his arms about, and
yelled with all the power of his lungs, ably assisted by the
others. But the bear came on quite undisturbed. The situation
was becoming critical. Each snatched up his weapon—Hansen
an ice staff, Johansen an ax, and Blessing nothing. They
screamed with all their strength, 'Bear! bear!' and set off for
the ship as hard as they could tear. But the bear held on
his steady course to the tent, and examined everything there
before (as we have seen) he went after them.

"It was a lean he-bear. The only thing that was found in
its stomach when it was opened was a piece of paper, with
the names 'Lütken and Mohn.' This was the wrapping paper
of a 'ski' light, and had been left by one of us somewhere
on the ice. After this day some of the members of the
expedition would hardly leave the ship without being armed
to the teeth.

"Wednesday, October 4. Northwesterly wind yesterday and
today. Yesterday we had −16°, and today −14° C. I have
worked all day at soundings and got to about 800 fathoms
depth. The bottom samples consisted of a layer of gray clay
4 to 4½ inches thick, and below that brown clay or mud. The

temperature was, strangely enough, just above freezing point
(+0.18° C.) at the bottom, and just below freezing point
(−0.4° C.) 75 fathoms up. This rather disposes of the story of
a shallow polar basin and of the extreme coldness of the water
of the Arctic Ocean.

"While we were hauling up the line in the afternoon the
ice cracked a little astern of the *Fram,* and the crack increased in breadth so quickly that three of us, who had to
go out to save the ice anchors, were obliged to make a bridge
over it with a long board to get back to the ship again.
Later in the evening there was some packing in the ice,
and several new passages opened out behind this first one.

"Thursday, October 5. As I was dressing this morning, just
before breakfast, the mate rushed down to tell me a bear
was in sight. I was soon on deck and saw him coming from
the south, to the lee of us. He was still a good way off,
but stopped and looked about. Presently he lay down, and
Henriksen and I started off across the ice, and were lucky
enough to send a bullet into his breast at about 310 yards,
just as he was moving off.

"We are making everything snug for the winter and for
the ice pressure. This afternoon we took up the rudder. Beautiful weather, but cold, −18° C. at eight P.M. The result of
the medical inspection today was the discovery that we still
have bugs on board; and I do not know what we are to do.
We have no steam now, and must fix our hopes on the cold.

"I must confess that this discovery made me feel quite ill.
If bugs got into our winter furs, the thing was hopeless. So
the next day there was a regular feast of purification, according to the most rigid antiseptic prescriptions. Each man
had to deliver up his old clothes, every stitch of them, wash
himself, and dress in new ones from top to toe. All the old
clothes, fur rugs, and such things, were carefully carried up
on to the deck, and kept there the whole winter. This was
more than even these animals could stand; −53° C. proved
to be too much for them, and we saw no more of them. As the
bug is made to say in the popular rhyme:

"'Put me in the boiling pot, and shut me down tight;
But don't leave me out on a cold winter night!'

"Friday, October 6. Cold, down to 11° below zero (Fahr.). Today we have begun to rig up the windmill. The ice has been packing to the north of the *Fram's* stern. As the dogs will freeze if they are kept tied up and get no exercise, we let them loose this afternoon, and are going to try if we can leave them so. Of course they at once began to fight, and some poor creatures limped away from the battlefield scratched and torn. But otherwise great joy prevailed; they leaped, and ran, and rolled themselves in the snow. Brilliant aurora in the evening.

"Saturday, October 7. Still cold, with the same northerly wind we have had all these last days. I am afraid we are drifting far south now. A few days ago we were, according to the observations, in 78°47' north latitude. That was 16' south in less than a week. This is too much; but we must make it up again; we *must* get north. It means going away from home now, but soon it will mean going nearer home. What depth of beauty, with an undercurrent of endless sadness, there is in these dreamily glowing evenings! The vanished sun has left its track of melancholy flame. Nature's music, which fills all space, is instinct with sorrow that all this beauty should be spread out day after day, week after week, year after year, over a dead world. Why? Sunsets are always sad at home too. This thought makes the sight seem doubly precious here and doubly sad. There is red burning blood in the west against the cold snow—and to think that this is the sea, stiffened in chains, in death, and that the sun will soon leave us, and we shall be in the dark alone! 'And the earth was without form and void'; is this the sea that is to come?

"Sunday, October 8. Beautiful weather. Made a snowshoe expedition westward, all the dogs following. The running was a little spoiled by the brine, which soaks up through the snow from the surface of the ice—flat, newly frozen ice, with older, uneven blocks breaking through it. I seated myself on a snow hummock far away out; the dogs crowded round to be patted. My eye wandered over the great snow plain, endless and solitary—nothing but snow, snow everywhere.

"The observations today gave us an unpleasant surprise; we are now down in 78°35' north latitude; but there is a

simple enough explanation of this when one thinks of all the
northerly and northwesterly wind we have had lately, with
open water not far to the south of us. As soon as everything
is frozen we must go north again; there can be no question
of that; but none the less this state of matters is unpleasant.
I find some comfort in the fact that we have also drifted
a little east, so that at all events we have kept with the wind
and are not drifting down westward.

"Monday, October 9. I was feverish both during last night
and today. Goodness knows what is the meaning of such
nonsense. When I was taking water samples in the morning
I discovered that the water lifter suddenly stopped at the
depth of a little less than eighty fathoms. It was really the
bottom. So we have drifted south again to the shallow water.
We let the weight lie at the bottom for a little, and saw
by the line that for the moment we were drifting north. This
was some small comfort, anyhow.

"All at once in the afternoon, as we were sitting idly
chattering, a deafening noise began, and the whole ship shook.
This was the first ice pressure. Every one rushed on deck
to look. The *Fram* behaved beautifully, as I had expected
she would. On pushed the ice with steady pressure, but down
under us it had to go, and we were slowly lifted up. These
'squeezings' continued off and on all the afternoon, and were
sometimes so strong that the *Fram* was lifted several feet;
but then the ice could no longer bear her, and she broke
it below her. Toward evening the whole slackened again, till
we lay in a good-sized piece of open water, and had hurriedly
to moor her to our old floe, or we should have drifted off.
There seems to be a good deal of movement in the ice here.
Peter has just been telling us that he hears the dull booming
of strong pressures not far off.

"Tuesday, October 10. The ice continues disturbed.

"Wednesday, October 11. The bad news was brought this
afternoon that 'Job' is dead, torn in pieces by the other dogs.
He was found a good way from the ship, 'Old Suggen' lying
watching the corpse, so that no other dog could get to it.
They are wretches, these dogs; no day passes without a fight.
In the daytime one of us is generally at hand to stop it,
but at night they seldom fail to tear and bite one of their

comrades. Poor 'Barabbas' is almost frightened out of his wits. He stays on board now, and dares not venture on the ice, because he knows the other monsters would set on him. There is not a trace of chivalry about these curs. When there is a fight, the whole pack rush like wild beasts on the loser. But is it not, perhaps, the law of nature that the strong, and not the weak, should be protected? Have not we human beings, perhaps, been trying to turn nature topsy-turvy by protecting and doing our best to keep life in all the weak?

"The ice is restless, and has pressed a good deal today again. It begins with a gentle crack and moan along the side of the ship, which gradually sounds louder in every key. Now it is a high plaintive tone, now it is a grumble, now it is a snarl, and the ship gives a start up. The noise steadily grows till it is like all the pipes of an organ; the ship trembles and shakes, and rises by fits and starts, or is sometimes gently lifted. There is a pleasant, comfortable feeling in sitting listening to all this uproar and knowing the strength of our ship. Many a one would have been crushed long ago. But outside the ice is ground against our ship's sides, the piles of broken-up floe are forced under her heavy, invulnerable hull, and we lie as if in a bed. Soon the noise begins to die down; the ship sinks into its old position again, and presently all is silent as before. In several places round us the ice is piled up, at one spot to a considerable height. Toward evening there was a slackening, and we lay again in a large, open pool.

"Thursday, October 12. In the morning we and our floe were drifting on blue water in the middle of a large, open lane, which stretched far to the north, and in the north the atmosphere at the horizon was dark and blue. As far as we could see from the crow's-nest with the small field glass, there was no end to the open water, with only single pieces of ice sticking up in it here and there. These are extraordinary changes. I wondered if we should prepare to go ahead. But they had long ago taken the machinery to pieces for the winter, so that it would be a matter of time to get it ready for use again. Perhaps it would be best to wait a little. Clear weather, with sunshine—a beautiful, inspiring winter day—but the same northerly wind. Took soundings, and found fifty fathoms of water (ninety meters). We are drifting slowly southward. Toward evening the ice packed together again with much force; but the *Fram* can hold her own. In the afternoon I fished in a depth of about twenty-seven fathoms (fifty meters) with Murray's silk net, and had a good take, especially of small crustaceans (*Copepoda, Ostracoda, Amphipoda,* etc.) and of a little Arctic worm (*Spadella*) that swims about in the sea. It is horribly difficult to manage a little fishing here. No sooner have you found an opening to slip your tackle through than it begins to close again, and you have to haul up as hard as you can, so as not to get the line nipped and lose everything. It is a pity, for there are interesting hauls to be made. One sees phosphorescence in the water here whenever there is the smallest opening in the ice. There is by no means such a scarcity of animal life as one might expect.

"Friday, October 13. Now we are in the very midst of what the prophets would have had us dread so much. The ice is pressing and packing round us with a noise like thunder. It is piling itself up into long walls, and heaps high enough to reach a good way up the *Fram's* rigging; in fact, it is trying its very utmost to grind the *Fram* into powder. But here we sit quite tranquil, not even going up to look at all the hurly-burly, but just chatting and laughing as usual. Last night there was tremendous pressure round our old dog floe. The ice had towered up higher than the highest point of the floe and hustled down upon it. It had quite spoiled a well, where we till now had found good drinking water, filling it with brine. Furthermore, it had cast itself over our stern ice anchor and part of the steel cable which held it, burying them so effectually that we had afterwards to cut the cable. Then it covered our planks and sledges, which stood on the ice. Before long the dogs were in danger, and the watch had to turn out all hands to save them. At last the floe split in two. This morning the ice was one scene of melancholy confusion, gleaming in the most glorious sunshine. Piled up all round us were high, steep ice walls. Strangely enough, we had lain on the very verge of the worst confusion, and had escaped with the loss of an ice anchor, a piece of steel cable, a few planks and other bits of wood, and half of a

Samoyede sledge, all of which might have been saved if we had looked after them in time. But the men have grown so indifferent to the pressure now that they do not even go up to look, let it thunder ever so hard. They feel that the ship can stand it, and so long as that is the case, there is nothing to hurt except the ice itself.

"In the morning the pressure slackened again, and we were soon lying in a piece of open water, as we did yesterday. Today, again, this stretched far away toward the northern horizon, where the same dark atmosphere indicated some extent of open water. I now gave the order to put the engine together again; they told me it could be done in a day and a half or at most two days. We must go north and see what there is up there. I think it possible that it may be the boundary between the ice drift the *Jeannette* was in and the pack we are now drifting south with—or can it be land?

"We had kept company quite long enough with the old, now broken-up floe, so worked ourselves a little way astern after dinner, as the ice was beginning to draw together. Toward evening the pressure began again in earnest, and was especially bad round the remains of our old floe, so that I believe we may congratulate ourselves on having left it. It is evident that the pressure here stands in connection with, is perhaps caused by, the tidal wave. It occurs with the greatest regularity. The ice slackens twice and packs twice in twenty-four hours. The pressure has happened about four, five, and six o'clock in the morning, and almost at exactly the same hour in the afternoon, and in between we have always lain for some part of the time in open water. The very great pressure just now is probably due to the spring tide; we had new moon on the 9th, which was the first day of the pressure. Then it was just after mid-day when we noticed it, but it has been later every day, and now it is at eight P.M."

The theory of the ice pressure being caused to a considerable extent by the tidal wave has been advanced repeatedly by arctic explorers. During the *Fram's* drifting we had better opportunity than most of them to study this phenomenon, and our experience seems to leave no doubt that over a wide region the tide produces movement and pressure of the ice. It occurs especially at the time of the spring tides, and more at new moon than at full moon. During the intervening periods there was, as a rule, little or no trace of pressure. But these tidal pressures did not occur during the whole time of our drifting. We noticed them especially the first autumn, while we were in the neighborhood of the open sea north of Siberia, and the last year, when the *Fram* was drawing near the open Atlantic Ocean; they were less noticeable while we were in the polar basin. Pressure occurs here more irregularly, and is mainly caused by the wind driving the ice. When one pictures to one's self these enormous ice masses, drifting in a certain direction, suddenly meeting hindrances—for example, ice-masses drifting from the opposite direction, owing to a change of wind in some more or less distant quarter—it is easy to understand the tremendous pressure that must result.

Such an ice conflict is undeniably a stupendous spectacle. One feels one's self to be in the presence of titanic forces, and it is easy to understand how timid souls may be overawed and feel as if nothing could stand before it. For when the packing begins in earnest it seems as though there could be no spot on the earth's surface left unshaken. First you hear a sound like the thundering rumbling of an earthquake far away on the great waste; then you hear it in several places, always coming nearer and nearer. The silent ice world re-echoes with thunders; nature's giants are awakening to the battle. The ice cracks on every side of you, and begins to pile itself up; and all of a sudden you too find yourself in the midst of the struggle. There are howlings and thunderings round you; you feel the ice trembling, and hear it rumbling under your feet; there is no peace anywhere. In the semidarkness you can see it piling and tossing itself up into high ridges nearer and nearer you—floes ten, twelve, fifteen feet thick, broken, and flung on the top of each other as if they were featherweights. They are quite near you now, and you jump away to save your life. But the ice splits in front of you, a black gulf opens, and water streams up. You turn in another direction, but here through the dark you can just see a new ridge of moving ice blocks coming toward you. You try another direction, but there it is the same. All round there is thundering and roaring, as of some enormous waterfall, with explosions like cannon salvos. Still nearer you it comes. The floe you are standing on gets smaller and smaller; water pours over it; there can be no escape except by scrambling over the rolling ice blocks to get to the other side of the pack. But now the disturbance begins to calm down. The noise passes on, and is lost by degrees in the distance.

This is what goes on away there in the north month after month and year after year. The ice is split and piled up into mounds, which extend in every direction. If one could get a bird's-eye view of the ice fields, they would seem to be cut up into squares or meshes by a network of these packed ridges, or pressure dikes, as we called them, because they reminded us so much of snow-covered stone dikes at home, such as, in many parts of the country, are used to enclose fields. At first sight these pressure ridges appeared to be scattered about in all possible directions, but on closer inspection I was sure that I discovered certain directions which they tended to take, and especially that they were apt to run at right angles to the course of the pressure which produced them. In the accounts of arctic expeditions one often reads descriptions of pressure ridges or pressure hummocks as high as fifty feet. These are fairy tales. The authors of such fantastic descriptions cannot have taken the trouble to measure. During the whole period of our drifting and of our travels over the ice fields in the far north I only once saw a hummock of a greater height than twenty-three feet. Unfortunately, I had not the opportunity of measuring this one, but I believe I may say with certainty that it was very nearly thirty feet high. All the highest blocks I measured—and they were many—had a height of eighteen to twenty-three feet; and I can maintain with certainty that the packing of sea ice to a height of over twenty-five feet is a very rare exception.

"Saturday, October 14. Today we have got on the rudder; the engine is pretty well in order, and we are clear to start north when the ice opens tomorrow morning. It is still slackening and packing quite regularly twice a day, so that we can calculate on it beforehand. Today we had the same open channel to the north, and beyond it open sea as far as our view extended. What can this mean? This evening the pressure has been pretty violent. The floes were packed up against the *Fram* on the port side, and were once or twice on the point of toppling over the rail. The ice, however broke below; they tumbled back again, and had to go under us after all. It is not thick ice, and cannot do much damage; but the force is something enormous. On the masses come incessantly without a pause; they look irresistible; but slowly and surely they are crushed against the *Fram's* sides. Now (eight-thirty P.M.) the pressure has at last stopped. Clear evening, sparkling stars, and flaming northern lights."

I had finished writing my diary, gone to bed, and was lying reading, in *The Origin of Species*, about the struggle for existence, when I heard the dogs out on the ice making more noise than usual. I called into the saloon that some one ought to go up and see if it was bears they were barking at. Hansen went, and came back immediately, saying that he believed he had seen some large animal out in the dark. "Go and shoot it, then." That he was quite ready to do, and went up again at once, accompanied by some of the others. A shot went off on deck above my head, then another; shot followed shot, nine in all. Johansen and Henriksen rushed down for more cartridges, and declared that the creature was shot, it was roaring so horribly; but so far they had only indistinctly seen a large grayish-white mass out there in the dark, moving about among the dogs. Now they were going on to the ice after it. Four of them set off, and not far away they really did find a dead bear, with marks of two shots. It was a young one. The old one must be at hand, and the dogs were still barking loudly. Now they all felt sure that they had seen two together, and that the other also must be badly wounded. Johansen and Henriksen heard it groaning in the distance when they were out on the ice again afterward to fetch a knife they had left lying where the dead one had lain. The creature had been dragged on board and skinned at once, before it had time to stiffen in the cold.

"Sunday, October 15. To our surprise, the ice did not slacken away much during last night after the violent pressure; and, what was worse, there was no indication of slackening in the morning, now that we were quite ready to go. Slight signs of it showed themselves a little later, upon which I gave orders to

get up steam; and while this was being done I took a stroll
on the ice, to look for traces of yesterday evening. I found
tracks not only of the bear that had been killed and of a larger
one that might be the mother, but of a third, which must have
been badly wounded, as it had sometimes dragged itself on its
hind quarters, and had left a broad track of blood. After
following the traces for a good way and discovering that I
had no weapon to despatch the animal with but my own fists,
I thought it would be as well to return to the ship to get a gun
and companions who would help to drag the bear back. I had
also some small hope that in the meantime the ice might have
slackened, so that, in place of going after game, we might go
north with the *Fram*. But no such luck! So I put on my
snowshoes and set off after our bear, some of the dogs with
me, and one or two men following. At some distance we
came to the place where it had spent the night—poor beast,
a ghastly night! Here I also saw tracks of the mother. One
shudders to think of her watching over her poor young one,
which must have had its back shot through. Soon we came up
to the cripple, dragging itself away from us over the ice as
best it could. Seeing no other way of escape, it threw itself
into a small water opening and dived time after time. While
we were putting a noose on a rope, the dogs rushed round the
hole as if they had gone mad, and it was difficult to keep
them from jumping into the water after the bear. At last we
were ready, and the next time the creature came up it got a
noose round one paw and a ball in the head. While the others
drew it to the ship, I followed the mother's tracks for some
way, but could not find her. I had soon to turn back to see if
there was no prospect of moving the *Fram;* but I found that
the ice had packed together again a little at the very time
when we could generally calculate on its slackening. In the
afternoon Hansen and I went off once more after the bear.
We saw, as I expected, that she had come back, and had
followed her daughter's funeral procession for some way, but
then she had gone off east, and as it grew dark we lost her
tracks in some newly packed ice. We have only one matter
for regret in connection with this bear episode, and that is
the disappearance of two dogs—'Narrifas' and 'Fox.' Probably
they went off in terror on the first appearance of the three

bears. They may have been hurt, but I have seen nothing to suggest this. The ice is quiet this evening also, only a little pressure about seven o'clock.

"Monday, October 16. Ice quiet and close. Observations on the twelfth placed us in 78°5′ north latitude. Steadily southward. This is almost depressing. The two runaways returned this morning.

"Tuesday, October 17. Continuous movement in the ice. It slackened a little again during the night; some way off to starboard there was a large opening. Shortly after midnight there was strong pressure, and between eleven and twelve A.M. came a tremendous squeeze; since then it has slackened again a little.

"Wednesday, October 18. When the meteorologist, Johansen, was on deck this morning reading the thermometers, he noticed that the dogs, which are now tied up on board, were barking loudly down at something on the ice. He bent over the rail astern, near the rudder, and saw the back of a bear below him, close in at the ship's side. Off he went for a gun, and the animal fell with a couple of shots. We saw afterward by its tracks that it had inspected all the heaps of sweepings round the ship.

"A little later in the morning, I went for a stroll on the ice. Hansen and Johansen were busy with some magnetic observations to the south of the ship. It was beautiful sunshiny weather. I was standing beside an open pool a little way ahead, examining the formation and growth of the new ice, when I heard a gun go off on board. I turned, and just caught a glimpse of a bear making off toward the hummocks. It was Henriksen who had seen it from the deck coming marching toward the ship. When it was a few paces off, it saw Hansen and Johansen, and made straight for them. By this time Henriksen had got his gun, but it missed fire several times. He has an unfortunate liking for smearing the lock so well with vaseline that the spring works as if it lay in soft soap. At last it went off, and the ball went through the bear's back and breast in a slanting direction. The animal stood up on its hind legs, fought the air with its forepaws, then flung itself forward and sprang off, to fall after about thirty steps; the ball had grazed the heart. It was not till the shot went off that Hansen saw the bear, and then he rushed up and put two revolver balls into its head. It was a large bear, the largest we had got yet.

"About midday I was in the crow's-nest. In spite of the clear weather, I could not discover land on any side. The opening far to the north has quite disappeared; but during the night a large new one has formed quite close to us. It stretches both north and south, and has now a covering of ice. The pressure is chiefly confined to the edges of this opening, and can be traced in walls of packed ice as far as the horizon in both directions. To the east the ice is quite unbroken and flat. We have lain just in the worst pressure.

"Thursday, October 19. The ice again slackened a little last night. In the morning I attempted a drive with six of the dogs. When I had managed to harness them to the Samoyede sledge, had seated myself on it, and called 'Pr-r-r-r, pr-r-r-r!' they went off in quite good style over the ice. But it was not long before we came to some high pack ice and had to turn. This was hardly done before they were off back to the ship at lightning speed, and they were not to be got away from it again. Round and round it they went, from refuse heap to refuse heap. If I started at the gangway on the starboard side, and tried by thrashing them to drive them out over the ice, round the stern they flew to the gangway on the port side. I tugged, swore, and tried everything I could think of, but all to no purpose. I got out and tried to hold the sledge back, but was pulled off my feet, and dragged merrily over the ice in my smooth sealskin breeches, on back, stomach, side—just as it happened. When I managed to stop them at some pieces of pack ice or a dust heap, round they went again to the starboard gangway, with me dangling behind, swearing madly that I would break every bone in their bodies when I got at them. This game went on till they probably tired of it, and thought they might as well go my way for a change. So now they went off beautifully across the flat floe until I stopped for a moment's breathing space. But at the first movement I made in the sledge they were off again, tearing wildly back the way we had come. I held on convulsively, pulled, raged, and used the whip; but the more I lashed the faster they went on their own way. At last I got them stopped by sticking my legs down into the snow between the sledge shafts, and driving a strong seal hook into it as well. But while I was off my guard for a moment they gave a tug. I lay with my hinder part where my legs had been, and we went on at lightning speed—that substantial part of my body leaving a deep track in the snow. This sort of thing went on time after time. I lost the board I should have sat on, then the whip, then my gloves, then my cap—these losses not improving my temper. Once or twice I ran round in front of the dogs, and tried to force them to turn by lashing at them with the whip. They jumped to both sides and only tore on the faster; the reins got twisted round my ankles, and I was thrown flat on the sledge, and they went on more wildly than ever. This was my first experience in dog driving on my own account, and I will not pretend that I was proud of it. I inwardly congratulated myself that my feats had been unobserved.

"In the afternoon I examined the melted water of the newly formed brownish-red ice, of which there is a good deal in the openings round us here. The microscope proved this color to be produced by swarms of small organisms, chiefly plants— quantities of diatomae and some algae, a few of them very peculiar in form.

"Saturday, October 21. I have stayed in today because of an affection of the muscles, or rheumatism, which I have had for some days on the right side of my body, and for which the doctor is 'massaging' me, thereby greatly adding to my sufferings. Have I really grown so old and palsied, or is the whole thing imagination? It is all I can do to limp about; but I just wonder if I could not get up and run with the best of them if there happened to be any great occasion for it: I almost believe I could. A nice arctic hero of thirty-two, lying here in my berth! Have had a good time reading home letters, dreaming myself at home, dreaming of the home-coming—in how many years? Successful or unsuccessful, what does that matter?

"I had a sounding taken; it showed over seventy-three fathoms (135 meters), so we are in deeper water again. The sounding line indicated that we are drifting southwest. I do not understand this steady drift southward. There has not been much wind either lately; there is certainly a little from the north today, but not strong. What can be the reason of it? With all my information, all my reasoning, all my putting of two and two together, I cannot account for any south-going current here—there ought to be a north-going one. If the current runs south here, how is that great open sea we steamed north across to be explained? and the bay we ended in farthest north? These could only be produced by the north-going current which I presupposed. The only thing which puts me out a bit is that west-going current which we had against us during our whole voyage along the Siberian coast. We are never going to be carried away south by the New Siberian Islands, and then west along the coast of Siberia, and then north by Cape Chelyuskin, the very way we came! That would be rather too much of a good thing—to say nothing of its being dead against every calculation.

"Well, who cares? Somewhere we must go; we can't stay here forever. 'It will all come right in the end,' as the saying goes; but I wish we could get on a little faster wherever we are going. On our Greenland expedition, too, we were carried south to begin with, and that ended well."

"Sunday, October 22. Henriksen took soundings this morning, and found seventy fathoms (129 meters) of water. 'If we are drifting at all,' said he, 'it is to the east; but there seems to be almost no movement.' No wind today. I am keeping in my den.

"Monday, October 23. Still in the den. Today, five fathoms shallower than yesterday. The line points southwest, which means that we are drifting northeastward. Hansen has reckoned out the observation for the nineteenth, and finds that we must have got ten minutes farther north, and must be in 78° 15′ N. lat. So at last, now that the wind has gone down, the north-going current is making itself felt. Some channels have opened near us, one along the side of the ship, and one ahead, near the old channel. Only slight signs of pressure in the afternoon.

"Tuesday, October 24. Between four and five A.M. there was strong pressure, and the *Fram* was lifted up a little. It looks as if the pressure were going to begin again; we have springtide with full moon. The ice opened so much this morning that the *Fram* was afloat in her cutting; later on it closed again, and about eleven there was some strong pressure; then came a quiet time; but in the afternoon the pressure began once more, and was violent from four to four-thirty. The *Fram* was shaken and lifted up; didn't mind a bit. Peter gave it as his opinion that the pressure was coming from the northeast, for he had heard the noise approaching from that direction. Johansen let down the silk net for me about eleven fathoms. It was all he could do to get it up again in time, but it brought up a good catch. Am still keeping in.

"Wednesday, October 25. We had a horrible pressure last night. I awoke and felt the *Fram* being lifted, shaken, and tossed about, and heard the loud cracking of the ice breaking against her sides. After listening for a little while I fell asleep again, with a snug feeling that it was good to be on board the *Fram;* it would be confoundedly uncomfortable to have to be ready to turn out every time there was a little pressure, or to have to go off with our bundles on our backs like the *Tegethoff* people.

"It is quickly getting darker. The sun stands lower and lower every time we see it; soon it will disappear altogether, if it has not done so already. The long, dark winter is upon us, and glad shall we be to see the spring; but nothing matters much if we could only begin to move north. There is now southwesterly wind, and the windmill, which has been ready for several days, has been tried at last and works splendidly. We have beautiful electric light today, though the wind has not been especially strong (5–8 m. per second). Electric lamps are a grand institution. What a strong influence light has on one's spirits! There was a noticeable brightening-up at the dinner table today; the light acted on our spirits like a draught of good wine. And how festive the saloon looks! We felt it quite a great occasion—drank Oscar Dickson's health, and voted him the best of good fellows.

"Wonderful moonshine this evening, light as day; and along with it aurora borealis, yellow and strange in the white moonlight; a large ring round the moon—all this over the great stretch of white, shining ice, here and there in our neighborhood piled up high by the pressure. And in the midst of this silent silvery ice-world the windmill sweeps round its dark wings against the deep blue sky and the aurora. A strange contrast: civilization making a sudden incursion into this frozen ghostly world.

"Tomorrow is the *Fram*'s birthday. How many memories it recalls of the launch-day a year ago!

"Thursday, October 26. Fifty-four fathoms (ninety meters) of water when the soundings were taken this morning. We are moving quickly north—due north—says Peter. It does look as if things were going better. Great celebration of the day, beginning with target shooting. Then we had a splendid dinner of four courses, which put our digestive apparatus to a severe test. The *Fram*'s health was drunk amidst great and stormy applause. The proposer's words were echoed by all hearts when he said that she was such an excellent ship for our purpose that we could not imagine a better (great applause), and we therefore wished her, and ourselves with her, long life (hear, hear!). After supper came strawberry and lemon punch, and prizes were presented with much ceremony and a good deal of fun; all being 'taken off' in turn in suitable mottoes, for the most part composed by the ship's doctor. There was a prize for each man. The first prize taker was awarded the wooden cross of the Order of the *Fram*, to wear suspended from his neck by a ribbon of white tape; the last received a mirror, in which to see his fallen greatness. Smoking in the saloon was allowed this evening, so now pipes, toddy, and an animated game of whist ended a bright and successful holiday.

"Sitting here now alone, my thoughts involuntarily turn to the year that has gone since we stood up there on the platform, and she threw the champagne against the bow, saying: '*Fram* is your name!' and the strong, heavy hull began to glide so gently. I held her hand tight; the tears came into eyes and throat, and one could not get out a word. The sturdy hull dived into the glittering water; a sunny haze lay over the whole picture. Never shall I forget the moment we stood there together, looking out over the scene. And to think of all that has happened these four last months! Separated by sea and land and ice; coming years, too, lying between us—it is all just the continuation of what happened that day. But how long is it to last? I have such difficulty in feeling that I am

not to see home again soon. When I begin to reflect, I know
that it may be long, but I will not believe it.

"Today, moreover, we took solemn farewell of the sun. Half
of its disk showed at noon for the last time above the edge
of the ice in the south, a flattened body, with a dull red
glow, but no heat. Now we are entering the night of winter.
What is it bringing us? Where shall we be when the sun
returns?

We Reach the Pole

ROBERT E. PEARY

"The true explorer does his work not for any hope of reward or honor, but because the thing he has set for himself to do is a part of his being, and must be accomplished for the sake of the accomplishment. And he counts lightly hardships, risks, obstacles, if only they do not bar him from his goal.

"To me the final and complete solution of the polar mystery which has engaged the best thought and interest of some of the best men of the most vigorous and enlightened nations of the world for more than three centuries, and today quickens the pulse of every man or woman whose veins hold red blood, is the thing which must be done for the honor and credit of his country, the thing which it is intended that I should do, and the thing that I must do."

With these words, spoken before a National Geographic Society audience, Robert E. Peary turned away from civilization to make his final polar journey, reaching the North Pole triumphantly in 1909. His success crowned a career of driving ambition and dedication that had begun with his first northern trip in 1886. Defeated time and again, Peary was drawn on to new efforts by what he called "the lure of the North."

THE LAST march northward ended at ten o'clock of the forenoon of April sixth. I had now made the five marches planned from the point at which Bartlett turned back, and my reckoning showed that we were in the immediate neighborhood of the goal of all our striving. After the usual arrangements for going into camp, at approximate local noon, on the Columbia meridian, I made the first observation at our polar camp. It indicated our position as 89°57′.

We were now at the end of the last long march of the upward journey. Yet with the Pole actually in sight I was too weary to take the last few steps. The accumulated weariness of all those days and nights of forced marches and insufficient sleep, constant peril and anxiety, seemed to roll across me all at once. I was actually too exhausted to realize at the moment that my life's purpose had been achieved. As soon as our igloos had been completed, and we had eaten our dinner and double-rationed the dogs, I turned in for a few hours of absolutely necessary sleep, Henson and the Eskimos having unloaded the sledges and got them in readiness for such repairs as were necessary. But, weary though I was, I could not sleep long. It was, therefore, only a few hours later when I woke. The first thing I did after awaking was to write these words in my diary: "The Pole at last. The prize of three centuries. My dream and goal for twenty years. Mine at last! I cannot bring myself to realize it. It seems all so simple and commonplace."

Everything was in readiness for an observation at six P.M., Columbia meridian time, in case the sky should be clear, but at that hour it was, unfortunately, still overcast. But as there were indications that it would clear before long, two of the Eskimos and myself made ready a light sledge carrying only the instruments, a tin of pemmican, and one or two skins; and drawn by a double team of dogs, we pushed on an estimated distance of ten miles. While we traveled, the sky cleared, and at the end of the journey, I was able to get a satisfactory series of observations at Columbia meridian midnight. These observations indicated that our position was then beyond the Pole.

Nearly everything in the circumstances which then surrounded us seemed too strange to be thoroughly realized, but one of the strangest of those circumstances seemed to me to be the fact that, in a march of only a few hours, I had passed from the western to the eastern hemisphere and had verified my position at the summit of the world. It was hard to realize that, on the first miles of this brief march, we had been traveling due north, while, on the last few miles of the same march, we had been traveling south, although we had all the time been traveling precisely in the same direction. It would be difficult to imagine a better illustration of the fact that most things are relative. Again, please consider the uncommon circumstance that, in order to return to our camp, it now became necessary to turn and go north again for a few miles and then to go directly south, all the time traveling in the same direction.

As we passed back along that trail which none had ever seen before or would ever see again, certain reflections intruded themselves which, I think, may fairly be called unique. East, west, and north had disappeared for us. Only one direction remained and that was south. Every breeze which could possibly blow upon us, no matter from what point of the horizon, must be a south wind. Where we were, one day and one night constituted a year, a hundred such days and nights constituted a century. Had we stood in that spot during the six months of the Arctic winter night, we should have seen every star of the northern hemisphere circling the sky at the same distance from the horizon, with Polaris (the North Star) practically in the zenith.

All during our march back to camp the sun was swinging around in its ever-moving circle. At six o'clock on the morning of April seventh having again arrived at Camp Jesup, I took another series of observations. These indicated our position as being four or five miles from the Pole, toward Bering Strait. Therefore, with a double team of dogs and a light sledge, I traveled directly toward the sun an estimated distance of eight miles. Again I returned to the camp in time for a final and completely satisfactory series of observations on April seventh at noon, Columbia meridian time. These observations gave results essentially the same as those made at the same spot twenty-four hours before.

I had now taken in all thirteen single, or six and one-half double, altitudes of the sun, at two different stations, in three different directions, at four different times. All were under satisfactory conditions, except for the first single altitude on the sixth. The temperature during these observations, had been from minus 11° Fahrenheit to minus 30° Fahrenheit, with clear sky and calm weather (except as already noted for the single observation on the sixth). I give here a facsimile of a typical set of these observations.

In traversing the ice in these various directions as I had done, I had allowed approximately ten miles for possible errors in my observations, and at some moment during these marches and countermarches, I had passed over or very near the point where north and south and east and west blend into one.

Of course there were some more or less informal ceremonies connected with our arrival at our difficult destination, but they were not of a very elaborate character. We planted five flags at the top of the world. The first one was a silk American flag which Mrs. Peary gave me fifteen years ago. That flag has done more traveling in high latitudes than any other ever made. I carried it wrapped about my body on every one of my expeditions northward after it came into my possession, and I left a fragment of it at each of my successive "farthest norths": Cape Morris K. Jesup, the northernmost point of land in the known world; Cape Thomas Hubbard, the northernmost known point of Jesup Land, west of Grant Land; Cape Columbia, the northernmost point of North American lands; and my farthest north in 1906, latitude 87°6′ in the ice of the polar sea. By the time it actually reached the Pole, therefore, it was somewhat worn and discolored.

A broad diagonal section of this ensign would now mark the farthest goal of earth—the place where I and my dusky companions stood.

It was also considered appropriate to raise the colors of the Delta Kappa Epsilon fraternity, in which I was initiated a member while an undergraduate student at Bowdoin College, the "World's Ensign of Liberty and Peace," with its red, white, and blue, in a field of white, the Navy League flag, and the Red Cross flag.

After I had planted the American flag in the ice, I told Henson to time the Eskimos for three rousing cheers, which they gave with the greatest enthusiasm. Thereupon, I shook hands with each member of the party—surely a sufficiently unceremonious affair to meet with the approval of the most democratic. The Eskimos were childishly delighted with our success. While, of course, they did not realize its importance fully, or its worldwide significance, they did understand that it meant the final achievement of a task upon which they had seen me engaged for many years.

Then, in a space between the ice blocks of a pressure ridge,

I deposited a glass bottle containing a diagonal strip of my flag and records of which the following is a copy:

90 N. LAT., NORTH POLE,
6th April, 1909.

Arrived here today, 27 marches from C. Columbia.

I have with me 5 men, Matthew Henson, colored, Oo-tah, E-ging-wah, See-gloo, and Oo-ke-ah, Eskimos; 5 sledges and 38 dogs. My ship, the S.S. *Roosevelt*, is in winter quarters at C. Sheridan, 90 miles east of Columbia.

The expedition under my command which has succeeded in reaching the Pole, is under the auspices of the Peary Arctic Club of New York City, and has been fitted out and sent north by the members and friends of the club for the purpose of securing this geographical prize, if possible, for the honor and prestige of the United States of America.

The officers of the club are Thomas H. Hubbard, of New York, President; Zenas Crane, of Mass., Vice-President; Herbert L. Bridgman, of New York, Secretary and Treasurer.

I start back for Cape Columbia tomorrow.

ROBERT E. PEARY,
United States Navy.

90 N. LAT., NORTH POLE,
6th April, 1909.

I have today hoisted the national ensign of the United States of America at this place, which my observations indicate to be the North Polar axis of the earth, and have formally taken possession of the entire region, and adjacent, for and in the name of the President of the United States of America.

I leave this record and United States flag in possession.

ROBERT E. PEARY,
United States Navy.

If it were possible for a man to arrive at 90° north latitude without being utterly exhausted, body and brain, he would doubtless enjoy a series of unique sensations and reflections. But the attainment of the Pole was the culmination of days and weeks of forced marches, physical discomfort, insufficient sleep, and racking anxiety. It is a wise provision of nature that the human consciousness can grasp only such degree of intense feeling as the brain can endure, and the grim guardians of earth's remotest spot will accept no man as guest until he has been tried and tested by the severest ordeal.

Perhaps it ought not to have been so, but when I knew for a certainty that we had reached the goal, there was not a thing in the world I wanted but sleep. But after I had a few hours of it, there succeeded a condition of mental exaltation which made further rest impossible. For more than a score of years that point on the earth's surface had been the object of my every effort. To attain it my whole being, physical, mental, and moral, had been dedicated. Many times my own life and the lives of those with me had been risked. My own material and forces and those of my friends had been devoted to this object. The journey was my eighth into the arctic wilderness. In that wilderness I had spent nearly twelve years out of the twenty-three between my thirtieth and my fifty-third year, and the intervening time spent in civilized communities during that period had been mainly occupied with preparations for returning to the wilderness. The determination to reach the Pole had become so much a part of my being that, strange as it may seem, I long ago ceased to think of myself save as an instrument for the attainment of that end. To the layman this may seem strange, but an inventor can understand it, or an artist, or any one who has devoted himself for years upon years to the service of an idea.

But though my mind was busy at intervals during those thirty hours spent at the Pole with the exhilarating thought that my dream had come true, there was one recollection of other times that, now and then, intruded itself with startling distinctness. It was the recollection of a day three years before, 21 April 1906, when after making a fight with ice, open water, and storms, the expedition which I commanded had been forced to turn back from 87°6′ north latitude because our supply of food would carry us no further. And the contrast between the terrible depression of that day and the exaltation of the present moment was not the least pleasant feature of our brief stay at the Pole. During the dark moments of that return journey in 1906, I had told myself that I was only one in a long list of arctic explorers, dating back through the centuries, all the way from Henry Hudson to the Duke of the Abruzzi, and including Franklin, Kane, and Melville— a long list of valiant men who had striven and failed. I told myself that I had only succeeded at the price of the best years of my life in adding a few links to the chain that led from the parallels of civilization toward the polar center, but that, after all, at the end the only word I had to write was failure.

But now, while quartering the ice in various directions from our camp, I tried to realize that, after twenty-three years of struggles and discouragement, I had at last succeeded in placing the flag of my country at the goal of the world's desire. It is not easy to write about such a thing, but I knew that we were going back to civilization with the last of the great adventure stories—a story the world had been waiting to hear for nearly four hundred years, a story which was to be told at last under the folds of the Stars and Stripes, the flag that during a lonely and isolated life had come to be for me the symbol of home and everything I loved—and might never see again.

The thirty hours at the Pole, what with my marchings and countermarchings, together with the observations and records, were pretty well crowded. I found time, however, to write to Mrs. Peary on a United States postal card which I had found on the ship during the winter. It had been my custom at various important stages of the journey northward to write such a note in order that, if anything serious happened to me, these brief communications might ultimately reach her at the hands of survivors. This was the card, which later reached Mrs. Peary at Sydney:

"90 NORTH LATITUDE, 7th April.
"My dear Jo,
"I have won out at last. Have been here a day. I start for home and you in an hour. Love to the 'kidsies.'
"BERT."

In the afternoon of the seventh, after flying our flags and taking our photographs, we went into our igloos and tried to sleep a little, before starting south again.

I could not sleep and my two Eskimos, See-gloo and E-ging-wah, who occupied the igloo with me, seemed equally restless. They turned from side to side, and when they were quiet I could tell from their uneven breathing that they were not asleep. Though they had not been specially excited the day before when I told them that we had reached the goal, yet they also seemed to be under the same exhilarating influence which made sleep impossible for me.

Finally I rose, and telling my men and the three men in the other igloo, who were equally wakeful, that we would try to make our last camp, some thirty miles to the south, before we slept, I gave orders to hitch up the dogs and be off. It seemed unwise to waste such perfect traveling weather in tossing about on the sleeping platforms of our igloos.

Neither Henson nor the Eskimos required any urging to take to the trail again. They were naturally anxious to get back to the land as soon as possible—now that our work was done. And about four o'clock on the afternoon of the seventh of April we turned our backs upon the camp at the North Pole.

Though intensely conscious of what I was leaving, I did not wait for any lingering farewell of my life's goal. The event of human beings standing at the hitherto inaccessible summit of the earth was accomplished, and my work now lay to the south, where four hundred and thirteen nautical miles of ice floes and possibly open leads still lay between us and the north coast of Grant Land. One backward glance I gave—then turned my face toward the south and toward the future.

Flight Over the Pole

RICHARD E. BYRD

School annuals, when looked back upon, often record lost hopes, but occasionally it is interesting to track down the early education of a great man. Here is the Naval Academy summation of Richard Evelyn Byrd:

"Athlete, leader in all right things, Friend, Gentleman. From the time we entered as plebes until the present, Dick has been putting his whole heart into everything he does. . . . Most of the time, Dick moves around with a faraway look in his eyes. But go where he may, he cannot hope to find the truth and beauty of which he dreams. He has always lived a life rich in experience and he will live a life richer still. But he will always give to life more than he takes."

To Byrd goes the credit for many polar firsts: he was the first to fly over both the North and South Poles and the first to coax age-old secrets from the polar ice. His flight over the North Pole took place in 1926. It was a difficult feat in those days: oil had to be thinned for lubrication, spare parts had to be carried laboriously through the snow—a take-off was almost impossible. Byrd tried to take off three times—and three times he damaged his plane. Finally, he made it, covering a 1440-mile round trip in sixteen hours.

THERE is one thing at least, which I can truly say of my career: it is that from the moment I became a full-fledged Navy pilot my ambition was to make a career in aviation. Not merely in the sense of routine flying, but rather in the pioneering sense. At the time I was learning to fly, the airplane was just on the verge of becoming a tool which mankind could fit to its hand. My ambition was to test the tool to the utmost and, through a series of long-range flights, help to show the way, if I could, toward improving technologies. That was a common ambition among pilots of my day, I must confess; for once you have tasted the heady satisfactions of flight, you never lose the love of them, nor the desire to make them known to others.

I found myself transferred to Nova Scotia, where I was given command of two air stations, one at North Sydney and the other at Dartmouth. My job was scouting for submarines in the northwest Atlantic. All the while I hammered at the Bureau of Aeronautics in the Navy Department for permission to fly the Atlantic in one of the long-range flying boats which the Navy was building. That came to nothing. But my research work in air navigation landed me the job of navigation officer of the NC flying boats that were to attempt a crossing of the Atlantic. I accompanied the planes for the first two legs of the flight as navigator.

For several years I was marooned in Washington as the Navy's liaison with Congress. Important and even instructive as this work was, it failed to appease my appetite for aviation. From this vacuum I received reprieve in the shape of an order to report to England for duty aboard the dirigible ZR-3, which was to be flown to the United States. But a few days after I reached England, that ship, while on a test cruise, exploded over the Humber River, killing forty-five men. I missed being aboard that day by what seemed to me to be a miracle. Instead of flying the Atlantic, I had the sad duty of recovering the bodies of my shipmates.

These disappointments convinced me that my naval career was headed toward futility. On my return from England, I found that along with the rest of my class at Annapolis I was to be demoted back to lieutenant from the war-time rank of lieutenant commander. Whereupon, I asked to be transferred to the inactive list, believing that I could better hasten my career in aviation outside the Service.

Now I turned toward the polar regions, which had drawn my interest from boyhood. With my great friend, Captain Bob Bartlett, I organized in 1925 an expedition for aerial exploration in North Greenland. At the request of the Navy Department, whose planes were to be used, we subsequently combined forces with Commander Donald B. MacMillan, who was preparing to lead a similar expedition into approximately the same region. That expedition, my first to the polar regions, was as exciting a trip as I ever made. It gave me my initiation into polar flying. It introduced to me Floyd Bennett, assigned to me by the Navy as a pilot-mechanic, as noble a character as I have ever found among men. Altogether Bennett and I flew some 2500 miles over the Greenland Ice Cap and the pack-strewn waters to the westward. As polar flights are reckoned today, this may not seem impressive; but the kind of plane we flew twelve years ago was at best a doubtful and dangerous vehicle; and, considering the severity of conditions around Greenland—the lack of landing places, the sudden squalls and snowstorms—we were lucky to do as much as we did without accident. More, we learned enough, Bennett and I, during the Greenland initiation, to become convinced that, with the new improvements being built into airplanes, a flight to the North Pole was no longer a crazy notion but a reasonable and practicable project.

This time, however, we resolved to base at Spitzbergen, near the northern tip of Norway. It had many advantages over other likely hopping-off places, foremost among which were the facts: (1) that it was only 720 miles from the Pole and (2) the Gulf Stream thereabouts starts wafting the pack ice away from the coast as early as April, which meant we could get into Kings Bay at a seasonable time with a supply ship. True, we realized the hazardous nature of the flight. Experienced polar travelers told us we were fools. The fog which lies over the Arctic Ocean would add to the already great risks; and, if we came a cropper, it would take us, they said, at least two years to walk back to land, if we ever made land at all. Nevertheless, these were risks we were prepared to take.

Neither Bennett nor I was able to begin serious work of preparation as easily as we had hoped. Official duties engaged us both until the middle of January, 1926. Then Secretary of the Navy Wilbur and my Chief Admiral Moffett allowed us leave. We were going this time on our own hook. We didn't ask the Navy to send us, as we felt the hazardous nature of the undertaking would make it unfair to do so. From then on came a crescendo of toil which culminated when we finally sailed.

After carefully weighing our own experience at Etah, as

well as the opinion of aeronautical experts, we selected for our
flight a Fokker, three-engine monoplane.

One was available that had already flown 20,000 miles. It
had 200 horsepower, Wright air-cooled motors, any two of
which would keep it up in the air (provided the load was not
too heavy) if the third failed. That, of course, added to our
chances of success.

The plane was 42 feet 9 inches long in body, with a wing
spread of 63 feet 3 inches. Two 100-gallon gasoline tanks were
set in each wing; and two others, each holding 110 gallons,
were carried in the fuselage. Whatever additional gasoline we
might need could be carried in five-gallon cans in the fuselage.

We named the plane *Josephine Ford* in honor of the daughter of my friend Edsel Ford. Careful tests of the plane were
made before we sailed. Its fuel consumption at cruising speed
was twenty-seven or twenty-eight gallons per hour—lower than
was anticipated, and therefore most encouraging. It was capable of a speed as high as 120 miles an hour.

Through the generosity of the Shipping Board I was able to
secure the steamer *Chantier*. She was of about 3500 tons
displacement and had ample space for our flying gear.

There were half a hundred members of the expedition,
nearly all volunteers, all young and adventurous. I selected
some from the list of men in the Naval Reserve who had
had sixteen and twenty years' service in the Navy. We obtained the others by culling out the best of the thousands of
volunteers.

After months of toil, we left New York on April 5, 1926,
with half a hundred men and six months' food supply aboard.
I suspect to this day that Captain Brennan and his three mates
from the Merchant Marine had many misgivings in starting
out on a 10,000 mile cruise with a ship's company made up
mostly of landlubbers.

We arrived at Kings Bay, Spitzbergen, at 4 P.M. April 29
and found the Amundsen-Ellsworth-Nobile Expedition members making preparations to receive the great Italian dirigible
Norge soon to leave Italy for a flight to the Pole.

Fate lost no time in placing serious obstacles in our path.
The little harbor of Kings Bay was choked with ice, but

skillful work by Captain Brennan brought the *Chantier* to anchor within 900 yards of the shore.

To my dismay, I found that there were no facilities for landing my heavy plane. I had counted on the dock at the coaling station. Previous inquiry told me the water there was deep enough for our ship; and permission was only a matter of asking the local manager.

Now we found tied up to this sole landing a small Norwegian gunboat, the *Heimdahl*, taking on coal. Of course, I went ashore immediately and asked if we could have the dock for a few hours, at least.

"Sorry but our ship was nearly lost a few days ago," I was informed. "Drifting ice caught her and carried her helplessly toward the land." I knew the danger from the drifting ice, and could see it was no use to argue.

The only thing to do was to anchor as close as possible to the shore and send our plane through the drift ice on some kind of raft. When the Norwegians heard about the plan, they urged us to desist. "You know nothing about ice," was the gist of their warning, "or you would not attempt such a thing. The ice is almost certain to start moving before you can get ashore."

By laying heavy planks across the gunwales of our four whaleboats the crew constructed a big raft. Of course that left the *Chantier* without boats, which I did not like on account of the constant threat from drifting ice. It began to snow; and the air was cold and raw as all hands worked at top speed.

In the midst of a snow squall, the First Mate, de Lucca, hoisted the fuselage of the *Josephine Ford* from the ship's hold, and lowered it safely and skillfully on the raft. A change in tide began to close the lane we had opened among the heavy cakes of ice blocking the way to the shore. Yet, by tireless work and unswerving determination our men managed to prop the awkward body of the plane on its frail support.

We were taking a tremendous chance in doing this; for, had a wind sprung up, the raft might have been crushed by ice or blown out to sea. It was either get our personnel and equipment ashore this way or come back to the States as ignominious

failures. We preferred to risk the first rather than weakly
accept the alternative.

Just as we finished the raft, the very thing we dreaded
happened. The ice started moving with great force, and we
had quite a struggle saving the raft and even the steamer itself.
An iceberg came whooping down on the tide. Drifting snow
concealed it, and we did not see the danger until the berg
was almost upon us. It threatened the ship's rudder, and we
had to land dynamite on a corner of the oncoming monster
and blow it into pieces small enough to be fended off or swept
clear by the current.

My relief was great when we at last reached the ice foot
protruding from the beach. Luck was with us—we must admit
that.

No one knew how efficiently a big plane like the *Josephine
Ford* would perform on skis. We had much to learn.

The edge of the landing field was about a mile from the
ice foot. If it was a big undertaking for the men to get the
plane ashore it was an equally difficult job for them to get
the plane and equipment up to the top of the long incline
through the deep snow in a temperature fifteen degrees below
zero.

Not having a level stretch smooth enough for a take-off with
a heavy load, we were forced to try another new stunt—to take
off going down hill. Smoothing the surface of the take-off
runway was the biggest job of all. The men had to work
eighteen hours a day, but I never heard a single complaint.

The plane's first attempt to get off on a trial flight ended
in a snowdrift. A ski was broken to bits and the landing gear
bent and broken.

Things then looked black, but the men refused to lose heart.
Then twice again we tried to get off, and each time a ski
collapsed in pretty much the same way. If this was the best
we could do with the plane lightly loaded, how could we
expect to lift the polar load of 10,000 pounds?

Noville, Mulroy, and "Chips" Gould, the carpenter, worked
two days and two nights making new skis. No other hard
wood being available in all Kings Bay, they reinforced the skis
with wood from the oars of the *Chantier*'s life boats. Profiting
from our first experience, we treated the bottom of the skis

with a mixture of rosin and tar. The runway was fairly smooth for the second attempt, and the plane was lightly loaded. We held our breaths.

This time the airplane moved forward rapidly, then rose gracefully into the air. With Lieutenant Noville and Lieutenant Parker aboard, in addition to Bennett, she made a trial flight of more than two hours and showed a remarkably low gas consumption. The cold-weather cowling on the engines came up to our highest expectations. Our worst fears were at an end.

Final preparations were completed on May 8. Meterologist Haines told us that the weather was right.

We warmed the motors; heated the oil; put the last bit of fuel and food aboard; examined our instruments with care. Bennett and I climbed in, and we were off. Off, but alas, not up. Our load proved too great, the snow too "bumpy," the friction of the skis too strong a drag. The plane simply would not get into the air. We overran the runway at a terrific speed, jolting over snow hummocks and landing in a snowdrift; the plane just missed turning over on her back.

A dozen men came up, weary, heartsick, and speechless. They had worked almost to the limit of their endurance to give us our chance. I waded through the deep snow to the port landing gear. Great! Both it and the ski were O.K. Then I stumbled to the other side and found that they also had withstood the terrible pounding.

My apprehension turned to joy, for I knew that if the landing gear would stand that strain we could eventually take off for the Pole with enough fuel to get there and back.

We dug the plane out of the snowdrift and taxied up the hill to try again. We held another council, and concluded to work through the night lengthening and smoothing the runway. Meanwhile, with the idea of reducing the load, we jettisoned some emergency equipment and a little reserve fuel.

The weather still held good. We decided to try to get off as near midnight as possible, when the cold of night would harden the snow and give a better run to the skis. Finally, at a half hour past midnight (Greenwich time), all was in readiness. Bennett and I had had almost no sleep for thirty-six hours, but that did not bother us.

We carefully iced the runway in front of the skis (so that

we could make a faster start), while Bennett and Kinkaid made their motor preparations.

Bennett came up for a last talk, and we decided to stake all on getting away—to give the *Josephine Ford* full power and full speed—and get off or crash at the end of the runway in the jagged ice.

With a total load of nearly 10,000 pounds we raced down the runway, dangerously close to the broken ice at the end. Just when it seemed we must crash into it as we had done before, Bennett, with a mighty pull on the wheel, lifted the plane cleanly into the air, and we were clear at last.

For months previous to this hour, utmost attention had been paid to every detail that would assure safety in case of accident. We had a short-wave radio set operated by a hand dynamo for use in the event of a forced landing. A handmade sledge, presented by Amundsen, was stowed in the fuselage, on which to carry food and clothing should we be compelled to walk to Greenland. We had food for ten weeks.

The first stage of the flight carried us past the well-known landmarks in the vicinity of Kings Bay. We climbed to 2000 feet to get a good view of the coast and the magnificent snow-covered mountains inland. Within an hour of taking the air we crossed the edge of the polar ice pack. It was much nearer the land than we had expected.

Ahead, the sea ice shone in the rays of the midnight sun—a fascinating scene whose lure had drawn men into its clutches, never to return. It was with a feeling of exhilaration that we felt that for the first time two men, aloof in a plane, could gaze upon its charms, and discover its secrets, out of reach of those sharp claws.

Though it was important to hit the Pole from the standpoint of achievement, it was more important to do so from that of our lives, so that we could get back to Spitzbergen, a target none too big. We could not fly back to land from an unknown position. We must put every possible second of time and our best concentration on the job of navigating and of flying a straight course—our lives depended on it.

We could see mountains astern gleaming in the sun at least a hundred miles behind us. That was our last link with civilization. The unknown lay ahead.

Bennett and I took turns piloting. At first, and for some unaccountable reason, the plane veered time and time again, to the right. Bennett could glance back to where I was working, through a door leading to the two pilots' seats. Every minute or two he would look at me, to be checked if necessary, on the course by the sun compass. If he happened to be off the course, I would wave him to the right or left until he got on it again. Once every three minutes while I was navigating, I checked the wind drift and ground speed, so that in case of a change in wind I could detect it immediately and allow for it.

We had three sets of gloves which I constantly changed to fit the job in hand, and sometimes removed entirely for short periods to write or figure on the chart. I froze my face and one of my hands in taking sights with the instruments from the trapdoors. But I noticed these frostbites at once and was more careful thereafter in the future. Ordinarily a frostbite need not be dangerous if detected in time and if the blood is rubbed back immediately into the affected parts. We also carried leather helmets that would cover the whole face when necessary to use them.

Finally, when certain of our course, I turned my attention to the ice pack, which I had wondered about ever since I was a youngster. We were flying at about 2000 feet, and I could see at about 50 miles in every direction. There was no sign of land. The pack was crisscrossed with pressure ridges, but here and there were stretches that appeared long and smooth enough to land on. However, from 2000 feet pack ice is extraordinarily deceptive.

I now turned my mind to wind conditions, for I knew they were a matter of interest to all those contemplating the feasibility of a polar airway. We found them smooth. This was as we had anticipated, for the flatness of the ice and the arctic temperature are not conducive to air currents, such as are sometimes found over land. Had we struck an arctic gale, I cannot say what the results would have been as far as air roughness is concerned. Of course, we still had the advantage of spring and twenty-four-hour daylight.

It was time now to relieve Bennett again at the wheel, not only that he might stretch his legs, but so that he could pour gasoline into the tanks from the five-gallon tins stowed all over the cabin. Empty cans were thrown overboard to get rid of the weight, small though it was.

On one occasion, as I turned to look over the side, my arm struck some object in my left breast pocket. It was filled with good-luck pieces!

I am not superstitious, I believe. No explorer, however, can go off without such articles. Among my trinkets was a religious medal put there by a friend. It belonged to his fiancée, and he firmly believed it would get me through. There was also a tiny horseshoe made by a famous blacksmith. Attached to the pocket was a little coin carried by Peary, pinned to his shirt, on his trip to the North Pole.

We were now getting into areas never before viewed by mortal eye. The feelings of an explorer superseded the aviator's. I became conscious of that extraordinary exhilaration which comes from looking into virgin territory. At that moment I felt repaid for all our toil.

At the end of this unknown area lay our goal, somewhere beyond the shimmering horizon. We were opening unexplored regions at the rate of nearly 10,000 square miles an hour, and were experiencing the incomparable satisfaction of searching for new land. Once, for a moment, I mistook a distant, vague, low-lying cloud formation for the white peaks of a faraway land.

To the right, somewhere, the rays of the midnight sun shone down on the scenes of Nansen's heroic struggles to reach the goal that we were approaching at the rate of nearly 100 miles an hour. To our left, lay Peary's trail.

When our calculations showed us to be about an hour from the Pole, I noticed through the cabin window a bad leak in the oil tank of the starboard motor. Bennett wrote on a note: "That motor will stop."

Bennett then suggested that we try a landing to fix the leak. But I thought that more dangerous still. We decided to keep on for the Pole. We would be in no worse fix should we come down near the Pole than we would be if we had a forced landing where we were.

When I took to the wheel again, I kept my eyes glued on that oil leak and the oil-pressure indicator. Should the pressure drop, we would lose the motor immediately. It fascinated me.

There was no doubt in my mind that the oil pressure would drop any moment. But the prize was actually in sight. We could not turn back.

At 9:02 A.M., May 9, 1926, Greenwich civil time, our calculations showed us to be at the Pole! The dream of a lifetime had at last been realized.

We headed to the right to take two confirming sights of the sun, then turned and took two more.

After that we made some moving and still pictures, then went on for several miles in the direction we had come, and made another larger circle to be sure to take in the Pole. Thus we made a non-stop flight around the world in a very few minutes. In doing that we lost a whole day in time; and, of course, when we completed the circle, we gained that day back again.

Two great questions confronted us now: Were we exactly where we thought we were? If not—and could we be absolutely certain?—we should miss Spitzbergen. And, even if we were on a straight course, would that engine stop?

As we flew there at the top of the world, we saluted the gallant, indomitable spirit of Peary and verified his report in every detail.

At 9:15 A.M. we headed for Spitzbergen, abandoning the plan to return via Cape Morris Jesup on account of the oil leak.

The reaction coming from the realization that we had accomplished our mission, together with the narcotic effect of the motors, made us drowsy when we were steering. I dozed off at the wheel and in turn had to relieve Bennett several times because of his sleepiness.

I quote from my impressions cabled to the United States on our return to Kings Bay:

"The wind began to freshen and change direction soon after we left the Pole, and soon we were making over 100 miles an hour.

"The elements were surely smiling that day on us, two insignificant specks of mortality flying over that great, vast white area in a small plane with only one companion, speechless and deaf from the motors, just a dot in the center of 10,000 square miles of visible desolation.

"We felt no larger than a pinpoint and as lonely as the tomb; as remote and detached as a star.

"Here, in another world, far from the herds of people, the smallnesses of life fell from our shoulders. What wonder that we felt no great emotion of achievement or fear of death that lay stretched beneath us, but instead, impersonal, disembodied. On, on we went. It seemed forever onward.

"Our great speed had the effect of quickening our mental processes, so that a minute appeared as many minutes, and I realized fully then that time is only a relative thing. An instant can be an age, an age an instant."

We were aiming for Grey Point, Spitzbergen, and finally when we saw it dead ahead, we knew that we had been able to keep on our course! That we were exactly where we had thought we were!

But, to our astonishment, a miracle was happening. That motor was still running. It is a hundred to one shot that a leaky engine such as ours means a motor stoppage. It is generally an oil lead that breaks. We afterward found out the leak was caused by a rivet jarring out of its hole; and when the oil got down to the level of the hole is stopped leaking. Flight Engineer Noville had put an extra amount of oil in an extra tank.

It was a wonderful relief not to have to navigate any more. We came into Kings Bay flying at about 4000 feet. The tiny village was a welcome sight, but not so much so as the good old *Chantier*, which looked so small beneath. I could see the steam from her welcoming and, I know, joyous whistle.

On my return to New York I sent a radiogram asking that an officer-messenger come for my charts and records. The Navy Department complied. Through the Secretary of the Navy I submitted everything to the National Geographic Society. The papers were referred to a special committee of the Society, consisting of its President, Dr. Gilbert Grosvenor, the Chairman of its Research Committee, Dr. Frederick Coville, and Colonel E. Lester Jones, a member of the Board of Trustees, who was also Director of the United States Coast and Geodetic Survey.

This committee appointed a subcommittee of expert mathematicians and calculators. The final report was submitted to the Secretary of the Navy and read in part as follows:

"We have the honor of submitting the following report of our examination of Lieutenant Commander Richard Evelyn Byrd's 'Navigation Report of Flight to Pole.' We have carefully examined Commander Byrd's original records of his observations en route to and from the North Pole. . . . We have verified all his computations. We have also made a satisfactory examination of the sextant and sun compass used by Commander Byrd.

"It is the opinion of your committee that at very close to 9 hours 3 minutes, Greenwich civil time, May 9, 1926, Lieutenant Commander Richard Evelyn Byrd was at the North Pole, insofar as an observer in an airplane, using the most accurate instruments and methods available for determining his position, could ascertain."

Nautilus 90 North

COMMANDER WILLIAM R. ANDERSON, WITH CLAY BLAIR, JR.

The Northwest Passage—a sea route from the Atlantic to the Pacific via the Arctic has lured discoverers from the days of the earliest mariners. They included Henry Hudson and Sir John Franklin, both of whom were lost looking for the "easy" way to the Orient.

Ship after ship was defeated by polar ice until one ship, the Nautilus, *went* under *the ice, blazing a submerged northwest passage, sailing* through *the North Pole in 1958 and opening a new era in polar achievement.*

PEARY describes the polar pack near the North Pole as a "trackless, colorless chaos of broken and heaved-up ice." Sir John Ross had this to say: "But let them remember that sea ice is stone, a floating rock in the stream, a promontory or an island when aground, not less solid than if it were a land of granite." They were right. But little did they dream of *Nautilus*, U. S. Navy, nuclear power, 1958.

Saturday morning, August 2, found 116 people running along at four hundred feet at cruising speed on course 000 true, just about forty-four hours short of culminating the most thrilling and adventurous cruise any sailor ever embarked upon. Overhead the ice was almost solid and incredibly rough, projecting downward as much as sixty-five feet from the surface, but averaging ten to fifteen feet thick. It would be less than honest to say that one can submarine under it with total abandon.

At first Frank Adams and I stood "watch and watch," which meant that one of us was up and about at all times. When my co-skipper took over, I could turn in for a few hours of sleep, knowing that the ship was in experienced and capable hands.

As we plunged deeper under the pack, I thought: *Where is*

the point of no return? Here? A hundred miles from here? A day's journey away? At the Pole itself, perhaps? Frankly, I did not know. But I had computed it to be at the "Pole of Inaccessibility," the geographic center of the ice pack, about four hundred miles below the true Pole. But who cared? We were safe, warm, and comfortable in our home beneath the sea.

Morale was high and excitement at fever pitch. Once we had reached deep water beneath the pack, all hands felt that from then on out it was a run for "home." Although our ship's log read eighteen knots, Chief Machinist's Mate Stuart Nelson, who by then was nicknamed "Stop Leak," scampered forward from the Engine Room to ask if the engineers couldn't make "just a couple more going-home turns." I ordered twenty knots. The whole ship seemed to purr along contentedly.

"Boy, this is the way to explore," remarked Robert N. Jarvis, Hospitalman First Class. Pipe in hand, a cup of coffee beside him, he took his ease between atmosphere analyses. "Pinging up and down and all around at twenty knots, fresh air all day long, a warm boat, and good hot food—we sure have the situation in hand. I'd hate to walk across these ice fields up there to the Pole the way Admiral Peary did it."

Though most of us considered the North Pole a desirable objective, our primary mission was to cross from the Pacific Ocean to the Atlantic Ocean, blazing a new northwest passage. Actually, from the standpoint of compass performance, it might have been preferable to avoid the Pole, to ease around it at lower latitude. However, the route across the Pole was the shortest and fastest. Besides, who could resist the temptation to cross the North Pole when it was so close at hand?

Dr. Lyon remained glued to his sonar equipment hour after hour, watching the recording pens trace the contour of the underside of the ice. His new instruments displayed the ice in far greater detail, and with much greater accuracy, than the machines we had used in 1957. In fact, it was at this point that we discovered that the ice pack was far thicker than we had estimated in 1957, and that pressure ridges (ice forced downward when two massive floes press against one another) projected down to 100 or 125 feet. As we sped along, Dr. Lyon's instruments collected in each hour more precise data on the ice and the Arctic Basin floor than have been assembled in all history. When he finally left the ship, he had accumulated two trunkfuls of data.

And what of peaks rising abruptly from the uncharted ocean floor? Our detection equipment kept a sharp "eye" on these obstacles. We found several. At latitude 76 degrees 22 minutes north, in a region where there are no charted soundings, our fathometer, which had been running along fairly steadily at about 2100 fathoms, suddenly spiked up to 1500 fathoms, and then, to my concern, to less than 500.

I camped alongside the fathometer for several hours, intently watching the rugged terrain as it unfolded beneath us. I saw incredibly steep cliffs—undersea ranges—rise thousands of feet above the ocean floor. Several times I ordered speed slackened, then resumed, as a promontory leveled off or descended as rapidly as it had risen. The shape of these undersea mountains appeared phenomenally rugged, and as grotesque as the craters of the moon.

As I paced from instrument to instrument, Chief Hospitalman Aberle arrived with the latest atmosphere analysis. He reported our air vitalization machines were working well enough to maintain an atmosphere averaging 20 to 30 parts per million carbon monoxide, 1.0 to 1.5 per cent carbon dioxide, and between 20 and 21.5 per cent oxygen. These figures were all within, or below, safe limits.

At latitude 83 degrees 20 minutes north we passed abeam of the geographical center of the ice pack, the "Ice Pole" or "Pole of Inaccessibility." Before the day of nuclear-powered submarines, the name was probably fitting. It may now have to be changed.

It has been reported that for the crew Nautilus "hung motionless in time and space." Nothing could be further from the truth. Every man aboard was acutely aware of our rapid and inexorable movement north. As the hours passed, each watch squad gasped at our astounding progress. Men remained transfixed at the electronic machines clocking our track mile by mile, or before the television set on which they could watch the ice passing overhead like beautiful moving clouds. A mixture of suspense, anticipation, and hope was discernible throughout the ship. Few could sleep. Many of us had been praying for the successful attainment of our goal, and now, God willing, it appeared within our reach.

Our psychiatrist, Dr. Kinsey, went about his work methodically and mysteriously, probing for, I suppose, those men who were afraid. Each day, to a random group of volunteers, he distributed cards containing a series of questions, such as "Do you feel happy?" If a man did not feel happy, he was supposed to indicate by writing a single "V" on the card. If he felt slightly happy, he wrote "VV." Three V's meant that he was in fine spirits, and four V's signified total enchantment. Personally, it made no sense to me. I was not one of the select volunteers.

The main fear within me was that which we all shared: a materiel failure, such as that which occurred in 1957, which would force us to turn back. Every man on board examined and re-examined his instruments and equipment. Vigilance, they all knew, would prevent a small fault from becoming a casualty that would terminate the voyage or leave us stranded beneath the ice.

I did not—could not—sleep. I wandered restlessly about the ship, occasionally taking a peek through the periscope. I was surprised on these observations to see phosphorescent streaks in the water. This is a phenomenon common in tropic waters. It seemed unusual to me to find these streaks in water so cold that the outside of our Engine Room sea-water pipes was covered with thick layers of rime ice.

As I walked about the ship, taking the measure of the crew, I listened as the men spun tales and cracked jokes.

One crewman, recalling the time when *Nautilus* paid a memorable visit to New Orleans, captivated his shipmates with this story:

"I was headed back for the ship early in the morning. We'd spent most of the evening in the Monkey Bar in the French Quarter. Well, it's about dawn, and I'm walking down this deserted street. Suddenly, out of the corner of my eye, I saw a panhandler crossing the street headed full speed in my direction. He stopped me and asked for a quarter. I looked this bird in the eye and said, 'Look, bud. I'm working this

side of the street. You stay on your own side.' Well, I wish
you could have seen his face. He was really shook."

In another compartment, two crewmen on watch were talking.

"Joe, do you know who man's best friend is?" Bill asked.

"Well, I always heard it was a dog," Joe said.

"That's not so," Bill said.

"Well, if the dog isn't, then who is?" Joe asked.

"Lady alligators," Bill explained. "You see, every year these
lady alligators come up on the beach and they lay about 1000
eggs. Then, they tell me, the lady alligator turns around and
devours about 999 of the eggs she laid."

"How does that make her man's best friend?" asked Joe.

"Well, Joe, it's like this. If that lady alligator didn't eat those
999 eggs, we'd be up to our neck in alligators."

In spite of this lighthearted talk, every man was alert for
an emergency. The leads or polynyas were infrequent, but
the position of each was carefully plotted, so that if it became
necessary to surface, we would know where to find an
opening. James H. Prater stood watch in the Torpedo Room,
carefully bleeding just the right amount of oxygen into the
hull. Nearby was Richard M. Jackman, prepared to make all
torpedo tubes ready on an instant's notice, if it became necessary to blast a hole through the ice. We were ready, but
the possibility of a casualty seemed remote. Indeed, I had
never seen the ship's machinery function so perfectly. Our
"out of commission" list reached a new low. It was as if
Nautilus herself had found peace and contentment beneath
the ice. If she could have filled out one of Dr. Kinsey's
cards, it would have contained four V's, or five, or six, for
every question.

Shortly after midnight, August 3, we passed latitude 84
degrees north. Since we had entered compass-baffling waters,
we made preparations to guard against longitude roulette. At
that time we placed our auxiliary gyrocompass in a directional
gyro mode so that instead of seeking north, it would tend
to seek the line we were following, a Great Circle course
up the Western Hemisphere, across the Pole, and south again
to the Eastern Hemisphere. This was the track I intended to
cruise. When our master gyrocompass began to lose its north-

14. Dr. Elisha Kent Kane, who led an expedition to investigate the mysterious disappearance of Sir John Franklin.

15. Members of the Lady Franklin Bay Expedition. *Standing:* Whisler, Ellis, Bender, Cross, Frederick, Lynn, Biederbick, Henry, Long, Ralston, Salor, Dr. Pavy, Gardner, Ellison. *Seated:* Connell, Brainard, Lieutenant Kislingbury, Lieutenant Greely, Lieutenant Lockwood, Israel, Jewell, Rice.

16. Long and Jens killing a bear.

17. Fridtjof Nansen, who described the experience of being adrift on the Polar Seas.

18. Nansen's ship the *Fram* leaving Bergen, Norway.

19. Robert E. Peary, the first man to reach the North Pole, on the deck of his ship *Roosevelt*.

20. Amundsen congratulates Richard E. Byrd and Floyd Bennett at the completion of their flight over the North Pole.

21. USS *Nautilus,* a nuclear-powered submarine, the first ship to pass under the arctic ice cap: August 5, 1958.

22. The transpolar route of the USS *Nautilus.*

23. Lenticular (shaped like a lentil) clouds in the Antarctic.

24. Mountains of granite five degrees from the South Pole.

25. Whaling in the Southern Ocean: The killer ship.

26. The factory ship.

27. Flensing the whale (stripping off the blubber).

28. The bird that walks like a man—emperor penguins at the
rookery near Hallett Station.

29. Antarctica today: a U. S. Geological Survey base camp.

30. Isolation today: the scientist in his laboratory.

31. Roald Amundsen, the first man to reach the South Pole.

32. Sir Douglas Mawson of the Antarctic.

33. Mawson emerging from his makeshift tent.

34. The half-sledge used in the last stage of Mawson's journey.

35. Sir Ernest Shackleton, the antarctic explorer.

36. Captain Robert Falcon Scott and members of his expedition at Amundsen's tent at the South Pole. (Captain Scott, Dr. E. A. Wilson, Captain L. E. Oates, Lieutenant H. R. Bowers)

seeking ability, as it would when we approached the northern-most point on earth, then we intended to shift to the auxiliary. Thus we would have something to steer by in the darkness below—something to lead us out on our track south.

In order to ensure that all of the gyrocompasses remained properly oriented, we made all course, speed, and depth changes extremely slowly. For example, when we came near the surface to decrease water pressure on the hull (this is desirable in operating the garbage ejector), we rose with an angle of one or two degrees, instead of the usual twenty to thirty degrees. Once we changed course twenty-two degrees. So gradual was the shift that six minutes elapsed before we had settled on the new heading. Some wag had suggested that when we neared the Pole we might put the rudder hard over and make twenty-five tight circles, thus becoming the first ship in history to circle the earth nonstop twenty-five times. Any such maneuver was, of course, out of the question.

As we rapidly closed in on the North Pole, Tom Curtis, manning the inertial navigator, which constantly plotted our position by electronics, made minute adjustments to ensure that his complex instrument was operating properly. At 1000 we crossed latitude 87 degrees north, breaking our record of last year, and with the passing of each new mile, we moved farther north than any other ship in history.

Two hours south of the Pole, a wave of unchecked excitement swept through *Nautilus*. Every man was up and about, and unabashedly proud to be aboard. Frank Adams, staring intently at the electronic gear, uttered a word often employed by *Nautilus* men who have exhausted all ordinary expressions to sum up their reaction to the never-ending *Nautilus* triumphs: "Fan-damn-tastic."

When we crossed the Pole, of course, no bells would ring, nor would we feel a bump. Only our instruments could tell us how close we had come. Since we had made the decision to cross the Pole, we were determined to hit it precisely on the nose. Along with Navigator Shep Jenks and his assistant, Chief Petty Officer Lyle B. Rayl, I had stationed myself in the Attack Center, and although we were almost as far north as man can go on this planet, we were literally sweating

over the charts and electronic position-indicators, making minute, half-degree adjustments at the helm.

The hour by *Nautilus* clocks, which were still set on Seattle
time, was 1900, or seven o'clock in the evening. Our nuclear
engine, which up to then had pushed Nautilus more than
124,000 miles, was purring smoothly. Our electronic log, or
speedometer needle, was hovering above twenty knots, the
depth-gauge needle about four hundred feet. Our sensitive
sonar indicated that the endless polar ice pack was running
between eight and eighty feet thick. Above the ice, we imagined,
the polar wind was howling across its trackless, barren stamping
ground, grinding massive floes one upon the other.

By then we had been under ice for sixty-two hours. Obviously,
it was not possible to take the usual fix on heavenly bodies
to determine our position, so we were navigating primarily
by dead reckoning. This means that we were spacing our
speed and course on the chart and plotting our position
every half hour or so, accordingly. Our bottom soundings,
sometimes useful in submerged navigating, did not help, of
course, in this uncharted, unsounded area. Our precision fathometer had indicated differences of as much as eight thousand
feet at those rare points where soundings were made, so we
could not rely on it. Our only check on our navigating was
the inertial navigator. At the exact moment we crossed the
Pole, we knew, the instrument would give a positive indication.
Tom Curtis moved closer to his dials and scopes as we drew
near.

A mile south of the Pole, I told Jenks to inform me when
we were four tenths of a mile from the Pole as indicated
by the electronic log. The mileage indicator was moving
rapidly. It was only a matter of seconds. *Nautilus* crewmen
had gathered in the Attack Center and the Crew's Mess.

On Jenk's mark, I stepped up to the mike of the ship's
public address system:

"All hands—this is the Captain speaking. . . . In a few
moments *Nautilus* will realize a goal long a dream of mankind
—the attainment by ship of the North Geographic Pole. With
continued Godspeed, in less than two days we will record
an even more significant historic first: the completion of a
rapid transpolar voyage from the Pacific to the Atlantic Ocean.

"The distance to the Pole is now precisely four tenths of a mile. As we approach, let us pause in silence dedicated with our thanks for the blessings that have been ours during this remarkable voyage—our prayers for lasting world peace, and in solemn tribute to those who have preceded us, whether in victory or defeat."

The juke box was shut off, and at that moment a hush literally fell over the ship. The only sound to be heard was the steady staccato of pinging from our sonars steadily watching the bottom, the ice, and the dark waters ahead.

I glanced again at the distance indicator, and gave a brief countdown to the crew. "Stand by. 10 . . . 8 . . . 6 . . . 4 . . . 3 . . . 2 . . . 1. MARK! August 3, 1958. Time, 2315 (11:15 Eastern Daylight Saving Time). For the United States and the United States Navy, the North Pole." I could hear cheers in the Crew's Mess.

I looked anxiously at Tom Curtis. He was smiling. The inertial navigator had switched precisely as expected, positively confirming that we had crossed the exact North Pole. Curtis sang out: "As a matter of fact, Captain, you might say we came so close we pierced the Pole."

I stood for a moment in silence, awe-struck at what *Nautilus* had achieved. She had blazed a new submerged northwest passage, vastly decreasing the sea-travel time for nuclear submarines from the Pacific to the Atlantic, one that could be used even if the Panama Canal were closed. When and if nuclear-powered cargo submarines are built, the new route would cut 4900 miles and thirteen days off the route from Japan to Europe. *Nautilus* had opened a new era, completely conquered the vast, inhospitable Arctic. Our instruments were, for the first time, compiling an accurate and broad picture of the Arctic Basin and its approaches. *Nautilus'* achievement was dramatic proof of United States leadership in at least one important branch of science; and it would soon rank alongside or above the Russian sputnik in the minds of millions. Lastly, for the first time in history a ship had actually reached the North Pole. And never had so many men—116—been gathered at the Pole at one time.

I was proud of what *Nautilus* had done, yet I felt no sense of personal triumph or achievement. That we had reached

the Pole was the work and support of many people. My
reaction, frankly, was an overwhelming feeling of relief that
after months and months of preparation and two unsuccessful
probes we had finally made it.

Precisely at the Pole, for the record, I made note of some
statistics which may or may not prove useful. The water
temperature was 32.4 degrees Fahrenheit. The depth of the
sea was 13,410 feet, exactly 1927 feet deeper than reported
by Ivan Papanin, a Russian who landed there, he claims,
in an airplane in 1937. (In 1909 Admiral Peary had found
the depth "greater than 9000 feet.") At the exact Pole our
ice detectors noted a pressure ridge extending twenty-five feet
down.

After crossing the Pole, I made my way forward to join
in the "North Pole Party" in the Crew's Mess. My first act
was to pay modest tribute to the man who, more than any
other, had made our historic voyage possible: the President
of the United States. A few minutes before, I had written
him a message. It concluded: "I hope, sir, that you will
accept this letter as a momento of a voyage of importance to
the United States." In the Mess, before seventy crew members
of Nautilus, I signed this letter, and one to Mrs. Eisenhower,
who had christened the ship.

Other events followed. A "North Pole" cake, prepared especially by leading Commissaryman Jack L. Baird, was cut,
distributed, and wolfed down. Electrician's Mate First Class
James Sordelet raised his right hand and became the first
man in history to re-enlist at the North Pole. In a special
North Pole ceremony eleven other men, having passed the
rigid written and oral examinations, were "qualified in nuclear
submarines." The prize-winning title to correspond to Shellbacks
and Bluenoses was announced: Panopo, short for "Pacific to the
Atlantic via the North Pole." A "North Pole" post card, stamped
with the special North Pole cachet, was distributed to all
hands. On the reverse side was a cartoon by McNally showing
a sailor in a bathing suit standing on a small block of ice
leaning against a striped "North Pole." The card read: "Greet-
ings from Sunny Panama." All during these proceedings, movie
and still cameras whirred and clicked.

Then a distinguished citizen "came aboard." It was our

talented McNally, dressed as Santa Claus. What a sight he made! Red vegetable coloring was splattered on his face. His whiskers were made of medical cotton, and a pillow was stuffed inside his Santa Claus suit, made of flag bunting.

Santa berated us for entering his private domain during the vacation season. He chided us particularly for failure to abide by his restriction on the use of garbage disposal units by submerged transiting submarines! I pleaded ignorance and promised on behalf of all the ship's company children to abide by all his rules henceforth.

That done, Santa Claus relaxed and became his usual jovial self. He listened very patiently as one of the fathers in the crew, Chief Engineman Hercules H. Nicholas, argued that the behavior of our children was absolutely beyond reproach. Santa promised, in light of our personal visit to the North Pole, that the coming Christmas season would be merry and lucrative for all our children.

Perspiring heavily, Santa finally said. "Well, I've got to go back to the Pole to make sure the elves are working." And with that our extraordinary party ended. The juke box was turned back on; men drifted to their bunks for a little rest.

An "extra" edition of the ship's newspaper was published that day, entitled "*Nautilus* Express—North Pole Edition." It was unusually mild in tone and contained nothing libelous, which is an indication, I believe, that all hands were deeply moved by *Nautilus'* triumph. The feeling of the crew was summed up in an article by the paper's editor, John H. Michaud. He wrote:

At Nautilus' *Greatest Moment*

The crew of the USS *Nautilus* (SS[N]571) have at this time accomplished one of the greatest feats that is possible for a peaceful nation composed of average citizens. We have reached a point that has never been attained before this time. Many courageous men have tried, few succeeded. Of all those men that have tried we humbly ask their forgiveness. They had courage and fortitude that many of us never had, never will have in our lifetime. To those men this is dedicated. We have arrived at the North Pole. The very last region of the earth that has never been explored. True we came to this region in a habitat that is not normal for man. We came with the best equipment, the best men, and a relative new form of power. Without this power we would have never attained the goal we set out for, now that we have reached that goal this same power will take us home to our loved ones, who have endured many hardships that will never be told to us. They bid us goodbye, some with tears, others with strained look and always a question in their eyes. Is it this time? They know the goal that we have been striving for, since our return of last year, but the time and place we cannot say. We have left our loved ones not unlike the explorers of other times, with prayers to bring us Godspeed and a safe return. We are on that return now with much rejoicing and many happy thoughts for those we left behind. To my fellow shipmates this has been one of the most enjoyable trips I have ever been on, and without a doubt the most important. May God be with you on all other voyages that you make.

THE MYSTERY OF THE
ANTARCTIC

What the Antarctic Is: Land of Ghosts

THOMAS R. HENRY

The Arctic is the home of many peoples but the forbidding Antarctic has no permanent human inhabitants. Despite the work of many explorers and scientists, it still has many mysteries—illusions of strange rainbows, startling skies, a white darkness. Thomas R. Henry, science editor and writer, was a member of the U. S. Navy's operation High Jump expedition in the winter of 1946–47.

THE TRUE picture of the Antarctic Continent has taken shape slowly during the century following the early voyages of exploration. It is a picture composed of such fabulous elements that they often outweigh the fancy of the pre-explorer imagination, for in the land at the bottom of the earth are encountered phenomena of nature so far outside ordinary experience as to suggest supernatural manifestations. They are eerie and beautiful and terrible, and science still gropes for understanding of many of these mysteries.

In the Antarctic the sky frequently is green when the sun is low on the horizon. The greenness, which is like that of a lawn in early spring, extends from the horizon halfway to the zenith; the closest analogy would be to a vivid green sunset. An extraordinary example of this was observed from the deck of the Coast Guard icebreaker *Northwind*, pushing southward through the ice pack on New Year's Eve, 1946. On the southern horizon appeared a green shore; close-mown lawns, bordered by hedges, sloped gently upward into eiderdown clouds. The effect was like a Chinese landscape painting, fifty miles long and ten miles high, suspended over the horizon.

No physical explanation of this is entirely satisfactory, but the phenomenon is believed caused in part by the reflection of white light from the sun at a different wavelength—it may be an "earthset," instead of a sunset, seen from the earth itself. Another factor may be the effect on white light of vast numbers of snow crystals in the atmosphere.

The late Dr. William J. Humphreys of the U. S. Weather Bureau has described green moons and green suns seen in middle latitudes, but he explains these as caused by very thick clouds of dust in the air. This explanation, of course, could not hold for the Antarctic, where dust does not exist. Again, meteorologists long have been puzzled by the "green flash" reported as a rare occurrence in the sub-Arctic. The flash, which usually appears in the sky just over the horizon shortly before sunset and lasts only a few seconds, is thought to be due to an electrical discharge from ice particles. It is possible that the green sky of the Antarctic is one of these green flashes lasting for a much longer period of time.

Of quite common occurrence in the Antarctic are halos around the sun and moon, caused by refraction and reflection through and from ice crystals. And strangest of all, men breathe rainbows. The moisture in the breath freezes instantly when it leaves the mouth, forming clouds of millions of floating ice crystals. Sunlight through these clouds creates a succession of rainbow-colored circles which appear to come from one's own lungs.

When a blizzard arose suddenly over the Antarctic one evening several winters ago, the drivers of two tractored jeeps became lost while attempting to make their way from the gasoline dump to the base camp—a distance of only two hundred yards. The drivers floundered helplessly in the dense whiteness where there were no landmarks and no shadows.

After about fifteen minutes the men remembered the instructions given them for such an emergency and were about to stop until the blizzard ended. Suddenly they found themselves back at the gasoline dump, in almost exactly the same spot from which they had started. Later examination of the tracks showed that they had made a complete circle, nearly a mile in radius, always turning left although both men insisted they had meant to bear to the right, in the direction of the camp.

This instinctive left-turning is a common phenomenon in Antarctica. Here everything which turns, naturally turns left. Lost men and dogs always circle to the left. Snow always swirls to the left. The sun in summer moves twenty-four hours a day around the high horizon, always from right to left. The remarkable fact is that even when men try consciously to turn right the sum of several turns is always to the left so that, without landmarks, it is almost impossible to avoid returning to one's starting point from the left.

The exact opposite is true in north polar regions where everything naturally turns right. There is an instinct, deeply rooted in the conscious, to turn right north of the equator and left south of the equator. The instinct appears to become more pronounced the farther north or south one goes; circles traversed by lost men sometimes reach extreme exactitude. The person who goes astray in the Antarctic and keeps on walking is almost certain to return to his starting point, if he lives long enough. Members of Rear Admiral Richard E. Byrd's expeditions recall instances where men tried deliberately to move with the wind, which was blowing in a right direction. In a short time they found themselves turned left and facing the wind, unable to understand how they had got themselves in this position. The instinct for downwind travel of course is very slight but the left-turning instinct is powerful.

This drive appears to be shared by all antarctic animals. Penguin tracks in the snow always bear left; seals "swim" in left-turning circles over the névé; flocks of the voracious skuas which fly at a man as soon as he steps on the ice shelf seem always to approach from a leftward direction.

In some complex fashion the consciousness of man, bird, and seal is integrated with the whirling of a planet in space which in turn is integrated with the mechanics of solar system and galaxy. The lost jeep drivers returned to the gasoline dump because of the direction in which a mass of fiery gas torn loose from the sun was started rotating.

The left-turning mechanism in the brain is, of course, entirely subconscious. The men themselves had no more realization of it than of the fact that since crossing the Antarctic Circle each of them had gained almost a pound in weight—

without putting on any extra flesh. This was due to the greater pull of gravity in the south polar region than in middle latitudes. Very close to the pole the pull is sufficient to cause a difference of about ten pounds per ton.

The weight of anything on the surface of the earth is measured by the gravitational pull of the earth itself which pulls everything toward the center balanced against the centrifugal force of the planet's rotation which tends to throw any loose object into space.

The distance to the earth's center is slightly less at either pole than at the equator. Hence, since the gravitational attraction between objects varies inversely with the square of their distance apart, the pull downward is greater by an infinitesimally minute amount. For an object weighing a ton it would be barely measurable with the most refined instruments. The balancing centrifugal force, however, disappears almost completely. The speed of the earth's rotation is about a thousand miles an hour at the equator; it is close to zero at either pole.

Weight also is increased slightly by the gravitational pull of such an enormous mass of ice and rock as the Antarctic Continent. It would be somewhat greater here than at the North Pole. Here the combination of factors meant an increase of nearly five hundred tons in the total weight of the Navy expedition and an increase of about a ton and a half in the combined weight of the four thousand men.

This unsensed weight increase has considerably more significance than a mere curiosity in the calculations of geophysics, for the figures become astronomical when applied to the polar icecap itself. Ice weighs about fifty pounds a cubic foot in middle latitudes. On this basis a minimum estimate of the total weight of the antarctic ice would be about 10,000,000,-000,000,000—that is, ten quadrillion—tons. The lessening of centrifugal force should increase this mass by two or three trillion tons. This is minute when compared with the total mass of the planet but there is a possibility that it has some bearing on the physics of the atmosphere in which small variations sometimes have far-reaching chains of effects. There is no such titanic ice mass in the Northern Hemisphere, which fact tends to make the planet very slightly "bottom heavy."

Awesome phenomena of Antarctica are the "flying seas," found in the windiest region in the world, Commonwealth Bay off the coast of Wilkes Land. Across this bay, about twenty-seven miles wide and twelve miles deep, an almost constant blizzard blows from the South Pole. Great whirlpools of snow on the continental plateau are raised to altitudes of as much as a thousand feet and blown northward at from fifty to ninety miles an hour. On the surface, though, it is calm; no snow falls. There is only the tumultuous snowstorm in the sky which accentuates the strange white darkness of a cloudy day.

This snow is precipitated over the sea and ice pack either as snow or rain. The Australian explorer, Sir Douglas Mawson, one of whose camps was established near Commonwealth Bay, estimated that in a year these swift-moving snow masses represent an area of water over the bay region about one and a quarter miles deep. In other words, an area of water one-fourth the size of Chesapeake Bay takes wings and flies.

Mawson and his men stayed at the bay all winter when the sea-carrying blizzards were at their worst. They found that wind velocities as high as a hundred miles an hour were not rare. Often the air traveled forward in a series of cyclonic gusts, with the greatest velocities at the centers. For months at a time the drifting snows never ceased; many days passed, Mawson reported, when it was impossible to see one's hand at arm's length. It was a ghostly place in the bitter winter cold. The wind-blown snow became charged with electricity and in the perpetual darkness all pointed objects, such as one's nose and fingertips, glowed with the pale blue phantom light of St. Elmo's fire. All around, the white darkness was filled with these flitting blue will-o'-the-wisps.

The region is important because it may afford one of the best approaches to the South Pole for a land party. Beyond Commonwealth Bay the land appears to slope gently upward to the pole without the presence of mountain ranges such as the Queen Mauds which block off polar parties at the foot of the Ross Shelf. Here, however, an area of pack ice extends north from the continental shores almost to the circle, which has remained essentially unchanged for a hundred years.

Somewhat analogous to the flying-seas region are the "hell holes" found along the coast of the Bellingshausen Sea which was surveyed by planes of Admiral Byrd's 1939 expedition. Here great glaciers flow through high mountain passes and empty into bays which cut far into the land. The heavy, cold wind from the south polar plateau falls from the stratosphere over these glaciers and mixes with the warmer air from the seas. The result is nearly constant winds of from fifty to eighty miles an hour velocity which whip through the bays like exhaust from funnels. Mouths for such bays are almost impossible for navigation; twenty miles farther north, however, there may be dead calm.

Two of the most celebrated of these "hell holes" are near Cape Colbeck at the foot of the Rockefeller Mountains and near Marguerite Bay on the eastern side of the Bellingshausen Sea. But similar exhaust valves of the enormous energies stored up over the continent are found all along the coast. The unbroken howling of the wind for days sometimes has driven men crazy.

A little farther to the east is the country of ice volcanoes. These strange formations in the shelf ice west of the Palmer Peninsula are gigantic bowls of ice, with floors as much as a mile in diameter surrounded by walls a hundred feet high; from above they look like miniatures of craters on the surface of the moon. Inside the bowls are little mountains of ice blocks thirty to forty feet high. The common explanation is that some sort of gas became entrapped in the shelf ice, resulting finally in an explosion with the formation of the craters; later explosions piled up the blocks inside them. Thus the phenomenon seems nearly to duplicate that of the volcano in solid ice, but on a much smaller scale.

Perhaps the most terrifying of Antarctic phenomena was reported by British explorers on one of the nearly motionless glaciers a few miles inland from the west coast of the Ross Sea. Over this glacier towers a lofty mountain. At almost the moment a shadow of the mountain falls on the ice on a sunny day there starts a succession of loud explosions, like mortar fire in battle. Sometimes the detonations last for a half hour; it is as if a titanic photoelectric reaction had been set off by the shadow. Networks of tiny crevasses, some of them as much as a hundred feet long and ten inches deep, appear.

One of the curiosities of the southern seas is a poison island. This is Zavodovski Island near South Georgia. From its numerous caves issue thin, reddish-brown clouds of sulphur-filled mist. Penguins, abundant on other islands near by, stay strictly away from this volcanic ice-covered rock. All efforts to land have been defeated by the poisonous fumes, which were as bad as ever when Frank Wild, who succeeded Sir Ernest Shackleton in command of his last expedition after the leader's death at sea, passed near the place in 1922.

The weirdest of all Antarctic phenomena are associated with light and some of them are at present inexplicable—such as sudden veils of blueness that fall over the world and vanish in a few minutes. A venerable gentleman now living in Washington, Dr. Henryk Arctowski, one evening in 1898 stood on the deck of the exploring ship *Belgica* which was entirely surrounded by pack ice in the Bellingshausen Sea somewhere west of the Palmer Peninsula. He was the physicist of the Belgian expedition of which Roald Amundsen, future discoverer of the South Pole, and Dr. Frederick A. Cook, later discredited claimant to the discovery of the North Pole, were members, and which drifted for more than a year in the Bellingshausen pack.

"At a given moment," says Dr. Arctowski, "the ice suddenly assumed an intense blue color of extraordinary purity, a little tinged with purple near the horizon. Fog and ice were colored alike, hence they must have been illuminated with blue light. It was clear enough to see floating ice a mile away."

Officers on watch on the deck of the Navy's flagship *Mount Olympus* early one morning while she was anchored in the Bay of Whales observed for about four hours a hitherto unrecorded optical phenomenon—the sudden appearance of an enormous ink-black patch in a clear blue sky. The ship's radar had just detected a gigantic iceberg somewhere outside the bay about four miles away. A sharp watch was ordered but the monster remained invisible. Then, over the approximate position indicated by the radar for the berg, appeared a single black spot. It bore no resemblance to a cloud. A few minutes later five similar black spots appeared extended in a straight line many miles to the north. All slowly changed shape during the four hours, after which they faded away almost as suddenly as they had appeared. The top of the iceberg was glimpsed only after the phenomenon had been in progress for two hours. A probable explanation for the first inkspot was the mirroring of this floating ice mountain in the sky directly above it, but the other spots were unexplainable, unless caused by smaller icebergs not located by the radar.

Quite frequently white rainbows were seen from the ship's deck above the bay ice. These appeared as broad, milk-white bands in a solid blue sky; they are similar to ordinary rainbows and are caused by refraction of light by water droplets in fog. The smaller the droplets, the lighter the colors, with more refractions from the violet end of the solar spectrum where radiation becomes invisible. Finally the blueness fades entirely, leaving only shimmering bands of whiteness.

The Southern Ocean

R. B. ROBERTSON

Whalers were among the first to explore the Southern Ocean, and the ice of the Antarctic Seas was often blood stained with the slaughter. The largest animals in creation, the blue whales, as well as many smaller whales and seals, migrate there during the summer months in incredible numbers to feed upon the rich shrimp life.

Even today, whaling ships know the terrors of the Southern Ocean. Dr. R. B. Robertson sailed as a senior medical officer for one of the largest whaling expeditions of modern times.

LEAVING South Georgia and heading due south, with the last human habitation astern of us and no living man ahead, was a bracing experience. It was so at least for me, and for young Evans and the other greenhorns on the ship, and I suspect it was also even for the old whalemen like Mansell and Burnett who had done it twenty or thirty times before. For we knew when we cast off the last rope from the filthy little wharf of Leith Harbor and saw the South Georgia mountains fading over the northern horizon that for the next few months we and our six-hundred-and-fifty-strong team were utterly dependent on ourselves and the resources we carried with us; that the world of men could bring us no aid if anything went wrong; and that we had turned our backs on man's last outpost and were entering that part of the earth from which the glacial period has not yet retreated, and where there is nothing but the fiercest of seas, surrounded by even fiercer ice, and sterile rock.

"Well! We're off—for better or for worse!" said Old Burnett in the saloon the night we sailed, presumably in a heavy-handed effort to cheer up the greenhorns. "And God alone

knows what will happen to us before we tie up anywhere
again."

"You stay sober and keep your engines running, old man,"
was Mansell's riposte. "Then we be all right. Mark sail the
ship safely if you give him plenty steam; I make plenty whale
oil and earn big bonus for you; and doctor try to keep you
alive until you get home; so you no need to worry."

Whether Old Burnett and the other departmental heads of
the expedition really did worry about the huge and unalleviated
responsibility they would have to carry for the next few
months, I do not know. I can speak only for myself. I tried
not to overdramatize the situation, and repeatedly reminded
myself that our well-equipped expedition of seventeen ships
and six hundred and fifty men moving into the fringe of
the polar seas was a minor venture compared with the enterprises of the explorers like Shackleton who took small parties
of men and single wooden ships hundreds of miles farther
into the ice than we proposed to go. Nevertheless, I saw
the departure from our last land station through the eyes of
the doctor responsible for whatever might happen to my shipmates in the way of accident or injury or disease in the next
five months. My exhilaration was tinged by some anxiety about
the grave accidents that are bound to happen when modern
industry is pursued at the uttermost and most dangerous end
of the earth, and the illness that would undoubtedly occur
among my hundreds of shipmates. No doctor is medically
and surgically omniscient, and a whaling trip into the Southern
Ocean is the only situation in the modern world where he
is expected so to be, both by his employers and by his
patients.

But worries fade rapidly if one goes into the company of
another whose worries are much greater, so the first few days
out of South Georgia I spent much of my time on the bridge
with Mark, who carried the legal responsibility for our ship
and our men and everything that would happen to us until
we dropped anchor again. He was always ready to talk to
the ignorant and was an unending and never repetitive source
of nautical and polar information. From him I learned the
lore of ice and frigid sea, and of the birds and beasts and

monstrosities and men that frequent the ocean—Mark's major study during an intelligent and keenly observant life.

I was with him on the bridge the day we sighted our first large iceberg. Needless to say, I dashed down aft to get my camera, and met the other greenhorns on the same errand as I did so.

Mark smiled when he saw our enthusiasm. "You'll see plenty of them before the trip's finished," he told me, "and I wouldn't waste any film on that little half-mile-long one if I were you. We'll get in among the big ones when we get farther south, and, anyway, they're very unsatisfactory objects to photograph."

He advised me—rightly, as I know today—that, if I wanted to take good pictures of the antarctic bergs, the best way to do so was to float ice cubes in my bath and take close-ups of them, for all the southern bergs had the same flat-topped sugar-cake shape. To find the fairy-castle and cathedral-shaped icebergs that artists love to draw, it is necessary to go to the other end of the earth, to the Arctic, where the bergs are formed in a completely different way.

Mark's course of instruction to me on icebergs lasted for days, and I can reproduce only the highlights of it. The biggest antarctic berg he had seen, he told me, was about thirty-five miles by ten, and a hundred feet high, but much bigger ones have been reported. But, rather than in the size, he was interested—and he got me to share his interest—in the extreme age and apparently (from the human point of view) futile life history of the antarctic icebergs.

All of them are formed of glacier ice. Snow falls through the centuries on the antarctic continent, perhaps many hundreds of miles inland. Further falls of snow, assisted by a sloping of the land from the plateau around the Pole to the periphery of the continent, push the older snow, now squeezed by un-believable pressures into hard crystalline ice, in mighty glacial streams down toward the sea. The outcrops of these glaciers form huge ice shelves jutting into the sea, afloat but still attached to the continent—"many of them bigger than the whole of Scotland," as Mark put it. Then chunks start break-ing off and become floating islands of ice, which drift northward and in general eastward in the antarctic currents, away from the polar seas up to the warmer waters. "The whole process," to quote Mark again, "takes, not hundreds, but thousands of years. The snow which went to make that small berg out there fell on Antarctica maybe six thousand years ago—about the time Tutankhamen was king of Egypt. And no man's ever seen it during those six thousand years. And, once it breaks away from the ice shelf, what's its fate? To drift up here and be seen once by you and me before it melts; for it's very unlikely any other ship will ever sight it. At most, it will drift nor'east and become a menace to shipping on the Cape-to-New-Zealand run for a week or two, then dissolve into the sea. It all seems kind of pointless, doesn't it? Or it makes you wonder whether we're the all-important things on this planet we imagine we are."

Mark, who was by no means a bigot, but, like most Shelties, held strong religious views, was inclined to lead such discussions into theological arguments, so I headed him off and brought the conversation round to the dangers of navigation in the polar seas in modern times.

Big bergs are no longer a danger to whaleships. Radar has eliminated their menace. As we went farther south, it was nothing unusual to have twenty or thirty large bergs in sight around the ship at the same moment, and, though fog or heavy weather might obscure them in a few minutes, every piece of ice sizable enough to sink our ship for thirty miles around remained clearly visible on the radar screen, and the bearing and distance of each could be read off in a moment. International sea law still demands that, when a ship is fog-bound, it shall drop to half-speed and sound a siren or other warning device every two minutes. When Mark was on the bridge, this regulation was still complied with, even on occasions when the radar showed no catcher within thirty miles and showed the large ice so clearly that we could have steamed full-speed with complete safety among it. Some of the other whalemen, more concerned with the catch of whales and the size of their bonus than with the safety of the ship, would razz Mark for being overcautious, and would compare his retention of the old precautions of pre-radar days with the six buckets of water on the flying bridge for fire fighting. But their criticism did not perturb him, for he knew that, in not trusting entirely to one gadget or means of navigation, he had the approval of all the really experienced old sailors on the ship, such as Gyle and Adamson. And to those who advocated a blind faith in radar under ice conditions Mark would argue: "When you've used radar as much as I have, you'll often have seen large bergs on the radar screen that weren't there in the sea when you looked with your glasses; so maybe someday, if I wait long enough, I'll see a berg in the fog dead ahead which doesn't show any existence on the radar screen. But I'll be going half-speed the day I do, and I'll have heard the echo of the siren off it long before I come near hitting it."

Icebergs, Mark maintained, are objects that any real seaman respects and fears, even when he has the latest ice-detecting and navigating equipment to help him. But, he told me, expeditions paradoxically will often find the ice their best friend. If a gale is blowing—and a Southern Ocean gale is something very different from a gale in any other sea in the world—there is always a big berg somewhere handy for the whalecatchers and other small craft of a whaling expedition to run to for shelter in its lee. I was told, and later experienced it, that even a huge ship like ours, if it has whales on deck and on tow, may have to seek the shelter of an iceberg when the weather gets up.

I asked Mark if many ships were lost down in the ice nowdays.

"The whaling companies don't talk, and their policy is to avoid publicity of anything to do with modern whaling," he told me, "so it's difficult to get accurate information. I know there have been factory ships lost since steam whaling started, and there's a catcher or two lost by some company nearly every year—we lost one the year before last, and another the year before that—but it never gets into the papers. Many of the companies carry their own insurance, or sail their ships under peculiar foreign flags, and their relations with the shipping authorities of their respective countries are usually a bit strained at the best of times, so the less the public knows and the fewer questions people ask about whaling, the better the companies like it."

I often discussed with Mark and other old hands the comparative dangers of modern whaling and whaling in the heroic old days of the small boat and the hand harpoon. They were all agreed that, though a great many dangers have been eliminated from the industry, at least as many have been added. There are perils associated with modern whaling which would daunt the most daring harpooneer of old, just as killing whale from small boats is not a job any modern gunner would care to tackle.

"But always remember," Mark warned me as we talked on the bridge one day, "when you're seeking information about the dangers of whaling, new or old, remember that whalemen are and always have been mighty fine liars. Since the first Phœnician threw the first harpoon, every whaleman has considered it his right and one of the prerogatives of his trade to tell the landsmen, or even other seamen, the biggest whoppers he could get them to believe. Read any whaling yarn written in the English language, to listen to the whalemen, old or new, talking, and you can safely discount all but about ten per cent of what you hear. My people have been in whaling for five generations, so I've been reading and listening to nothing but whaling stories since I was a wean. There's always some truth in every whaling tale—unless it's a gunner that's telling it—but there's a good deal of exaggeration when it comes to the heroism of the job."

Mark used to refer to the great days of the sperm-whale fisheries from New Bedford and Dundee as the "Maybe Dick" days, and was always inclined to cry down the exploits of the whalemen of the last century—exploits in which his own ancestors had participated—but some of the comparisons he made between the dangers of old and new whaling were just.

Take the ships: The huge tub in which we were sailing south seemed the safest thing afloat; but she was not by any means, and all our ship's officers were agreed that they would rather weather out an antarctic gale in a Nantucket bark than on top of twenty thousand tons of industrial machinery in a blunt iron box. On the other hand, we had radar, echo-sounding gear, electric logs, and a thousand other safety devices that would make the old whaling skippers laugh us to scorn, and, best of all, we had double specially plated and reinforced bows, which could crash into and brush aside pieces of ice that would cause to founder the largest and strongest whaling ship of the last century.

But with our catchers and small craft it was different. They had no double bows or watertight bulkheads. They were about half the size of a whaling bark, and were little more than single-plated, over-engined steel speedboats that could not withstand a single squeeze from the pack ice or a hefty blow from a small growler. Yet they were ready and eager to go much deeper into the ice than the old barks normally ventured.

And, though no modern expedition would dream of lowering small boats to chase the whale, to counterbalance this the modern whalers go after mainly the blue and the fin whales. The old hands never attempted to catch these two species because, in the first place, they lacked a fourteen-knot engine and could never catch up with blues and fins, the fastest in the ocean. In the second place, these whales sink when they die, and a powerful modern winch or other mechanical means is needed to raise them and keep them afloat. Finally, the oldtimers would never have dared to attack blue and fin whales even if they came up alongside, for these two species fight in a way no monster sperm ever did.

Again, though the size of the craft that hunt the whale has increased, everything else has increased in proportion, and often enough the danger increases with the size. Take the ropes. The three-quarter-inch hemp line that the old whalemen used was dangerous enough as it smoked past the loggerhead and burned the hand of any man who grasped it. There are on record at least three authentic cases of men being hauled out of the whaleboat and lost through being entangled in the line. But compare the modern eight-inch Manila whale line, and the damage that results when anything goes wrong with that. As Mark said to me: "Jesus! I'd like to see my grandfather try to handle some modern cordage, and I'd like to see his face and hear the stories he'd tell afterward if ever he were present when a three-inch nylon rope with a strain of a thousand tons on it and stretched to half its length again fouls and is cut by a catcher's propeller!"

Not all my time on the bridge with Mark as we headed south was spent in the discussion of polar navigation and

whaling, for the Southern Ocean had much other diversion
to offer us. I began to find that my instructor was a well-in-
formed authority on most of the things we saw as we yarned
together, leaning over the dodger. The birds were always the
most obvious diversion, and on these he would talk for hours.
I carried in my pocket all the time a little handbook of ocean
birds which supplied the scientific data, but Mark would back
this up with innumerable whalemen's legends and much accurate information based on his own observation of the birds
of the Southern Ocean.

As with all who are new to the southern seas, it was the
albatrosses that interested me most. There was invariably one
of these great birds, and often enough twenty or more,
gliding over and around our ship as we steamed toward the
ice pack. The first sight of them had been disappointing. They
looked no bigger and no more inspiring than large sea gulls,
and the color of most of them was not the evil white so often
described, but a patchy, mundane brown.

But occasionally, as we stood motionless on the wing of
the bridge, one of them would glide down to skim the water
far below us. There it would coast along, undulating its
flight to fit exactly the shape of the ocean swell and seeming
as though it would hit the crest of every wave that swept
from our bows, but never quite doing so. Then, when it
had kept up this surface-skimming for minutes or even hours,
a bigger and steeper swell would come along, and the bird
would rise without effort. It would veer toward the highest
part of the swell, approaching the advancing wall of water
so closely as to give the impression that its intention was
to burst through and come out the other side. Then, at the
last moment, an imperceptible muscular twitch would change
its direction, and the pressure ridge of air caused by the
advancing swell would do the rest. Without the flicker of a
wing tip, the bird would rise steeply from the water, and
in a moment would be gliding right alongside us by the
bridge, fifty feet high. And there, where we could have leaned
out and touched it, we saw this bird, greater than the eagle,
in its true dimension and grandeur.

Then we could see—and, had we wished, could have bent
over to measure—its astounding wing span: eight to ten feet

in the small ones, eleven to thirteen feet in the greater. And we could bear witness to its apparent utter immobility in the air—except for the eyes. My guidebook did not tell me, but Mark pointed out, that the eyes of the albatross are never still and fixed, as are the eyes of most birds in flight, but are continually flickering up, sideways, down, then ahead.

"They're seamen's eyes," Mark said, and I saw what he meant. For I had noted during our long hours on the bridge together that, though he would remain motionless except for a slight movement to compensate for the rolling of the ship, Mark's eyes were never still. Although he might be talking to me of birds or whales or ice, his eyes would never be on me, but would be moving up to the sky, then sweeping the horizon, then the bows of the ship below us, then straight ahead for their steadiest and most prolonged gaze.

"Would you kill an albatross?" I asked Mark suddenly one day as we were watching the great birds.

"Christ! No! . . . And don't you do so either, or I'll heave you over the side!" was his violent rejoinder. "I'm a religious man," he added, "though you might not think so at times by my language; and I believe in heaven and hell, and my church doesn't approve of superstitions—like the superstition that the souls of dead seamen enter into albatrosses. But if I were God" (a not uncommon and by no means intentionally blasphemous phrase on the lips of a Scot) "I wouldn't take seamen up to strum harps with their horny hands. But I *would* put their souls into albatrosses; and, you see, doctor, it's possible that God does have enough sense to do that. So don't you go killing any albatrosses around here!"

Partly from my bird book and partly from Mark I learned the explanation of the absence of the classical pure-white albatross from the vicinity of our ship. The book told me that in this part of the ocean we could expect to encounter mainly the sooty albatross, which breeds on South Georgia and will be found seeking its food hundreds of miles from its breeding-place. This species, as the name implies, is a smutty-looking bird. Only the great wandering albatross is pure white all over, except for his primaries (which are the feathers forming the tips of his wings). But it is only the adult that is pure white, and all birds under about two years in this species retain their dirty-brown fledgling feathers. Although we saw many hundreds of the young birds, we saw no adult white wandering albatrosses around our ship. This the book did not explain, but Mark took up the story from there:

"There are various theories," he said, "to explain why no whaling ship ever sights a pure-white adult wandering albatross. One is that the older members of the species are too delicate to stand the cold of the Southern Ocean and always head north from their nesting-grounds. The other is that, when they have turned pure white, they are old and wise enough to know that they'll find damned little grub thrown overboard from a British whaleship with a Norwegian chief steward, so they fly up astern of us, take one look at our port of registration, smell the Norwegian cooking, and sheer off in a panic to find an American ship with an Argentine chief steward."

One particular albatross that we met about a week out of South Georgia I shall never forget. We were still steaming due south, and loose pack ice was beginning to appear around us. From up on the bridge we first saw this bird as a tiny speck flying on a course northward, exactly opposite to ours. The wind was from the north, and he was gliding on it, mast high, in the effortless way of his species. We assumed with unconscious vanity that he was coming out of the ice to meet us, and would turn and join the dozen or so of his brethren which were already in our convoy. But, as we watched him approach, he showed no sign of turning, but maintained a steady course. Our courses crossed with about ten yards between us, and he sailed serenely over our right shoulders and past our rigging without the slightest deviation and without even, it seemed, a glance sideways, and continued on astern of us. When he had finally disappeared away into the evening haze behind us, Mark exploded. "Would you bloody well believe it!" he swore. "He didn't even notice us!"

When Mark was busy, I used to seek out Dornoch, the second steward, who was also an endless source of ornithological information, perhaps not as amusing but certainly as accurate as that of Mark. Dornoch introduced me to the smaller birds of the Antarctic, and many hours we spent hanging over the side of the ship with our cameras, he augmenting his already wonderful series of sea-bird photographs, and I taking a succession of pictures invariably the same, and invariably on development turning out to resemble the child photographer's first blurred and disappointing effort to catch a sea gull on the wing from the beach. However, I learned much about the little birds during these sessions. Two species in particular fascinated Dornoch, and he communicated his fascination to me.

The first was a little brownish fellow which fluttered low near the water below us. Like the albatrosses, this small bird and his kind stayed with us for weeks on end, though they seemed to lack all the advantages that enabled the albatrosses to do so. They could not glide like the great birds, and they never settled on the water, so that they were never at rest, but continued to flutter—flutter—flutter—day and night for weeks on end, occasionally darting down to the surface of the water to pick up a morsel of grub, but never alighting on the sea. It seemed, in fact, that they could not swim, though the bird book did not mention this. Their expenditure of energy in porportion to their size and the food they ate must have been tremendous, and we felt sorry for them as we watched, for it made one tired by empathy to look at them. Dornoch told me the whalemen's legend concerning them. It appears that, while the albatross is the seaman's soul in a state of bliss, the Wilson's petrel is the damned soul of a landsman, condemned forever to find his livelihood on the ocean, and denied any seagoing attributes to aid him. The myth was appropriate to the tormented little bird, and was rather frightening. It occurred to me that this was something Dante might have used, had he known about it, in his diabolic prescriptions for the disposal of damned souls.

Dornoch's other Southern Ocean pet was the prion, a small, graceful, slender bird that skims the wave tops and descends deep into the troughs seeking air currents, albatross fashion, but differing from its mighty cousin in that it occasionally dives deep below the surface seeking live fish. This sharp-winged, alert little bird has many aliases among seamen. Some call it the "ice bird" because the men of the old sailing ships believed that it indicated the presence of ice. This might be so, for certainly we never saw it except when there was ice about. And the old whalemen called it the "whalebird," for they reckoned it led them to the whales. This Dornoch disputed, and my own subsequent observation made me agree with him, for, when we were among the whales, we never saw a prion. The real "whalebird" is the Cape pigeon, a plump black-and-white bird sitting high and serene on the water, looking just like a pigeon, as its name implies. It seldom rises in flight for more than a yard or two. This bird, which has a most attractive appearance but a most unattractive personality, we never saw in passage anywhere, and it ignored our ship completely if we were whaleless. But, if whales were about, it would begin to appear, and, let one whale be killed, and the Cape pigeons would be on the sea all round us, literally by the thousands, waiting to share our spoils with us. They are surface feeders, preferring whale guts to any other diet, and neither Mark nor Dornoch nor the bird book could tell me what they could find to eat on the surface of the icebound Southern Ocean when no whalers were around. We could only speculate that they fol- lowed the schools of live whales, hungry but hopeful, anticipat- ing their early death at our hands, and a good feed to follow.

"They're like the whaleship-owners," Dornoch put it, express- ing the whaleman's age-old cynical opinion of his employers. "They only take an interest in us when there's some profits to be disbursed. Maybe we should call them the 'whaleowner birds'!"

I was again with Dornoch one evening when I had an unforgettable ornithological experience. The long twilight of high latitudes, when objects are still fairly clear but photog- raphy is impossible, had descended, and we were up in the bows. Dornoch was gazing hypnotically at the cleavage made by our ship through the icy water, and I was trying in a desultory way to find some subject of conversation which would make this interesting little character open up a bit more and reveal his philosophy.

Suddenly there came a loud "Ca-a-a-k! Ca-a-a-k!" from the sea, seemingly from about fifty yards out. It was a most unmarine and farmyardlike noise, and, when I looked quickly, I saw nothing but empty water. Dornoch noticed my astonish- ment, and explained. This was the noise made by the penguin when he is in his real home, the sea. I watched closely for a while, and soon I saw them: four flashing black shapes suddenly shot out of the water to a height of about a foot, projected themselves through the air in a graceful, streamlined curve, and re-entered the water without causing a ripple. A few seconds later, and a hundred feet ahead, they repeated the action. The glide and dive were smoother, faster, and more graceful than the surfacing of any dolphin, and my first glimpse of it changed immediately my opinion of the penguin as an awkward and ridiculous or frustrated and unnatural creature. For there was nothing ridiculous or unnatural in this astonishing progression through and over the water. I have seen it aptly described since as "flying in water" instead of in the air, and seeing it the first time produces the same effect as that moment in circus routine when the incredibly awkward and ludicrous clown who has been rolling in the sawdust, amusing the children, suddenly seizes the trapeze and swings gracefully to the top of the tent with a skill even greater than that of the beautiful lady and sleek, well-polished gentleman who earn their living by daring acrobatic feats. I had glimpsed the other side of the life of the sad little comic of the Antarctic, and, as the four glossy black shapes drew ahead at twice the speed of our ship, I saluted them. Maybe they had, as Gyle averred in South Georgia, earned our contempt for giving up their heritage of flight for a full belly of fish, but, if they had left the kingdom of the air, it was to claim regal dignity in the ocean. And, if Mansell was correct (and I began to hope he was) in theorizing that they would in some dim future age rise right out of the sea to return no more, then they fully deserved their elevation in the evolutionary scheme.

It might be thought, from my description, that a whaling expedition sailing south to the ice from its last port of call is tranquil and idle, the hands having nothing to do but hang over the side looking at the birds. Certainly the whalemen do spend much of their spare time examining and, according to their individual psychic states, communing with the other beings that make the Southern Ocean their home and hunting ground. But there is in fact little idle time for anyone as the whaling ground is approached. Even the senior medical officer, who,

next to the chief engineer, is reckoned by the average unap-
preciative whaleman to have the softest job on the expedition,
was very busy for the week or so after our expedition left
South Georgia. Although he spent as much time as he could
bird-watching, he spent rather more time during that period
in the sick bay.

For an epidemic of "influenza," as we called it, had broken
out on our ships, and the men were going down like the
traditional flies, with three-day fevers, coughs, and occasionally
a threatened pneumonia. I had been forewarned by predeces-
sors in my job of this peculiar outbreak, which attacks nearly
every whaling expedition leaving South Georgia. It had scared
the wits out of many a whaling doctor in the old days of
Dover's Powders, and had killed many a whaleman and explorer who had left the island (including the toughest of
them—Shackleton), but in these days of penicillin and various
-mycins, it was a troublesome but not frightening outbreak.
It would take an epidemiologist to explain properly the South
Georgia "flu" that was affecting us all at this time. I can
only say vaguely that it seems to be connected with the fact
that the resistance to all respiratory infections among the
island inhabitants drops sharply during the winter, when they
are cut off from all the coughs and sneezes of the rest of
the world. The whaling ships bring the bugs back to the
ill-prepared islanders in the southern spring, and the whole
immunity-starved island is knocked flat by germs that have
been browbeaten and rendered harmless in the crowded
northern hemisphere. Then, by what the bacteriologists call
"serial passage" through a succession of highly susceptible subjects, the germs resume their virulence—get back their self-
confidence, as it were, in their malevolent attack on the
human race—and, by the time the whaleships leave the island,
are malignant enough to make another assault on the men
who brought them to the island. So even I was busy as we
headed south.

But again, if I felt inclined to complain about my job, I
had only to go up to the bridge, where others, Mark chief
among them, were ten times busier than I was and had
responsibilities exceeding mine, and my complaints would be
silenced. For the whaling was about to start, and, though Mark

and the other bridge officers all had the flu, they were on their toes sixteen hours a day, with only occasional intermissions to talk to the doctor and watch the birds.

Mark took time off to show me what was going on (probably, I think, because I had remembered Mansell's advice to take special care of the health of this man, and had given him particular and discriminative treatment to keep him on his feet when the fever did hit him), and he took me into the chartroom often to explain the expedition's plans.

The general plan of attack on the cetacean world was this: One of our little whalecatching ships, commanded by Thor, that phenomenon among gunners, the former New York taxi-driver, had gone ahead of us by several days to "look for the whales." Thor had headed due south to the edge of the pack ice, which he was now skirting in an easterly direction, somewhere south of the South Sandwich Islands. Every few hours he reported back to the factory ship. Accompanying us were the other sixteen small vessels that made up our fleet: catchers, corvettes, and buoy boats. They were ahead, astern, and all around us. "Like a hen and her chickens" is the conventional metaphor for such occasions, but, though our huge ship may have behaved like a lumbering old hen, these vicious little hawklets around us were no chickens. In a day or two they would be biting, and biting hard and fatally, at the greatest of the mammals.

When we reached the whales in any quantity, the thirteen catchers, assisted by their superior speed of fifteen knots, would draw ahead of us and fan out over an arc of ocean that in the beginning would be about fifty miles across. Within this arc, between us and the catchers, would steam the two buoy boats, vessels almost identical with the catchers and armed like them. Their job would be to buoy and collect such whales as the catchers killed, and do a bit of hunting themselves if circumstances permitted. Also in the arc would be the two unarmed corvettes, which would form a fast connecting shuttle service between us and the fleet of small ships, and would tow in to us the dead whales. Communication within the fleet would be by a continuous day-and-night radio-telephone service.

"I'd better show you how that works, doc," Mark said.

"They'll be wanting to talk to you oftener than they talk to me, to yarn about their aches and pains and how to deal with their hangovers. All whaling gunners have stomach ulcers—have you found that out yet? And most of them will have the d.t.'s sometime during the trip, and the mates of the catchers will be calling you on the blower to ask what to do."

He took me over to a complicated gadget of the wire-and-dial-and-glowing-bulb type that always terrifies me. It turned out to be very simple, however, and in a few minutes I had got the hang of the one-way conversations and the "over to you."

"Now, the first thing to remember," Mark warned me, "is that the whole fleet will be listening to every word you say, and they'll be specially interested in any secrets you have to give away. There's a duplicate set in the wireless room, another in the manager's cabin, and speakers in the wheelhouse and the secretary's office; and every one of the small ships has a set which they leave on all the time to pick up what gossip they can. . . . Now let's talk to Thor on Number One catcher—he's about a hundred and fifty miles away, which is the extreme effective range of this machine—and see what he's got to say." He twisted the necessary knobs and buttons, the machine came to humming life, and he spoke into the handset:

"Hello, Number One! Hello, Number One! Factory calling! Factory calling! Is the gunner there? Is the gunner there? Good morning, Thor! Good morning, Thor! Over!"

He put in the "Over" switch, and the low, whining hum the machine was making changed into a mighty roar, in which I was eventually able to distinguish human words and syllables through the speakers. It bellowed through the chartroom, outside on the bridge, and from half a dozen points in the distance.

"U-u-u-rgh! 'Ullo! Fagdory! 'Ullo! Fagdory! Number One here! Number One here! Gutt mornig, Mark! Gutt mornig, Mark! You want to know about whales—u-u-u-rgh? You call at right time! We chasing sperm now—plenty sperm around here. Maybe we be 'fast-fish' in a few minutes. You send up other catchers now. We have gutt day's fishing tomorrow. . . . You talk to mate now. I go forrard and kill first whale of season!"

A few minutes later the radio telephone began to roar and crackle again, and we heard the voice of the catcher's mate: "Hello! Factory! Hello! Factory! Number One here! Number One here! 'Fast-fish.' Large sperm. Lots of others around; weather good. Lot of ice. We'll stick around here and wait for the corvettes to come up. Gunner reckons he'll get three or four sperm anyway. Get the other catchers up quickly. G'by!"

"Bloody fool might have told us where he is!" was Mark's unexcited comment. "Only he probably doesn't know himself. However, we should pick them up about midnight. Then you'll see your first whale close up, doc, and neither of us will have much time for watching the birds. I'll leave you to amuse yourself now, if you don't mind. I've got work to do."

He glanced at the chart, looked up at the gyrocompass over the table, turned the radar on a moment and gazed at the screen, read the speed from the electric log, shouted a word to the cadet out on the bridge, then picked up the telephone and informed the engineer of the watch profanely and dogmatically that it would be entirely his fault if we did not have a whale on the deck by nightfall.

Antarctica: The Urgency of Protecting Life on and Around the Great Southerly Continent

ROBERT CUSHMAN MURPHY

Dr. Robert Cushman Murphy, presently Lamont Curator Emeritus of Birds of the American Museum of Natural History made his first trip to Antarctica in 1912 and his most recent in 1960. He has been described as America's ambassador to the penguin, the petrel, and the tern, and his interests in conservation are worldwide. Here he describes the threats to the ecosystem of Antarctica.

BEYOND doubt, the Antarctic is the only facet of our world in which man has not yet lived long enough to have had an overwhelming effect upon the native ecosystem. Everywhere else he has transformed primordial conditions to such an extent that we have only a vague idea of what they once were. Man, throughout his latter cultural history, has shown that he is the sole insatiable predator because, unlike all other animals, he takes his prey mostly from motives other than those of personal survival. Places in which we can observe and experiment in a primitive climax grow scarcer year by year, or day by day, but in Antarctica they remain thus far at our service.

The water and land enclosed within the Antarctic Circle are unique in several ways. Their relationships with both higher and lower belts of latitude are different from those of corresponding areas around the northern end of the earth's axis. Southward from the North Pole and Arctic Ocean, for example, there is a relatively rapid climatic transition from polar to subarctic, to cold-temperate, to warm-temperate. In the Southern Hemisphere, however, we have to forget the equivalent positions of the two polar circles and to recognize that the antarctic environment is actually three times larger than the arctic environment.

The continental climate of high latitudes in the Northern Hemisphere assures mild summers and a rich diversity of plant and animal life. Antarctica, on the contrary, has a broad belt of oceanic climate surrounding the lofty and frozen interior. Instead of being closely rimmed by land masses such as Eurasia and North America it is by far the most isolated part of the world. The narrowest gap that separates it from other continents south of the Equator is the 700-mile reach across Drake Passage, from the Antarctic Peninsula to Cape Horn.

That Antarctica is by far the most insulated area on earth is equally meaningful. It is meteorologically buffered from all other land by a wide and permanently cold ocean and an overlying ring of circling winds. It has been well said that Antarctica has "trapped" its own cold—which is fortunate for air-breathing life everywhere else.

Site of a present-day ice age more stupendous than the northern Pleistocene glaciation, Antarctica thus far shows no sign of a coming interglacial stage. The twin factors of isolation and insulation seem to forestall that. Melting of the load of antarctic ice, which is ninety per cent of all the ice in the world, would raise the ocean level by at least 200 feet. But most glaciologists believe that the six or more million cubic miles of antarctic ice are not lessening, despite the recent worldwide trend toward climatic amelioration. Warming, indeed, may only supply more moisture from the north to swell the scanty antarctic precipitation and thus add to the ice cap. Russian glaciologists have found reasons for concluding that antarctic stored ice may be growing at a net rate of nearly 300 cubic miles a year. This possible, though not yet proven, gain would result even though immeasurable quantities of ice are carried outward from the glacial coasts in tabular icebergs, some of which are as big as the state of Connecticut. The principal effect of such transport is to maintain *status quo* by keeping the isolating and insulating ocean as cold as possible.

The respective differences between plant and animal life in the Arctic and the Antarctic are due, therefore, to the continental controls in the north and the isolation, insulation, and peripheral oceanic climate of the southern realm. In Antarctica we find no widely varied flora and fauna such as fill the lands around the North Pole. A hundred or more kinds of flowering plants thrive to the north of the Arctic Circle, whereas there are only two small and obscure species south of the Antarctic Circle. In spring the Arctic rings with birdsong. The land birds of Greenland include eagles, falcons, owls, ptarmigan, larks, wheatears, fieldfares, pipits, wagtails, redpolls, buntings, and ravens. The arctic mammals number lemmings, hares, ermines, foxes, wolves, bears, caribou, and musk-oxen. These —not to mention a counterpart of the Eskimo—are all missing from the south. The distinctions show us, as was long ago pointed out by Charles Darwin, that the periodic extreme temperatures of polar winter are less inimical to life than the unrelieved chill of antarctic, and even subantarctic, summer.

For food resources, the Antarctic claims the richest of all ocean waters, and despite the harsh climatic threshold, it has produced also a spectacular assemblage of life above sea level. Virtually all this life, however, subsists upon a food chain that extends from the sea. For higher animals, such as birds and mammals, there is no equivalent of the arctic food chains that stem from terrestrial vegetation. Antarctic life is manifest in enormous numbers of individual organisms, rather than in a wide range of kinds. The penguins, the hordes of flying sea-fowl, the seals of the drifting and the fast ice, the primitive yet highly specialized arthropods, the extraordinary inverte-brates of pools that remain frozen except for a few days in each year, the lichens, mosses, and other cryptogamic plants— all are there to be investigated by the methods of many scientific disciplines.

We need all these life forms for ecological, behavioristic, physiological, sociological, medical, and many other reasons. We need them likewise for esthetic and humanistic ends. Since the Antarctic is the only fragment of the world that still seems unsuited to what we euphemistically call "development," let us keep it as we found it.

Nobody any longer doubts the importance of national parks, even though New Zealand is probably the only nation that has dedicated an adequate proportion of its territory toward such use. The Antarctic should properly be regarded as an international park, a concept that would harmonize with agreements already concluded among the countries that began joint exploration and research during the International Geophysical Year.

In 1964 twelve nations, which had earlier signed the Antarctic Treaty and subscribed to co-operative endeavor, ratified a list of "Agreed Measures for the Conservation of Antarctic Fauna and Flora." This was an important step, even though the field was limited to land and water beyond 60° south latitude. This means that it does not cover the many islands to the north, along the Antarctic Convergence. Even more regrettable, it excludes whaling operations, which have long been the most shamefully short-sighted of overexploitations. More than 46,000 whales, a toll four or five times greater than the ocean population can safely endure, have been slaughtered in the Antarctic within a single season. Also, seals on high-seas ice receive no present protection under the "Agreed Measures." One seal, the crabeater, appears right now to be running the risk of a commercial threat. A list of specially protected species has, however, been drawn up, as well as a list of specially protected areas. But the official designation of these areas has been put off for further consideration. The document recognizes that protection of the limited vegetation, and of the great bulk of small animal organisms, can be achieved only through preservation of the habitat.

These slow-moving international intentions are commendable, as we all realize. But the representatives of the United States in Antarctica should on no account wait for their implementation. By precept and action it is up to us to make sure that the spirit of conservation prevails, most of all on the periphery of the continent, which harbors life for a hundred miles back from the sea.

This means that the pumping out of ships' bilges in coastal waters, and the ill-considered use of explosives, are no more tolerable in the Antarctic than elsewhere. It means that all resources are to be used only for truly cultural purposes. It means that life is never to be sacrificed for sport or "trophies." It means that colonies of penguins and other seabirds are never to be regarded as centers of amusement. We know too well that penguin populations decline if frequently and carelessly visited by groups of human beings, and especially if they are stampeded by helicopters. Even in the course of carefully controlled investigation of Adélie Penguins it has been learned that a bird seized and held briefly for banding may reveal the traumatic effect for a week thereafter, perhaps discontinuing the behavior appropriate for its reproductive stage, or failing to seek food in the sea at the normal time.

No one would want to deny workers at an antarctic station the privilege of watching penguins, but regulations should leave no doubt that the opportunity is a privilege, subject to necessary restrictions. Now that Antarctica seems inevitably destined to become an austral summer tourist realm, the point needs more stressing than ever before.

In short, a penguin colony cannot be a circus—not if it is to remain a penguin colony. Intentional damage, such as vandalism, is less to be feared than harm from well-intentioned trespass. Those who have spent patient weeks recording the seasonal cycle of breeding animals know this, to their sorrow. The same devoted researchers know likewise the murderous havoc that can and does result from heedless maneuvering of aircraft. At the Antarctic Symposium held at Buenos Aires in November, 1959, it was "conceded that each season the re-supply operations in support of antarctic scientific bases bring with them into the Antarctic a number of persons, members of ships' companies and others, who possess a minimum of interest in the natural life and its conservation and who, if not supervised and controlled, have made and will continue to cause serious damage to the flora and fauna."

And the time is past, except in emergencies, when we are entitled to rely upon antarctic resources for a significant proportion of station or shipboard food. Marine invertebrates and fish are perhaps an exception, but eggs and seals are not. Nobody need now complain because three hundred tons of seals were killed and cached as food for the sledge dogs of a former expedition. But today there are too many of us, coming too often, to warrant such a sacrifice. Let me quote from the minutes of the fourth meeting of the Special Committee on Antarctic Research, assembled at Cambridge in 1960. "In recent years the depredations of expeditions upon this traditional food source have become alarmingly heavy, and are now continued without respite from year to year. For example, near several stations the stocks of Weddell seals have been so disturbed that breeding rates have been affected and scientific research rendered difficult. Animals are killed without regard to age or sex, and even animals marked in the course of scientific studies have been taken. Without biological research it is impossible to assess the permissible annual crop which the various seal colonies would stand, but it is certain that this figure is being seriously exceeded in many areas."

We now have better use for the seals and, fortunately, decreasing need of the dogs. Dogs seem to me to pose one of the few threats of lasting contamination in the Antarctic. Rats, established for the better part of two centuries at some of the low-antarctic islands, are incapable of surviving in a feral state on the continent. Dogs, however, constitute a danger worthy of international consideration. There are rumors aplenty that parties from at least two co-operating countries have allowed their dogs to run free, with resulting butchery of penguins. No native antarctic animals are instinctively wary of terrestrial enemies. How could they be when they have never known them?

It is not absurdly unlikely that dogs might become acclimated in Antarctica and take on the role of arctic wolves. In February, 1958, the Japanese were forced to abandon fifteen Karafoto huskies when heavy ice prevented the relief vessel *Soya* from approaching their station, and a blizzard made recovery of the animals by helicopter out of the question. In the following spring, two of these dogs were found alive, and the information was headlined in Tokyo newspapers. The expedition leader radioed that when the advance party landed, "Taro" and "Jiro" bounded forward, wagging their tails. It was assumed that the thirteen lost dogs had fallen into crevasses, had been rafted out to sea on ice, or had been devoured by the surviving huskies.

When Sir Vivian Fuchs came aboard U.S.S. *Glacier* off Marguerite Bay, in March, 1960, he told me that he had lost one of his sledge dogs near the base of the Antarctic Peninsula. Sixty days later the truant turned up again at the ship not simply in good condition but fat, after journeying 150 miles across the ice. Dogs and wolves are of the same genus. Huskies and wolves are as close in habitus as in heritage. It is horrifying and not wholly chimerical to picture wild dogs surviving, breeding, and multiplying on a winter diet of Emperor Penguins and a summer diet of Adélies—for as long as the birds lasted!

And what of other domestic or laboratory animals? The importation of poultry into Antarctica was stopped in July, 1966, but guinea pigs and mice are still called for. Such creatures could not become feral, but they might introduce parasites and viruses to infect the indigenous fauna. If experimental animals are necessary at national stations, provision should be made for their hermetic isolation and for incineration of their excreta and bedding.

The transfer of contamination over long distances needs always to be kept in mind. No chlorinated hydrocarbons, so far as known, have been used within many hundreds of miles of Antarctica, yet Drs. Sladen and Reichel have recently detected residues of DDT in the tissues of Adélie Penguins and a crabeater seal from Cape Crozier. Other biologists have found the same substance in fish of the antarctic family Nototheniidae. Not one of these species ranges northward beyond the pack-ice zone. The DDT was doubtless acquired by way of a marine food chain, and ultimately from creatures that ingested it thousands of miles away, perhaps in the Northern Hemisphere. Although the compound in the antarctic animals was in concentrations believed to be insignificant, the circumstances should still serve as a warning.

Few persons are free from prejudice, and prejudices spring as freely from altruistic motives as from any other. An example in Antarctica is the enmity that the skua arouses in the tender breasts of men who come in the ships and planes. Skuas devour penguin eggs. They miss no opportunity to steal, swallow whole, or tear to bits young penguins at any stage of growth. They hang around, ghoulishly, every adult penguin that shows signs of being ready to depart this life, and at the favorable moment they are quick to hasten its demise. (I may add that the presence of indignant human observers usually adds to the skua's chances of doing such mischief to "friendly" creatures.) From an objective point of view, this relationship between skua and penguin is neither to be condemned nor condoned. Penguins live on euphausid shrimps; skuas on penguins. So it has been, presumably, throughout the latter half of the Tertiary and ever since. To make it a moral issue by clubbing skuas and smashing their eggs is of no benefit to the penguins or to anything else. A childish desire to upset an ecological regime should have no place in anyone who is to head southward. We are down there to learn the ways of nature, not to reform them.

Many animals of the Arctic rear large broods of offspring. This is true, for example, of some of the northern ducks. Among mammals such as lemmings, the litters may furthermore number several in a season. A similar high rate of fertility is unknown in the Antarctic, where the fauna may be said to exist on a marginal basis of stability. Two additional influences tend to assure a low reproductive rate, namely, the uniquely severe summer environment, and the fact that all the air-breathing vertebrates take their exclusively animal food directly or indirectly from the sea.

Heavy snowfall, extreme frost, storms, or winds that merely close leads and clog coastal waters with tight pack are always likely to make prey inaccessible and thus, in the case of birds, block the feeding of the young. Scientific literature teems with instances of how heavily the hazards of weather are weighted against the egg and nestling stages of antarctic birds. Data from the life histories of Emperor Penguin and Snow Petrel suggest that an unsuccessful annual breeding cycle may be statistically more "normal" than one in which a single chick per pair of adults is reared to fledging and departure. At the Argentine Islands, off the western coast of the Antarctic Peninsula, Roberts found the mortality of Wilson's Petrel chicks to be about sixty-five per cent. The well-advertised carcasses of ancient, desiccated, chiefly immature seals at localities far inland show in like manner how tardy departure, or premature freezing and closure of sea ice, can lead to aimless scattering, starvation, and death.

Other factors limiting exuberant multiplication include both disease and predators. The polar environment is regarded as singularly healthful, and yet we know that *Aspergillus,* a mold responsible for respiratory infections in birds, is liable to arrive with man's invasion, if it is not already there. Maladies grouped under the pathological term "ornithosis" sometimes take a heavy toll of bird life. Nor are the seals free from unpredictable holocausts. A report by Laws and Taylor describes mass deaths of crabeater seals during the season of the year that should be devoted to pupping. The mortality in a localized population of about 3000 animals was estimated to be eighty-five per cent. The proximate cause was a highly contagious virus infection. It was limited in the area of its ravages and also extraordinarily host-specific. Weddell seals in the same vicinity, but dependent upon dissimilar food, remained healthy. The sickness of the crabeaters was probably induced by shortage of krill (euphausids), but going back to prior causes, the mortality was of climatic origin.

Mature antarctic animals are less prone to catastrophic destruction than are eggs and young. The limited data we have on longevity and viability indicate that most of the birds and mammals, once past their vulnerable infancy, enjoy a notably favorable life expectancy. No more convincing support for this opinion need be sought than the findings of Roberts in a west antarctic colony of Wilson's Petrels. This author ringed nearly all the birds of twenty-three mated and nesting pairs. At the next breeding season, a year later, he recovered most of his marked petrels, linked with the identical mates and occupying the identical burrows of the previous year. In other words, there was no evidence of adult mortality among pelagic birds that, between reproductive periods, migrate far into middle latitudes of the Northern Hemisphere.

In such relative safety of adult antarctic animals we find an explanation of the very large numbers that some of their populations attain. Despite physical risks, predation by skuas, Giant Fulmars, leopard seals, killer whales, etc., despite proportional scarcity of reproductive sites vis-à-vis the vast extent of watery pasturage, we encounter in Antarctica some of the most abundant of all species of birds, as well as seal populations estimated to number six million or more individuals of at least one of the six kinds. Why then, it would be fair to ask, has conservation of the antarctic fauna suddenly become a matter of growing concern?

The answer is that in a long-isolated realm of tenuous balance, where broods are small (rarely more than a single annual replacement) and the dangers of immaturity extravagant, man, the new interloper, is the straw that can break the camel's back. We have seen the signs already in the overexploitation of Weddell seals in the neighborhoods of some stations. Around the periphery of the Antarctic, we have the appalling history of fur seal destruction—all but total—which is only now beginning to mend because of the half century of protection at South Georgia.

In the same outer oceanic ring of islands we note with foreboding that, although whales continue to decrease, the improved techniques of slaughter almost manage to maintain the scale of total return. The former, drastic wiping-out of the humpback has now been followed by similar extirpation of the blue whale stock. The percentage of blue whales in the antarctic catch is today only a twentieth of what it was in 1930. The finback, last of the unprotected whalebone whales, is in turn paying the costs. There is nothing to follow except the sperm whale, which is once again being harried throughout the world's warmer oceans.

Man has himself become the center of a potential demographic crisis in Antarctica. Proliferation of his occupancy and travel must be accepted. There may be a modest withdrawal during some years, but it appears certain that the remainder of the twentieth century will be mostly years of expansion in his numbers, and that pursuit of scientific information will be the main reason for his presence.

An establishment like McMurdo, the home of a thousand or more human beings in the austral summer and of a couple of hundred in winter, fairly bursts with conservation problems, of which the disposal of sewage, garbage, and other waste is only the first. There is no subsoil seepage, no rapid bacterial decomposition, such as come to our aid in the more familiar world. Each season the biologists find that they must go farther afield for their ecological studies. Even the bottom of Winter Quarters Bay is losing the semblance of a "natural area."

With a dozen nations engaged in antarctic research, over-collecting of organisms and unwitting repetition of studies that call for collecting require weighing. Penguins, as preserved specimens or as captives for zoological parks, are much sought after by different groups at even single national bases. Fewer examples, especially of killed birds, might be made to serve the purposes of several or many workers. Sladen, Penney, Prévost, and others have recently conducted penguin investigations of great significance with negligible sacrifice of life and minimum disturbance of the colonies.

The task of perpetuating antarctic life calls for long vision no less than for immediate control measures. We are in need of scientific forecasts such as only patient and cautious study can supply. We cannot preserve without an understanding of the regime. Sound foresight may then prevent us from making the slight overdrafts on resources that differ only in degree from the gross overdrafts that we can already see. For whether we use many times too much or only a little too much of things we cannot create, the result will still be depletion. We are already wise enough to discard the fallacy that a species is in no danger because it is still common. We need always to recall and heed the brilliant maxim of Paul-Emile Victor, made at the Antarctic Symposium of 1960 in Paris, namely that Antarctica represents a system of immense capital, yet of only small annual increment. If we fail to acknowledge this, we may find that the ecosystem can be wrecked even more speedily than those of the temperate regions.

The Antarctic: A Laboratory for Men Under Stress

FINN RONNE

The Antarctic now serves as a gigantic laboratory. Admiral Byrd predicted it would once become "a vast freezer" for the surplus food of the world. In time, too, minerals, from uranium to coal, may be mined there. Tomorrow's weather and yesterday's glacial past are constantly being studied there and many countries are exchanging information about the remaining secrets of the Antarctic—among them the United States, Britain, Japan, Russia, Australia, Belgium, New Zealand, Norway, Argentina, Chile, France, and South Africa.

More scientific expeditions to the South Polar regions mean more men there—and more men under stress. Perhaps the greatest laboratory aspect of the area is that human personality with all its strengths and weaknesses under stress and isolation can be studied there—often duplicating conditions for space exploration.

Captain Finn Ronne, an American whose father was Martin Ronne of Norway, one of the members of Amundsen's South Polar Expedition, has taken part in five antarctic expeditions. He speaks from the vantage point of having known both yesterday's polar heroes and today's polar scientists.

ACCOUNTS of problems in human relations on antarctic expeditions have been circulated and analyzed among explorers since the continent was first sighted. All expeditions suffer from the same malady, although few such stories and their causes have ever been widely publicized.

In order to appear more successful and heroic, expedition leaders (as well as their followers), have consistently minimized their difficulties in human relationship. Even on occasions when human relationship has become the balancing point between success or tragic failure, we have attempted invariably to cover or gloss over these frailties. Perhaps this has been a mistake and a distinct disservice to those who follow. It has certainly considerably delayed bringing any national focus on a very serious problem.

In my opinion, this area of human relationship under abnormal conditions should be a fundamental area for immediate intensified study. On the ability of humans to adapt themselves hangs the future success of undertakings under similar conditions. This application goes further than to the polar regions. The problems are the same as sending men into outer space. An analogy of the two fields will find many similarities between the necessary mental preparation required to deal with abnormal physical conditions. The Antarctic probably offers the best example of isolated stress and strain to be found on the face of this planet.

Never has sufficient interest been taken in this human problem, nor has much serious attempt been made to find the answer. Several summer transients have professed some understanding and have even had the courage to set forth their views. But the real answers will only come from those who have and will live through an antarctic winter night, not only once but several times. The psychiatrists should stay a year or two in the Antarctic, not merely visit and ask questions. The true answers to those questions change with the first sight of the relief ship.

Exploration of the Antarctic demands youth for aggressiveness, age for mature judgment, skilled technicians for specialized practical jobs, and well-rounded scientists to pursue the scientific objectives sought. In such diversified groups there will be divergent opinions regardless of where they are located.

In civilization long-established conventions have a controlling effect, whereas in the remote, cold, cramped, isolated, womanless, abnormal society of the polar regions views that would be mildly divergent elsewhere often become nearly irreconcilable.

Money has no place here, for there is nothing to buy.

First-timers are often unprepared and bitterly surprised by the lack of established tradition which has governed their life heretofore. The complete isolation from civilization makes a man lose interest in the outside world. Technically there is no set of laws to govern the actions of such a community. A new set of norms is needed. The world becomes a narrow daily life with limited associates. Man's basic animal instinct of survival is laid bare. Either he faces up to the challenge and gets along or he makes himself miserable and endangers the lives of his fellowmen.

Those who have gone through the ordeal of an antarctic winter tend to mellow. They are considerably more adaptable and stable the second winter. But regardless of all the flowery words that have been written to the contrary, I do not believe that the conditions experienced on antarctic wintering expeditions bring out the best in most men. The personnel of American expeditions in particular no longer seem to show the rugged resourcefulness, moral fiber, and mental discipline so often associated with the pioneers of this country less than 200 years ago. I have known only a dozen or so men who possessed the qualifications of the ideal expeditioner.

There are few life-long friendships among antarctic explorers —competition and jealousy become overwhelming somewhere along the way. It is possible that having been brought up in a hero-worshipping society, a man subconsciously identifies himself with the great-name explorers of the past when he ventures into the Antarctic himself. I have watched men suffer such delusions. Have they always been this way; or are life's frustrations so magnified in the isolation that man's common sense no longer governs his reasoning? Perhaps some day the answer will be found.

THE CHALLENGE OF THE SOUTH POLE

1773–75:   Captain James Cook, British explorer, reached the antarctic area at 71°10′ South. He was the first to cross the Antarctic Circle. The Antarctic had always been thought to be a land of mystery and Cook had been sent to find out if the continent actually existed. From the very earliest times it had been maintained that there would have to be two polar regions, north and south, to balance each other. Cook did not actually prove that the antarctic continent existed, but he was pretty sure that it would never be reached if it did, because it would be surrounded by ice. He declared, "I can be bold enough to say that no man will ever venture further than I have done and that the lands which may be the South will never be explored."

1819–21:   Captain Fabian von Bellingshausen was put in command of ships to sail to the Antarctic for Russia. He discovered Peter I and Alexander I islands.

              A young American, Nathaniel Palmer, a sailor from Stonington, Connecticut, with the ship *Sloop Hero* discovered the tip of Palmer Peninsula. For a while it was thought that Palmer was the first to discover the Antarctic Continent but the Russians feel that Bellingshausen discovered it and the British give credit to William Smith and Edward Mansfield who supposedly got there a few months earlier.

Bellingshausen made the first true landfall inside the Antarctic Circle on January 22, 1821. During this early period of antarctic activity it was generally sealers and whalers who were making the discoveries, although they frequently kept their discoveries to themselves because of the richness of the feeding grounds.

1823:   James Weddell, an Englishman, in an effort to find new sealing grounds, also tried to make scientific investigations of water currents, temperatures, and tides. He discovered the Weddell Sea.

1838:   Jules S. C. D. d'Urville of France was instructed to go further south than Weddell, for the glory of his country. Now began a period of competition in the polar areas. D'Urville went back to the Antarctic in 1840 and discovered Adélie Land (the Adélie penguins are called by the same name, both in honor of his wife).

1840:   James Clark Ross of England, who had determined the position of the North Magnetic Pole, in 1831, now tried to reach the South Magnetic Pole. He discovered one of the wonders of the world, the Great Ice Barrier, the Frozen Sahara of the Antarctic. His deep-sea soundings and magnetic and hydrographic observations were so exact that they opened up Antarctica for the explorers to come afterward.

Charles Wilkes of the United States announced the existence of the continent of Antarctica having followed the coast for 1500 miles. Wilkes' expedition was poorly prepared for the Antarctic and Wilkes himself was later court-martialed for the martinetlike treatment of his men which almost seems to have been necessary under the terrible circumstances of their journey. One hundred and twenty-seven men deserted.

1895: Leonard Kristensen, of Norway, a whaling captain, landed on the coast of Victoria Land in January. His party was the first ashore on the main continental mass.

1897: Lieutenant Adrien de Gerlache of Belgium spent the first winter below the Antarctic Circle. Roald Amundsen, who would be the first to reach the South Pole, was with him.

1899: C. E. Borchgrevin of Norway, who had been a member of Kristensen's party, returned to the Antarctic to winter with a British expedition.

1901–04: Robert Falcon Scott of England discovered Edward VII's Peninsula.

1907–08: Ernest Shackleton of Great Britain made a drive to the South Pole. His trip came only ninety-seven miles short of the Pole.

1908: Douglas Mawson of Australia made his remarkable sledge journey to the South Pole. With two companions he reached the Magnetic Pole and planted the Union Jack. Sir Douglas was a scientist who pioneered a variety of antarctic work, from oceanographic studies to studies of plankton.

1908–09: Ernest Shackleton explored the Antarctic with Manchurian ponies. In 1909 he discovered a route by way of the Beardmore Glacier that led to the Pole.

1911: Roald Amundsen of Norway used dog teams to reach the Pole on December 14.

The first Australian antarctic expedition under Sir Douglas Mawson.

1912:   Robert F. Scott reached the Pole with four companions, Dr. E. A. Wilson, Lieutenant Bowers, Captain Oates and Petty Officer Edgar Evans, only to discover that Amundsen had beat them. All were lost on the return voyage. Captain Scott probably died around March 29, 1912. His body was found on November 12, 1912.

1928:   Hubert Wilkins of England flew over Antarctica.

1929:   Richard E. Byrd of America established Little America and then made a 1600-mile airplane trip over the South Pole on November 29 with pilot Bernt Balchen and a radio operator-photographer. He dropped the United States Flag over the Pole.

1934–35:   Byrd led an extensive expedition to Little America, exploring 450,000 square miles of territory.

1940:   Byrd made extensive chartings of the coast of Antarctica.

1946–47:   The U. S. Navy's operation High Jump photomapped the coast line.

1946–48:   The Ronne Antarctic Research Expedition, under Commander Finn Ronne of the U. S. Navy, determined Antarctica to be only one continent. He discovered 250,000 square miles of land and made 14,000 aerial photographs over 450,000 square miles. Mrs. Ronne and Mrs. H. Darlington, whose husband was also on the expedition, were the first women to winter in the Antarctic.

1955–57:   Coastal stations were established under the U. S. Navy's operation Deepfreeze.

1957:   Vivian Fuchs of England crossed Antarctica.

1957–58:   The International Geophysical Year, July 1957 to December 1958, set up a sixty-station network to study arctic and antarctic life, including oceanography, glaciology, meteorology, and seismology. Captain Finn Ronne was also active during this year.

To date: Continued research in the South Polar regions: the establishment of a new earth science laboratory; extensive photographic mapping; investigation to help the space effort; communications efforts particularly on plastic-coated copper cable stretched across the icecap to study ice conditions.

The Serious Business of Exploration

ROALD AMUNDSEN

Roald Amundsen, the first man to reach the South Pole, was, as were so many of the great polar heroes, extremely articulate about how he became an explorer and just what the explorer's life meant.

Since he was fifteen years old, his path was clear to him. It was sometimes an extremely difficult path—one in which he had to make his own way— but his reward was the conquest of the South Pole in 1911.

How DID I happen to become an explorer? It did not just happen, for my career has been a steady progress toward a definite goal since I was fifteen years of age. Whatever I have accomplished in exploration has been the result of lifelong planning, painstaking preparation, and the hardest kind of conscientious work.

I was born a few miles south of Oslo in Norway, and when I was three months of age my parents removed to the capital, where I was reared and educated. I passed without incident through the usual educational routine of Norway, which is divided into a primary school for the ages of six to nine, a "gymnasium" for the ages of nine to fifteen, and college from the age of fifteen to eighteen. My father died when I was fourteen, and my older brothers went out into the world to care for themselves. I was thus left at home alone with my mother, by whom I was directed toward a course to prepare me to practice medicine. This ambition, however—which orig-inated with her and for which I never shared her enthusiasm— was never to be realized. When I was fifteen years old, the works of Sir John Franklin, the great British explorer, fell into my hands. I read them with a fervid fascination which has shaped the whole course of my life. Of all the brave Britishers who for 400 years had given freely of their treasure, courage, and enterprise to dauntless but unsuccessful attempts to negotiate the Northwest Passage, none was braver than Sir John Franklin. His description of the return from one of his expeditions thrilled me as nothing I had ever read before. He told how for three weeks he and his little band had battled with the ice and storms, with no food to eat except a few bones found at a deserted Indian camp, and how before they finally returned to the outpost of civilization they were reduced to eating their own boot leather to keep themselves alive.

Strangely enough the thing in Sir John's narrative that appealed to me most strongly was the sufferings he and his men endured. A strange ambition burned within me to endure those same sufferings. Perhaps the idealism of youth, which often takes a turn toward martyrdom, found its crusade in me in the form of arctic exploration. I, too, would suffer in a cause—not in the blazing desert on the way to Jerusalem, but in the frozen North on the way to new knowledge in the unpierced unknown.

In any event, Sir John's descriptions decided me upon my career. Secretly—because I would never have dared to mention the idea to my mother, who I knew would be unsympathetic—I irretrievably decided to be an arctic explorer.

More than that, I began at once to fit myself for this career. In Norway, in those days, there were no organized athletic sports as there are now everywhere. The only sports at all were football and skiing. Although I did not like football, I went in for it as part of the task of training my body to endure hardship. But to skiing I took with perfect naturalness and intense enthusiasm. At every opportunity of freedom from school, from November to April, I went out in the open, exploring the hills and mountains which rise in every direction around Oslo, increasing my skill in traversing ice and snow and hardening my muscles for the coming great adventure.

In those days, houses were kept tightly closed in winter, so I was regarded as an innovator and something of a freak because I insisted on sleeping with my bedroom windows wide open, even in the bitterest weather. My mother anxiously expostulated with me about this practice. To her I explained that I liked fresh air, but of course it was really a part of my conscientious hardening process.

At eighteen I graduated from the college, and, in pursuance of my mother's ambition for me, entered the university, taking up the medical course. Like all fond mothers, mine believed that I was a paragon of industry, but the truth is that I was a worse than indifferent student. Her death two years later, in my twenty-first year, saved her from the sad discovery which she otherwise would have made, that my own ambitions lay in another direction and that I had made but poor progress in realizing hers. With enormous relief, I soon left the university, to throw myself wholeheartedly into the dream of my life.

Before I could realize it, however, I had to discharge the duty of all young men in Norway, of performing my tour of military service. This I was eager to do, both because I wanted to be a good citizen and because I felt that military training would be of great benefit to me as further preparation for life. I had, however, one serious disqualification for a military career, which was unsuspected by most of my companions. My eyesight was especially powerful, but I was troubled by near-sightedness, which, to this day, though gradually improved, is not wholly corrected. If this defect were discovered by the medical examiner, I would not be admitted to military training. Fortunately, I had refused to wear the glasses that had been prescribed for me.

When the day came for me to take my physical examination for the army, I was ushered into an office where the chief examiner sat behind a desk with two assistants. He was an elderly physician, and, as I quickly discovered, to my extreme embarrassment, an enthusiastic student of the human body. I was, of course, stripped to the skin for the examination. The old doctor looked me over and at once burst into loud exclamations over my physical development. Evidently my eight years of conscientious exercise had not been without their effect. He said to me: "Young man, how in the world did you ever develop such a splendid set of muscles?" I explained that I had always been fond of exercise and had taken a great deal of it. So delighted was the old gentleman at his discovery, which he appeared to regard as extraordinary, that he called to a group of officers in the adjoining room to come in and view the novelty. Needless to say, I was embarrassed almost to extinction by this exhibition of my person in the altogether.

The incident, however, had its fortunate side. In his enthusiasm over the rest of my physical equipment, the good old doctor entirely forgot to examine my eyes. Consequently, I was passed with flying colors and got my training in the army.

Military service in Norway occupies only a few weeks of the year, so I had plenty of time to carry on my own course of special training for my future career of explorer. One incident of this training very nearly wrote "finis" to my life, and involved dangers and hardships fully as severe as any I was destined ever to encounter in the polar regions.

This adventure happened in my twenty-second year. It was in an effort to achieve a sort of arctic passage not many miles from Oslo itself. To the west of the capital there rises a line of steep mountainsides surmounted by a plateau of about six thousand feet elevation. This plateau extends westward nearly to the coast of Norway, in the neighborhood of Bergen, and is marked on that side by an even more abrupt descent—so difficult, in fact, that only two safe trails down its side exist. In summer the plateau was frequented only by Lapp herdsmen pasturing their nomadic herds of reindeer. No farmers lived there, so the only building of any sort in many miles was a hut erected by these herdsmen for shelter from cold rainstorms in the fall of the year. In the winter, the Lapps descended to the valleys, and the plateau was deserted. There was no record of any person having ever crossed the plateau in winter, from the mountain farm called Mogen on the east to the farm called Garen on the west coast. I determined to make this crossing.

Choosing a single companion, I proposed that we make the venture together. He agreed, and we left Oslo during the Christmas holidays. We made our way rapidly over the snow on our skis to the little farm called Mogen. Here we stopped at the last farmhouse that we expected to see on the whole trip. It was a tiny affair of only one room in which were crowded an old man and his wife and their two married sons—six people in all. They were, of course, of the simplest peasant type. There were no tourists in those days in any season of the year, so that our descent upon them would have been a surprise at any time. Coming as we did in the dead of winter, they were doubly astonished. We had no difficulty in persuading them to allow us to stay overnight with them. They were hospitable folk and made room for us on the floor near the fireplace, where we rolled ourselves up in our reindeer sleeping bags and slept very comfortably.

On the morrow, however, it was snowing, and this storm turned out to be a regular blizzard. It lasted for eight days, and we spent the whole of this time in the farmhouse.

Of course, our hosts were curious to know what errand could have brought us to their remote home. When we told them our plan to ascend to the plateau and cross it to the coast, they were first incredulous and then greatly alarmed for our safety. All three of the men were familiar with the plateau and joined in earnestly warning us not to attempt to cross it in winter. It had never been done, and they were sure it could not be done. Nevertheless, we were determined to push on and attempt it, so on the ninth day they accompanied us to the foot of the plateau at the head of their valley and showed us the best way to ascend. They bade us good-bye sadly, and we understood that they feared they would never see us again.

Of course, we were lighthearted about the enterprise. To us it seemed simple enough. The plateau was only about seventy-two English miles wide, and with our skill on skis and any decent luck with the weather, we counted at most on two days to make the crossing. Our equipment for the venture was based upon this theory, and accordingly was of the sketchiest character. Besides our skis and ski sticks, we each had a reindeer sleeping bag that we carried on our backs. We took no tent. Each of us had a small bag containing our provisions and a small alcohol lamp. This bag was rolled inside the sleeping bag. Our provisions consisted of a few crackers, some bars of chocolate, and a little butter—at the best scant rations for perhaps eight days. We had a pocket compass and a map of the region printed on paper.

We had no difficulty in ascending to the plateau. It was not a perfectly level plain that we found, but, for the practical purpose of travel, it might as well have been, for it offered no distinguishing landmarks to guide our course. There was nothing to be seen but an endless succession of small and indistinct hills.

We set our course by the compass. Our destination for our first day's travel was the herder's hut which was about in the middle of the plateau. At that time of the year in Norway, the daylight is little better than twilight, but with our compass we had no difficulty in getting along, and early in the evening we found the hut.

Our elation at this discovery was rather short-lived, for we found that the door and window of the hut had been nailed up and the top of the chimney covered over with heavy boards. We were pretty well tired with our day's exertions, the wind had started to blow again, and the thermometer was about ten degrees Fahrenheit below zero. With these handicaps, it was the hardest kind of work to get into the hut and later to clamber onto the roof and clear the top of the chimney so that we could start a fire. Both of us got our fingers badly frostbitten, and my companion, for some weeks after, was in grave danger of losing one of his.

We had the good fortune to find firewood stacked up in the hut. It took us some time, however, to make it of any use to us—if you have ever tried to build an open fire under a cold chimney with the thermometer below zero, you will understand the difficulty we had in getting a draught going. The cold air settles down on your fire like a blanket, and you have to get a pretty brisk blaze going before the heat displaces the column of cold air in the flue. Meanwhile, of course, in our efforts to do this, we had filled the little hut with smoke that got into our eyes and throats and caused us much discomfort.

We felt pretty good after we had the fire blazing and had eaten a supper. At length, we rolled up in our sleeping bags in the bunks on the opposite wall and slept very comfortably.

In the morning, we found that our troubles had only begun. The wind of the night before was still blowing, and it was now snowing heavily. The storm was so severe that it would obviously be folly to venture out in it. We therefore settled down to sit the storm out before the fireplace. Further exploration of the hut revealed another bit of good luck—it disclosed a small sack of rye flour that had been left behind

by some herdsman. As we now realized that our own provisions must be husbanded, we made a thin porridge of this
flour, which we cooked in an iron kettle over the open fire.
We spent two days in the hut, and the only food we took in
that time was this weak porridge. At best, it was not very
nourishing, and neither was it palatable.

On the third day, the storm had somewhat abated, and we
decided to resume our march westward toward Garen. We
now had to set our course very carefully, as there were only
two places on the west coast at which a descent from the
plateau was at all possible, and as these places were several
miles apart, we had now definitely to choose one of them and
reject the other. Having made this choice we set forward.

We had not gone far before it started snowing again and
the weather grew milder. We had frequently to consult the
map to take our bearings, and the wet snow falling on the
flimsy paper soon reduced it to pulp. After that, we had to
proceed as best we could by the compass alone.

Night overtook us before we reached the edge of the plateau
and, of course, there was nothing to do but to camp where it
found us, out in the open. That night nearly finished us.
When we had unrolled our sleeping bags, we took out our
provision bags and laid them at our feet. Alongside them we
set up our ski sticks as markers to indicate in the morning
where the bags were if the overnight snow should cover them.
We spent the night in extreme discomfort. The soft snow had
melted on our clothing and had saturated it with moisture.
When we got into our sleeping bags, the heat of our bodies
turned enough of this moisture into steam so that it permeated
the inside of the sleeping bags as well. It was a wretched
experience. Worse yet, it turned cold again in the night. I
woke up in the darkness feeling half frozen, and was so uncomfortable that I could not go back to sleep. It finally occurred to me that, if I got up and drank some of the alcohol
out of the lamp in my provision bag, it would restore my
circulation. I climbed out of the sleeping bag and felt around
in the dark until I got hold of my ski stick, and then I clawed
about for my provision bag. To my astonishment and chagrin,
it was not to be found. When morning broke, we both resumed the search and could find neither of the bags. To this

day I have not been able to make a reasonable conjecture that would explain what became of them. There was, however, no doubt of the fact—they were gone.

Our plight now was worse than uncomfortable, it was extremely dangerous. Unless we could speedily reach shelter and food, we should certainly freeze to death. With this alarming situation confronting us, we headed west again in hopes of reaching the edge of the plateau before night fell.

Luck was still against us. It soon began to snow so heavily that we could not see our way more than a few feet ahead. We decided now that the only thing to do was to turn around and try to make our way east across the plateau to our starting point. We made a few miles on this new course when night again overtook us.

Again the night was wet. We were drenched, and our bags were still heavy with moisture. Snow was still falling. When night came on, we had reached a small peak that thrust up out of the plateau. We sought out its lee side, figuring that we might be reasonably comfortable if we could keep out of the wind. We found that it did make a good deal of difference. I decided to improve even on that. I dug into the snow and made myself a small cave not much larger than my body, and into the cave I climbed head first and pulled my bag in after me. I soon congratulated myself on this idea, for I escaped altogether the gusts of wind outside.

In the night, the weather turned cold suddenly. The wet snow had settled down on me in my cave and over its entrance at my feet. When the temperature dropped, it froze. In the middle of the night I woke up. I was lying on my back with my right wrist across my eyes and the palm of my hand up—as one often sleeps to keep the morning light out of his eyes. My muscles felt cramped and I made the instinctive move to change my position. I could not move an inch. I was practically frozen inside a solid block of ice! I struggled desperately to free myself, but without the slightest effect. I shouted to my companion. Of course he could not hear.

I was now stricken with horror. In my panic, I naturally thought he likewise had been frozen in the wet snow that had fallen in the night and that he was in a like predicament with me. Unless a thaw immediately set in, we should both soon freeze to death in our ghastly coffins of ice.

My shouts quickly died away, as I found it impossible to breathe deeply. I realized that I must keep quiet or I would suffocate. I do not know whether it was the heaviness of the little air I had to breathe, or what was the reason, but I soon dropped off into either sleep or unconsciousness. When I came to I could hear faint sounds. My companion, after all, had not been imprisoned. Probably the only reason he had not emulated my example and built himself a cave the night before was that he was too tired, and from exhaustion too indifferent, to go to the trouble. In any event, his failure to do so saved our lives. When he awakened and looked about, he found himself alone in an ocean of snow. He called to me, and I did not answer. Then he began a frantic search for some trace that would show him where I had gone. There was only one, and providentially his eye fell upon it—a few hairs of the reindeer skin of my sleeping bag were visible in the snow. At once he began digging with his hands and ski stick to extricate me from my prison. It took him three hours to dig me out.

Both of us were now getting pretty weak. It was still night when he got me out, but we were too much upset to think of trying to rest further. Though it was still dark, the sky was clear and we were able to set a course and travel by the stars. We had been going two hours, with my companion in the lead, when suddenly he disappeared as if the earth had swallowed him up. Instinctively, I realized that he had gone over a precipice, and, instinctively, I acted instantly to save myself. I threw myself flat on the ground. A moment later, I heard his voice calling up, "Don't move. I have dropped over a precipice." He had indeed fallen about thirty feet. Fortunately, he had landed on his back, so that the sleeping bag which he carried as a pack on his shoulders had broken the force of the fall and he did not suffer more than a severe shaking up. Naturally, we did not attempt to go farther until daylight. Then we ploughed ahead on our seemingly hopeless travels.

We had now been four days without food of any sort, and the two days before that our diet of weak rye porridge had not been much better, so far as sustenance was concerned. We were getting nearly exhausted. The only thing that had saved us from collapse was our ability to get drinking water. On the plateau were numerous little lakes connected by small streams, and at these streams we had been able to keep our stomachs filled with water, and this saved us from the extreme effects of starvation.

At nightfall we came upon a little shanty filled with hay. There were ski tracks around the shanty. This discovery renewed our courage and proved that we were certainly back near civilization. It gave us hope, that, if we could keep ourselves going, on the morrow we might find food and shelter. The hay offered us a luxurious bed, and we spent the night burrowed into the heart of it.

The next morning I turned out to explore our surroundings. My companion was now so exhausted and dispirited that he seemed unequal to the effort and I left him in the haymow while I followed the ski tracks. After an hour's trudging, I saw a man in the distance. I surmised correctly that he was a peasant farmer making the morning rounds of the snares he had set for ptarmigan. I called loudly to him. He gave a startled look and, to my dismay, proceeded to run as fast as he could away from me. These lonely peasants are a superstitious folk. While they are courageous enough in the presence of real danger, they suffer many terrors of their own creation. Doubtless his first impression of me was of a ghostly apparition haunting the uninhabited plateau.

I called again and threw my whole soul into the cry. My tone must have conveyed my desperation, for the man stopped running and, after some hesitation, came back to meet me. I explained our plight and asked him where we were. I had a little difficulty in understanding his explanation, and even when I did, could hardly believe my senses, for it showed that we were now not more than an hour's travel from the farmhouse above Mogen from which, eight days before, we had started on our misadventure.

Heartened by this information, I hurried back for my companion. The news put fresh vigor in him, too, and soon, with no great trouble, we made our way down the little valley to the

familiar farmhouse. We knocked at the door, were invited
to enter, and went in. I was puzzled at our reception—until
later I saw myself in the mirror. In the single room of the
farmhouse the women were busy at their spinning and the
men at wood-carving. They looked up hospitably, but merely
greeted us with a brief "How do you do," in an entirely
impersonal and inquiring manner. It was soon apparent that
they did not recognize us. Little wonder, as I later realized,
for our scraggly beards had grown, our eyes were gaunt and
hollow, our cheeks were sunken, and the ruddy glow of color
had changed to a ghastly greenish yellow. We were a truly
awful spectacle. Our hosts at first would not believe us when
we explained that we were the two young fellows who had
left them eight days earlier. They could see no resemblance to
their former guests in the gaunt specters before them. At
length we convinced them, and they showed us every kindness.
We spent a couple of days with them, eating and sleeping
until our strength returned, and then, with many expressions
of gratitude, we took our leave of them and made our way
safe into Oslo.

The sequel of the story I did not myself learn until a year
later, when I discovered it was known that the farmer who
owned Garen, on the westerly edge of the plateau at the head
of the trail we had intended to descend, had come out of his
house one morning and found ski tracks within a few yards
of his doorway coming from the east and not from the west.
He could not credit his eyes, because he knew no one had
ever come that way in the winter, nor did he believe it was
possible. Those tracks could have been none other than ours,
for the date also matched.

Think of it! We had been unknowingly within a hundred
yards of our destination and had turned back to recross the
plateau after being within ten minutes' walk of a safe haven
on its western edge!

As I said when I started to describe this adventure, it
involved as many hardships and dangers as anything I later
encountered in my polar expeditions. It was a part of my
preliminary training for my polar career. The training proved
severer than the experience for which it was a preparation,
and it well-nigh ended the career before it began.

I find that most people think of "adventure" when the word "exploration" is used. It may, therefore, be well to explain in detail the difference between the two words from the explorer's point of view. I do not mean to belittle the thirst for adventure. It is a perfectly natural longing for excitement that affects any man in normal health. Doubtless, it is an inheritance of our race from those remote ancestors whose struggle for existence involved the uncertainties of the chase, the hazards of combat with wild beasts, and the perils of the unknown. To them, life was a constant adventure, and the thrill that suffuses us in reproducing their experience is the normal thrill of healthy nerves reacting to the natural struggle for self-preservation. Our ancestors had to take the chances of death to get their daily livelihood. When we "flirt with death," we are going back to the compensating nervous pleasure of primitive man, which protected and elevated him in his daily struggle.

To the explorer, however, adventure is merely an unwelcome interruption of his serious labors. He is looking, not for thrills, but for facts about the unknown. Often his search is a race with time against starvation. To him, an adventure is merely a bit of bad planning, brought to light by the test of trial. Or it is unfortunate exemplification of the fact that no man can grasp all the possibilities of the future. Every explorer has adventures. He gets a thrill out of them, and he takes pleasure in thinking back upon them. But he never goes about looking for them. Exploration is too serious a business.

Not all would-be explorers realize this truth. The result is many a grave needlessly occupied before its time, and many a blasted hope.

Serious work in exploration calls for as definite and as rigorous professional preparation as does success in any other serious work in life. Infinite harm has been done to the true profession of exploring by the entrance into the field of all sorts of people who have had no proper place in it. Some of these people are mere adventurers looking for another thrill. Some are notoriety seekers looking for a quick road to an empty fame. At least one whom I have known was crazy. Many of these men have lost their lives to no useful purpose whatsoever. This is bad enough, but the worst of it is that they have cast such a doubt in the minds of sober people upon the whole field of exploration that most of the world thinks of all exploration as mere foolhardiness. This state of mind has made it extremely difficult for serious explorers like Nansen, Peary, and others to obtain funds for their work, or even to secure an opportunity to explain their serious scientific intentions in undertaking it. Few people, except a few scientists who specialize in meteorology, oceanography, geography, etc., have the slightest idea of what explorers are accomplishing, or have the slightest ability to distinguish between serious workers in exploration and the host of adventurous publicity seekers and charlatans.

The first qualification of an explorer is a sound and trained body. Exploring involves the hardest kind of physical exertion, and the capacity to endure such exertion under stress both for long periods of sustained endeavor and in the trying moments of emergency. How preposterous, then, it is for men who have lived at desks to maturity suddenly to attempt these arduous enterprises! How absurd also for men whose whole experience of life has been among the conveniences of civilization suddenly to undertake a mode of life in which everything is primitive, and for which the training of the fur trader or the whaling seaman is of infinitely more value than a college education. A great part of my success in arctic work came from my carefully trained physique and from my hard-won apprenticeship to the actual life of the wilderness.

After the physical equipment essential to an explorer comes his mental equipment. I do not mean only the natural endowment of brains. With the exception of the one crazy man I have mentioned, all the men I have known who have led expeditions of any sort in the arctic regions have been men of good intelligence, and some of them have been men of very high education. What I have in mind, rather, is the specialized mental equipment, which is informed regarding the experience of all preceding expeditions. This knowledge in my own case has several times saved me from serious mistakes. For example, the reader may recall that my choice of a base in the Antarctic on the Bay of Whales, which so largely contributed to our success in reaching the South Pole, was made as a result of a careful comparison of every existing

description of that part of the antarctic glacier, from its discovery by Sir John Ross in 1842 down to the year before we
started south. Second-hand experience out of books is often as
good as first-hand, if the reader has had enough practical
experience in the same field to understand and apply what he
reads.

The explorer's mental equipment—I mean if he intends to
do serious work that justified the hazards of his undertaking—
must also include a thorough understanding of the scientific
problems in the solution of which his explorations can have
an essential part. And, finally, the explorer must understand
perfectly the use of scientific instruments with which he may
make observations of sufficient accuracy to be useful to the
scientists to whom he brings them home.

The foregoing sketch of the qualifications of a serious explorer will, I hope, convince the reader that exploring is a
highly technical and serious profession, calling for laborious
years of physical and mental preparation, and having for
its objective matters of importance far beyond the mere thrills
of the adventurer and the cheap, brief fame of charlatans
and notoriety seekers.

Arctic exploration of a serious character dates far back in
history. The British for four centuries had sent expeditions
to attempt the Northwest Passage. These expeditions were
carefully planned, and they were outfitted and managed according to the best knowledge of their times. Though they
invariably resulted in failure, and frequently in disaster, they
did not fail for lack of care in planning. And they achieved
scientific information of great value.

The search for the North Pole was likewise undertaken by
many serious-minded men. They, too, made a good deal of
progress. But the best that could be done by their methods
was Lockwood's achievement of reaching his farthest north.

Dr. Fridtjof Nansen revolutionized polar exploration. He
worked out new methods, based upon profound reasoning
about the nature of the problem. He invented practical means
to apply these measures. The result was his sensational advance
over Lockwood's record, to 86°14′N., or about 200 nautical miles
nearer the Pole than any man before him had ever been.

The story of Dr. Nansen and the *Fram*, as described in

his *Farthest North,* is familiar to practically everybody. Unless, however, one has read and pondered the technical details underlying the events described in that thrilling narrative, he cannot realize that Dr. Nansen's achievement in the technical methods of arctic exploration was vastly more important even than his sensational distance record, or than the actual scientific observations made on the *Fram* expedition.

Dr. Nansen's epochal achievement in polar work was his invention of a new method. He it was who first realized the value of dogs and light sleds as means of transport in the North. He first threw aside the heavy sledges that had broken the backs and the hearts of all previous explorers, substituting for them scientifically designed sledges of greater strength and infinitely less weight. By this invention, he easily doubled the traveling radius of men and dogs. The *Fram* expedition was a brilliant demonstration of the correctness of his theory and of the practical utility of his invention. Without his work, our capture of the South Pole would equally have been impossible. I realized the revolutionary importance of Nansen's method; I adapted it to my purposes; and I succeeded with it. No just appraisal of successful polar exploration can be made that leaves out of reckoning the fundamental importance of Dr. Nansen's work. He was the pioneer, both in theory and in practice, who made success possible.

Strangely enough, Dr. Nansen has lived to see his method become obsolete. Today, the dog and the sledge have wholly outlived their usefulness in the Arctic as instruments of exploration. Their place now, though forever glorious, is in the museum and the history books.

Aircraft has supplanted the dog. The Wright brothers and Count Zeppelin were the pioneers of the new method. The future of polar exploration lies in the air. I make bold to claim for myself the distinction of being the first serious polar explorer to realize this fact, and the first to give a practical demonstration of its future possibilities. I prepared, in 1909, to undertake geographical reconnaissance of polar regions from the air, and went so far as to employ a pilot for this purpose. In 1914, I bought a Farnam plane and learned to fly it myself. In 1921–22, I made several attempts to undertake this work again, this time from Point Barrow.

It was not, however, until 1925 that sufficient funds and the right planes became available, through the generosity of Mr. Lincoln Ellsworth, and we made our first flight from Spitzbergen. Though that expedition did not take us, as we had hoped, from continent to continent across the Pole, it did, nevertheless, indicate both the certainty that such a flight was only a matter of time and improved devices, and that geographical observations made from the air would be of the highest value.

In 1926, with Mr. Ellsworth, I commanded the expedition which made the first continent-to-continent flight across the North Pole. This flight was successful in every sense of the word, and proved, beyond further doubt, by practical demonstration, the permanent utility of aircraft in polar exploration.

"What is the good of arctic exploration?"

How many times that question has been put to me! Doubtless, every serious explorer has had it put to him numberless times.

The most practical value of polar exploration is the new knowledge it provides to science regarding the phenomena of terrestrial magnetism and regarding the nature of the climate and winds in those regions (which are the weather makers of the world). The greatest advance likely soon to be made in the accurate prediction of day-to-day weather in the North Temperate Zone will come from the erection and maintenance of permanent weather observatories on the north coasts of America, Europe, and Asia. These observatories, completely encircling the Polar Sea, and reporting several times daily by wireless to some central station, will provide far more reliable and valuable information upon which to base weather predictions than has heretofore ever been made available to man. I got some conception of how important such a chain of observatories could be by the excited gratitude of scientists that was aroused when twice daily wireless reports of the weather encountered by the *Maud* off the north coast of Asia were sent.

The other "good" of polar exploration cannot be so definitely translated into terms of human comfort or of money saved to the world. Personally, however, I have no doubt that it is of equal value. Whatever remains to man unknown, in this world of ours, is by so much a burden on the spirits of all men. It remains a something that man has not yet conquered—a continuing evidence of his weakness, an unmet challenge to his mastery over nature. By the same token, every mystery made plain, every unknown land explored, exalts the spirit of the whole human race—strengthens its courage and exalts its spirit permanently. The trail breaker is an indispensable ally of the spiritual values which advance and sustain civilization.

Alone

SIR DOUGLAS MAWSON

Stress and isolation are two of the key words in tomorrow's studies of the Antarctic, but perhaps no story ever to come out of the polar regions reflects isolation better than the extraordinary personal adventure of Sir Douglas Mawson, the great Australian scientist and explorer.

Mawson and two companions, Lieutenant B. E. S. Ninnis and Dr. Xavier Mertz, a Swiss skier and mountaineer, left their expedition's main base to undertake a research trip. Ninnis fell in a chasm and was killed, Mertz died of starvation and exposure, and Mawson was left to make the return trip alone.

OUTSIDE, the bowl of chaos was brimming with drift snow as I lay in the sleeping bag beside my dead companion. I wondered how, in such conditions, I would manage to break and pitch camp single-handed. There appeared to be little hope of reaching the Hut, still one hundred miles away. It was easy to sleep in the bag, and the weather was cruel outside. But inaction is hard to bear and I braced myself together determined to put up a good fight.

Failing to reach the Hut, it would be something done if I managed to get to some prominent point likely to catch the eye of a search party, where a cairn might be erected and our diaries cached. So I commenced to modify the sledge and camping gear to meet fresh requirements.

The sky remained clouded, but the wind fell off to a calm which lasted several hours. I took the opportunity to set to work on the sledge, sawing it in halves with a pocket tool and discarding the rear section. A mast was made out of one of the rails no longer required, and a spar was cut from the other. Finally, the load was cut down to a minimum by the elimination of all but the barest necessities, the abandoned articles including, sad to relate, all that remained of the exposed photographic films.

Late that evening, the eighth, I took the body of Mertz, still toggled up in his bag, outside the tent, piled snow blocks around it and raised a rough cross made of the two discarded halves of the sledge runners.

On January ninth the weather was overcast and fairly thick drift was flying in a gale of wind, reaching about fifty miles an hour. As certain matters still required attention and my chances of re-erecting the tent were rather doubtful, if I decided to move on, the start was delayed.

Part of the time that day was occupied with cutting up a waterproof clothes bag and Mertz's burberry jacket and sewing them together to form a sail. Before retiring to rest in the evening, I read through the burial service and put the finishing touches on the grave.

January tenth arrived in a turmoil of wind and thick drift. The start was still further delayed. I spent part of the time in reckoning up the food remaining and in cooking the rest of the dog meat, this latter operation serving the good object of lightening the load, in that the kerosene for the purpose was consumed there and then and had not to be dragged forward for subsequent use. Late in the afternoon, the wind fell and the sun peered among the clouds just as I was in the middle of a long job riveting and lashing the broken shovel.

The next day, January eleventh, a beautiful, calm day of sunshine, I set out over a good surface with a slight down grade.

From the start my feet felt curiously lumpy and sore. They had become so painful after a mile of walking that I decided to examine them on the spot, sitting in the lee of the sledge in brilliant sunshine. I had not had my socks off for some days for, while lying in camp, it had not seemed necessary. On taking off the third and inner pair of socks, the sight of my feet gave me quite a shock, for the thickened skin of the soles had separated in each case as a complete layer, and abundant watery fluid had escaped, saturating the sock. The new skin beneath was very much abraded and raw. Several of my toes had commenced to blacken and fester near the tips and the nails were puffed and loose.

I began to wonder if there was ever to be a day without some special disappointment. However, there was nothing to be done but make the best of it. I smeared the new skin and the raw surfaces with lanolin, of which there was fortunately a good store, and then with the aid of bandages bound the old skin casts back in place, for these were comfortable and soft in contact with the abraded surface. Over the bandages were slipped six pairs of thick woolen socks, then fur boots and finally crampon over-shoes. The latter, having large stiff soles, spread the weight nicely and saved my feet from the jagged ice encountered shortly afterward.

So glorious was it to feel the sun on one's skin after being without it for so long that I next removed most of my clothing and bathed my body in the rays until my flesh fairly tingled— a wonderful sensation which spread throughout my whole person, and made me feel stronger and happier.

Then on I went, treading rather like a cat on wet ground endeavoring to save my feet from pain. By five-thirty P.M. I was quite worn out—nerve-worn—though having covered but six and a quarter miles. Had it not been a delightful evening I should not have found strength to erect the tent.

The day following passed in a howling blizzard and I could do nothing but attend to my feet and other raw patches, festering fingernails and inflamed frostbitten nose. Fortunately there was a good supply of bandages and antiseptic. The tent, spread about with dressings and the meager surgical appliances at hand, was suggestive of a casualty hospital.

Toward noon the following day, January thirteenth, the wind subsided and the snow cleared off. It turned out a beautifully fine afternoon. Soon after I had got moving the slope increased, unfolding a fine view of the Mertz Glacier ahead. My heart leaped with joy, for all was like a map before me and I knew that over the hazy blue ice ridge in the far distance lay the Hut. I was heading to traverse the depression of the glacier ahead at a point many miles above our crossing of the outward journey and some few miles below gigantic ice cascades. My first impulse was to turn away to the west and avoid crossing the fifteen miles of hideously broken ice that choked the valley before me, but on second thought, in view of the very limited quantity of food left, the right thing seemed to be to make an airline for the Hut and chance what lay between. According, having taken an observation of the sun for position and selected what appeared to be the clearest route across the valley, I started downhill. The névé gave way to rough blue ice and even wide crevasses made their appearance. The rough ice jarred my feet terribly and altogether it was a most painful march.

So unendurable did it become that, finding a bridged crevasse extending my way, I decided to march along the snow bridge and risk an accident. It was from fifteen to twenty feet wide and well packed with winter snow. The march continued along it down slopes for over a mile with great satisfaction as far as my feet were concerned. Eventually it became irregular and broke up, but others took its place and served as well; in this way the march was made possible. At eight P.M. after covering a distance of nearly six miles a final halt for the day was made.

About eleven P.M. as the sun skimmed behind the ice slopes to the south I was startled by loud reports like heavy gun shots. They commenced up the valley to the south and trailed away down the southern side of the glacier toward the sea. The fusillade of shots rang out without interruption for about half an hour, then all was silent. It was hard to believe it was not caused by some human agency, but I learned that it was due to the cracking of the glacier ice.

A high wind which blew on the morning of the fourteenth diminished in strength by noon and allowed me to get away. The sun came out so warm that the rough ice surface underfoot was covered with a film of water and in some places small trickles ran away to disappear into crevasses.

Though the course was downhill, the sledge required a good deal of pulling owing to the wet runners. At nine P.M., after traveling five miles, I pitched camp in the bed of the glacier. From about nine-thirty P.M. until eleven P.M. "cannonading" continued like that heard the previous evening.

January fifteenth—the date on which all the sledging parties were due at the Hut! It was overcast and snowing early in the day, but in a few hours the sun broke out and shone warmly. The traveling was so heavy over a soft snowy surface, partly melting, that I gave up, after one mile, and camped.

At seven P.M. the surface had not improved, the sky was thickly obscured and snow fell. At ten P.M. a heavy snowstorm was in progress, and, since there were many crevasses in the vicinity, I resolved to wait.

On the sixteenth at two A.M. the snow was falling as thick as ever, but at five A.M. the atmosphere lightened and the sun appeared. Camp was broken without delay. A favorable breeze sprang up, and with sail set I managed to proceed in short stages through the deep newly fallen blanket of snow. It clung in lumps to the runners, which had to be scraped frequently. Riven ice ridges as much as eighty feet in height passed on either hand. Occasionally I got a start as a foot or a leg sank through into space, but, on the whole, all went unexpectedly well for several miles. Then the sun disappeared and the disabilities of a snow-blind light had to be faced.

After laboriously toiling up one long slope, I had just taken a few paces over the crest, with the sledge running freely behind, when it dawned on me that the surface fell away unusually steeply. A glance ahead, even in that uncertain light, flashed the truth upon me—I was on a snow cornice, rimming the brink of a great blue chasm like a quarry, the yawning mouth of an immense and partly filled crevasse. Already the sledge was gaining speed as it slid past me toward the gaping hole below. Mechanically, I bedded my feet firmly in the snow, and, exerting every effort, was just able to take the weight and hold up the sledge as it reached the very brink of the abyss. There must have been an interval of quite a minute during which I held my ground without being able to make it budge. It seemed an interminable time; I found myself reckoning the odds as to who would win, the sledge or I. Then it slowly came my way, and the imminent danger was passed.

The day's march was an extremely heavy five miles; so before turning in, I treated myself to an extra supper of jelly soup made from dog sinews. I thought at the time that the acute enjoyment of eating compensated in some measure for the sufferings of starvation.

January seventeenth was another day of overcast sky and steady falling snow. Everything from below one's feet to the sky above was one uniform ghostly glare. The irregularities in the surfaces not obliterated by the deep soft snow blended harmoniously in color and in the absence of shadows faded into invisibility. These were most unsuitable conditions for the crossing of such a dangerous crevassed valley, but delay meant a reduction of the ration and that was out of the question, so nothing remained but to go on.

A start was made at eight A.M. and the pulling proved easier than on the previous day. Some two miles had been negotiated in safety when an event occurred which, but for a miracle, would have terminated the story then and there. Never have I come so near to an end; never has anyone more miraculously escaped.

I was hauling the sledge through deep snow up a fairly steep slope when my feet broke through into a crevasse. Fortunately as I fell I caught my weight with my arms on the edge and did not plunge in further than the thighs. The outline of the crevasse did not show through the blanket of snow on the surface, but an idea of the trend was obtained with a stick. I decided to try a crossing about fifty yards further along, hoping that there it would be better bridged. Alas! it took an unexpected turn catching me unawares. This time I shot through the center of the bridge in a flash, but the latter part of the fall was decelerated by the friction of the harness ropes which, as the sledge ran up, sawed back into the thick compact snow forming the margin of the lid. Having seen my comrades perish in diverse ways and having lost hope of ever reaching the Hut, I had already many times speculated on what the end would be like. So it happened that as I fell through into the crevasse the thought "so this is the end" blazed up in my mind, for it was to be expected that the next moment the sledge would follow through, crash on my head and all go to the unseen bottom. But the unexpected happened and the sledge held, the deep snow acting as a brake.

In the moment that elapsed before the rope ceased to descend, delaying the issue, a great regret swept through my mind, namely, that after having stinted myself so assiduously in order to save food, I should pass on now to eternity without the satisfaction of what remained—to such an extent does food take possession of one under such circumstances. Realizing that the sledge was holding I began to look around. The crevasse was somewhat over six feet wide and sheer walled, descending into blue depths below. My clothes, which, with a view to ventilation, had been but loosely secured, were now stuffed with snow broken from the roof, and very chilly it was. Above at the other end of the fourteen-foot rope, was the daylight seen through the hole in the lid.

In my weak condition, the prospect of climbing out seemed very poor indeed, but in a few moments the struggle was begun. A great effort brought a knot in the rope within my grasp, and, after a moment's rest, I was able to draw myself up and reach another, and, at length, hauled my body on to the overhanging snow-lid. Then, when all appeared to be well and before I could get to quite solid ground, a further section of the lid gave way, precipitating me once more to the full length of the rope.

There, exhausted, weak and chilled, hanging freely in space and slowly turning round as the rope twisted one way and the other, I felt that I had done my utmost and failed, that I had no more strength to try again and that all was over except the passing. It was to be a miserable and slow end and I reflected with disappointment that there was in my pocket no antidote to speed matters; but there always remained the alternative of slipping from the harness. There on the brink of the great beyond I well remember how I looked forward to the peace of the great release—how almost excited I was at the prospect of the unknown to be unveiled. From those flights of mind I came back to earth, and remembering how Providence had miraculously brought me so far, felt that nothing was impossible and determined to act up to Service's lines:

> "Just have one more try—it's dead easy to die,
> It's the keeping-on-living that's hard."

My strength was fast ebbing; in a few minutes it would be too late. It was the occasion for a supreme attempt. Fired by the passion that burns the blood in the act of strife, new power seemed to come as I applied myself to one last tremendous effort. The struggle occupied some time, but I slowly worked upward to the surface. This time emerging feet

first, still clinging to the rope, I pushed myself out extended
at full length on the lid and then shuffled safely on to the
solid ground at the side. Then came the reaction from the
great nerve strain and lying there alongside the sledge my
mind faded into a blank.

When consciousness returned it was a full hour or two
later, for I was partly covered with newly fallen snow and
numb with the cold. I took at least three hours to erect
the tent, get things snugly inside and clear the snow from
my clothes. Between each movement, almost, I had to rest.
Then reclining in luxury in the sleeping bag, I ate a little
food and thought matters over. It was a time when the mood
of the Persian philosopher appealed to me:

> "Unborn Tomorrow and dead Yesterday,
>   Why fret about them if Today be sweet?"

I was confronted with this problem: whether it was better
to enjoy life for a few days, sleeping and eating my fill until
the provisions gave out, or to "plug on" again in hunger
with the prospect of plunging at any moment into eternity
without the supreme satisfaction and pleasure of the food.
While thus cogitating, an idea presented itself which greatly
improved the prospects and clinched the decision to go ahead.
It was to construct a ladder from a length of alpine rope
that remained; one end was to be secured to the bow of
the sledge and the other carried over my left shoulder and
loosely attached to the sledge harness. Thus if I fell into a
crevasse again, provided the sledge was not also engulfed, it
would be easy for me, even though weakened by starvation,
to scramble out by the ladder.

Notwithstanding the possibilities of the rope ladder, I could
not sleep properly, for my nerves had been overtaxed. All
night long considerable wind and drift continued.

On the nineteenth it was overcast and light snow falling;
very dispiriting conditions after the experience of the day before, but I resolved to go ahead and leave the rest to Providence.

My feet and legs, as they wallowed through the deep snow,
occasionally broke through into space. Then I went right under,

but the sledge held up and the ladder proved "trumps." A few minutes later I was down again, but emerged once more without much exertion, though half-smothered with snow. Faintness overcame me and I stopped to camp, though only a short distance had been covered.

All around there was a leaden glare and the prospect was almost unpromising. The sun had not shown up for several days and I was eager for it, not only that it might illuminate the landscape, but for its cheerful influence and life-giving energy. A few days previously my condition had been improving, but now it was relapsing.

During the night of the eighteenth loud booming noises, sharp cracks and muffled growls issued from the neighboring crevasses and kept waking me up. At times one could feel a vibration accompanying the growling sounds, and I concluded that the ice was in rapid motion.

The sun at last appeared on the nineteenth, and the march was resumed by eight-thirty A.M. The whole surface, now effectively lighted up, was seen to be a network of ice rifts and crevasses, some of the latter very wide. Along one after another of these, I dragged the sledge in search of a spot where the snow bridge appeared to be firm. Then I would plunge across at a run, risking the consequences.

After a march of three hours safer ground was reached. On ahead, leading to the rising slopes on the far side of the glacier, was a nearly level ice plain dotted over with beehive-shaped eminences usually not more than a few feet in height. Once on this comparatively safe wind-swept surface I became overreliant and in consequence sank several times into narrow fissures.

At length the glacier was crossed and the tent pitched on a snowy slope under beetling, crevassed crags which rose sheer from the valley level some five hundred feet. I had never dared to expect to get so far and now that it was an accomplished fact, I was intoxicated with joy. Somewhat to the right could be traced out a good path, apparently free from pitfalls, leading upward to the plateau which still remained to be crossed. This entailed a rise of some three thousand feet and led me to reconsider the lightening of the load on the sledge. The length of alpine rope was abandoned as also

were finnesko-crampons and sundry pairs of worn finnesko and
socks. The sledge was overhauled and sundry repairs effected,
finishing up by treating the runners to a coat of waterproofing
composition to cause them to glide more freely on moist snow.

January twentieth was a wretched overcast day and not at
all improved by considerable wind and light drift. In desperation a start was made at two P.M. and, though nothing was
visible beyond a few yards distant, I kept a steady course
uphill and, assisted by the wind, covered two and a half
miles as the day's work.

The next day, though windy, was sunny, and a stretch of
three miles of steep rise was negotiated. All that night and
until noon on the twenty-second, wind and drift prevailed,
but the afternoon came gloriously sunny. Away to the north
beyond Aurora Peak was a splendid view of the sea at Buchanan
Bay. It was like meeting an old friend and I longed to be
down near it. That evening six more miles had been covered,
but I felt very weak and weary. My feet were now much
improved and the old skin-casts after shriveling up a good
deal had been thrown away. However, prolonged starvation
aided by the unwholesomeness of the dog meat was taking
the toll in other ways. My nails still continued to fester and
numerous boils on my face and body required daily attention.
The personal overhaul necessary each day on camping and
before starting consumed much valuable time.

During the early hours of the twenty-third the sun was
visible, but about eight A.M. the clouds sagged low, the wind
rose and everything became blotted out in a swirl of drifting
snow.

I wandered through it for several hours, the sledge capsizing
at times owing to the strength of the wind. It was not
possible to keep an accurate course, for even the wind changed
direction as the day wore on. Underfoot there was soft snow
which I found comfortable for my sore feet, but which made
the sledge drag heavily at times.

When I halted at four P.M. to pitch camp I reckoned that
the distance covered in a straight line was but three and
a half miles. Then followed a long and difficult task erecting
the tent in the wind. It proved a protracted operation. When
the outside was finished off satisfactorily the inside was dis-

covered to be filled with drift snow and had to be dug out. Everything was stuffed with soft damp snow including the sleeping bag, and it took a rare time to put things right.

By this time I was doing a good deal of "thinking out loud" which, by the way, seemed to give some sort of consolation.

High wind and dense driving snow persisted throughout the twenty-fourth and I made a good five and a half miles. I was able to sit on the sledge much of the time and the wind and the good sail did the work. I was quite done up when at last the tent was up and everything snug for the night.

Torrents of snow fell throughout the twenty-fifth and it sizzled and rattled against the tent under the influence of a gale of wind. After the trying experience of the previous two days I did not feel well enough to go on. As the hours went by, the snow piled higher, bulging in the sides of the small, odd-shaped tent until it weighed down upon the sleeping bag and left practically no room at all. The threshing of the seething drift was no longer audible. I was buried indeed! The coffin shape of the bag lent a more realistic touch to the circumstances. With such a weight above there was no certainty that I would be able to get out when the time came to move. So, though the weather was just as bad on the twenty-sixth, I determined to struggle out and try another stage. It was a long and laborious work reaching the daylight from beneath the flattened tent and digging everything free. Then some hot food was prepared of which I was much in need. Only four or five pounds of food remained now and there was no guarantee that the weather would clear in the near future, so the position was most anxious. At that time the skin was coming off my hands, which were the last parts of my body to peel. A moulting of the hair followed the peeling of the skin. Irregular tufts of beard came out and there was a general shedding of hair from my head, so much so that at each camp thereabouts the snowy floor of the tent was noticeably darkened.

There was no need of a sail on the twenty-sixth. The wind, blowing from behind, caught the sledge and drove it along so that, though over a soft surface of snow, the traveling was rapid. The snow came down in the form of large pellets and rattled as it struck the sledge. For one in so poor a condition it was a very trying day, blindly struggling through the whirl of the seething snow; after covering nine miles and erecting the tent, I was thoroughly done up. The night was far spent before I had cleared the snow out of my clothes, sleeping bag, etc.: cooked some food and given myself the necessary medical attention.

As the twenty-seventh was just such another day as the twenty-sixth I decided to rest further to recuperate from the exertions of the previous day.

By the morning of January twenty-eighth the wind had moderated considerably, but the sky remained overcast and snow continued to fall. It was a difficult matter getting out of the tent and a long job excavating it, for the packed snow had piled up within a few inches of the peak. There was no sign of the sledge which with the harness and spars had all to be prospected for and dug out. It appeared that since pitching the tent the whole level of the country had been raised a uniform three feet by a stratum of snow packed so densely that in walking over it but little impression was left.

Soon after the start the sun gleamed out and the weather improved. The three-thousand-foot crest of the plateau had been crossed and I was bearing down rapidly on Common-wealth Bay, the vicinity of which was indicated by a dark water-sky on the northwest horizon.

The evening turned out beautifully fine and my spirits rose to a high pitch, for I felt for the first time that there was a really good chance of making the Hut. To increase the excitement, Madigan Nunatak showed up a black speck away to the right front. Eight good miles were covered that afternoon. The change in the weather had come most opportunely, for there now remained only about twenty small chips of cooked dog meat in addition to half a pound of raisins and a few ounces of chocolate which I had kept carefully guarded for emergencies.

However, the wind and drift got up in the night and the start next morning was made in disappointing weather. When five miles on the way another miracle happened.

I was traveling along on an even down grade and was

wondering how long the two pounds of food which remained would last, when something dark loomed through the haze of the drift a short distance away to the right. All sorts of possibilities raced through my mind as I headed the sledge for it. The unexpected had happened—in thick weather I had run fairly into a cairn of snow blocks erected by McLean, Hodgeman, and Hurley, who had been out searching for my party. On the top of the mound, outlined in black bunting, was a bag of food, left on the chance that it might be picked up by us. In a tin was a note stating the bearing and distance of the mound from Alladin's Cave (E. 30°S., distance twenty-three miles), and mentioning that the ship had arrived at the Hut and was waiting, and had brought the news that Amundsen had reached the Pole, and that Scott was remaining another year in Antarctica.

It certainly was remarkably good fortune that I had come upon the depot of food; a few hundred yards to either side and it would have been lost to sight in the drift. On reading the note carefully I found that I had just missed by six hours what would have been crowning good luck, for it appeared that the search party had left the mound at eight A.M. that very day (January 29). It was about 2 P.M. when I reached it. Thus, during the night of the twenty-eighth our camps had been only some five miles apart.

Hauling down the bag of food I tore it open in the lee of the cairn and in my greed scattered the contents about on the ground. Having partaken heartily of frozen pemmican, I stuffed my pocket, bundled the rest into a bag on the sledge and started off in high glee, stimulated in body and mind. As I left the depot there appeared to be nothing on earth that could prevent me reaching the Hut within a couple of days, but a fresh obstacle with which I had not reckoned was to arise and cause further delay, leading to far-reaching results.

It happened that after several hours' march the surface changed from snow to polished névé and then to slippery ice. I could scarcely keep on my feet at all, falling every few moments and bruising my emaciated self until I expected to see my bones burst through the clothes. How I regretted having abandoned those crampons after crossing the Mertz Glacier; shod with them, all would be easy.

With nothing but finnesko on the feet, to walk over such a sloping surface would have been difficult enough in the wind without any other hindrance; with the sledge sidling down the slope and tugging at one, it was quite impossible. I found that I had made too far to the east and to reach Aladdin's Cave had unfortunately to strike across the wind.

Before giving up, I even tried crawling on my hands and knees.

However, the day's run, fourteen miles, was by no means a poor one.

Having erected the tent I set to work to improvise crampons. With this object in view the theodolite case was cut up, providing two flat pieces of wood into which were stuck as many screws and nails as could be procured by dismantling the sledgemeter and the theodolite itself. In the repair bag there were still a few ice nails which at this time were of great use.

Late the next day, the wind which had risen in the night fell off and a start was made westward over the ice slopes with the pieces of nail-studded wood lashed to my feet. A glorious expanse of sea lay to the north and several recognizable points on the coast were clearly in view to east and west.

The crampons were not a complete success for they gradually broke up, lasting only a distance of six miles. Then the wind increased, and I got into difficulties by the sledge sidling into a narrow crevasse. It was held up by the boom at the foot of the mast. It took some time to extract and the wind continued to rise, so there was nothing for it but to pitch camp.

Further attempts at making crampons were more handicapped than ever, for the best materials available had been utilized already. However, from the remnants of the first pair and anything else that could be pressed into the service, a second pair was evolved of the nature of wooden-soled finnesko with spikes. This work took an interminable time, for the tools and appliances available were almost all contained in a small pocket knife that had belonged to Mertz. Besides a blade it was furnished with a spike, a gimlet, and a screw driver.

A blizzard was in full career on January thirty-first and I spend all day and most of the night on the crampons. On February first the wind and drift had subsided late in the afternoon, and I got under way expecting great things from the new crampons. The beacon marking Aladdin's Cave was clearly visible as a black dot on the ice slopes to the west.

At seven P.M. that haven within the ice was attained. It took but a few moments to dig away the snow and throw back the canvas flap sealing the entrance. A moment later I slid down inside, arriving amidst familiar surroundings. Something unusual in one corner caught the eye—three oranges and a pineapple—circumstantial evidence of the arrival of the *Aurora*.

The improvised crampons had given way and were squeezing my feet painfully. I rummaged about amongst a pile of food bags hoping to find some crampons or leather boots, but was disappointed, so there was nothing left but to repair the damaged ones. That done and a drink of hot milk having been prepared, I packed up to make a start for the Hut. On climbing out of the cave imagine my disappointment at finding a strong wind and drift had risen. To have attempted the descent of the five and a half miles of steep ice slope to the Hut with such inadequate and fragile crampons, weak as I still was, would have been only as a last resort. So I camped in the comfortable cave and hoped for better weather next day.

But the blizzard droned on night and day for over a week with never a break. Think of my feelings as I sat within the cave, so near and yet so far from the Hut, impatient and anxious, ready to spring out and take the trail at a moment's notice. Improvements to the crampons kept me busy for a time; then, as there was a couple of old boxes lying about, I set to work and constructed a second emergency pair in case the others should break up during the descent. I tried the makeshift crampons on the ice outside, but was disappointed to find that they had not sufficient grip to face the wind, so had to abandon the idea of attempting the descent during the continuance of the blizzard. Nevertheless, by February eighth my anxiety as to what was happening at the Hut reached such a pitch that I resolved to try the passage in spite of everything, having worked out a plan whereby I was to sit on the sledge and sail down as far as possible.

Whilst these preparations were in progress the wind slackened. At last the longed for event was to be realized. I snatched a hasty meal and set off. Before a couple of miles had been covered the wind had fallen off altogether, and after that it was gloriously calm and clear.

I had reached within one and a half miles of the Hut and there was no sign of the *Aurora* lying in the offing. I was comforted with the thought that she might still be at the anchorage and have swung inshore so as to be hidden under the ice cliffs. But even as I gazed about seeking for a clue, a speck on the northwest horizon caught my eye and my hopes went down. It looked like a distant ship. Was it the *Aurora?* Well, what matter! the long journey was at an end—a terrible chapter of my life was concluded!

Then the rocks around winter quarters began to come into view; part of the basin of the Boat Harbor appeared, and lo! there were human figures! They almost seemed unreal— was it all a dream? No, indeed, for after a brief moment one of them observed me and waved an arm—I replied— there was a commotion and they all ran toward the Hut.

The End Is in Sight

SIR ERNEST SHACKLETON

"We have done our best." Such refrains constantly reappear in the stories of the great polar explorations, when the emphasis was upon physical courage and endurance against terrible odds. These were the words that Sir Ernest Shackleton used when his company of men had to stop just ninety-seven geographical miles from the South Pole in 1908.

Shackleton died of influenza on a later expedition to the Antarctic on January 4, 1922, writing in his diary the night before:

> *"At last, we came to anchor in Grytviken . . . a wonderful evening."*

JANUARY 4—The end is in sight. We can only go for three more days at the most, for we are weakening rapidly. Short food and a blizzard wind from the south, with driving drift, at a temperature of 47° of frost [—15° F.] have plainly told us today that we are reaching our limit, for we were so done up at noon with cold that the clinical thermometer failed to register the temperature of three of us at 94°. We started at seven-forty A.M., leaving a depot on this great wide plateau, a risk that only this case justified, and one that my comrades agreed to, as they have to every one so far, with the same cheerfulness and regardlessness of self that have been the means of our getting as far as we have done so far. Pathetically small looked the bamboo, one of the tent poles, with a bit of bag sown on as a flag, to mark our stock of provisions, which has to take us back to our depot, one hundred and fifty miles north. We lost sight of it in half an hour, and are now trusting to our footprints in the snow to guide us back to each bamboo until we pick up the depot again. I trust that the weather will keep clear. Today we have done 12½ geographical miles, and with only

70 pounds per man to pull it is as hard, even harder, work than the 100-odd pounds were yesterday, and far harder than the 250 pounds were three weeks ago, when we were climbing the glacier. This, I consider, is a clear indication of our failing strength. The main thing against us is the altitude of 11,200 ft. and the biting wind. Our faces are cut, and our feet and hands are always on the verge of frostbite. Our fingers, indeed, often go, but we get them round more or less. I have great trouble with two fingers on my left hand. They have been badly jammed when we were getting the motor up over the ice face at winter quarters, and the circulation is not good. Our boots now are pretty well worn out, and we have to halt at times to pick the snow out of the soles. Our stock of sennegrass is nearly exhausted, so we have to use the same frozen stuff day after day. Another trouble is that the lamp wick with which we tie the finnesko is chafed through, and we have to tie knots in it. These knots catch the snow under our feet, making a lump that has to be cleared every now and then. I am of the opinion that to sledge even in the height of summer of this plateau, we should have at leasty forty ounces of food a day per man, and we are on short rations of the ordinary allowance of thirty-two ounces. We depoted our extra underclothing to save weight about three weeks ago, and are now in the same clothes night and day. One suit of underclothing, shirt and guernsey, and our thin Burberries, now all patched. When we get up in the morning, out of the wet bag, our Burberries become like a coat of mail at once, and our heads and beards get iced-up with the moisture when breathing on the march. There is half a gale blowing dead in our teeth all the time. We hope to reach within 100 geographical miles of the Pole; under the circumstances we can expect to do very little more. I am confident that the Pole lies on the great plateau we have discovered, miles and miles from any outstanding land. The temperature tonight is minus 24° Fahrenheit.

January 5—Today head wind and drift again, with 50° of frost [−18° F.] and a terrible surface. We have been marching through eight inches of snow, covering sharp sastrugi, which plays hell with our feet, but we have done 13⅓ geographical miles [the geographical mile is roughly thirteen per cent longer than our statute mile], for we increased our food, seeing that it was absolutely necessary to do this to enable us to accomplish anything. I realize that the food we have been having has not been sufficient to keep up our strength, let alone supply the wastage caused by exertion, and now we must try to keep warmth in us, though our strength is being used up. Our temperatures at five A.M. were 94° Fahrenheit. We got away at seven A.M. sharp and marched till noon, then from one P.M. sharp till six P.M. All being in one tent makes our camp-work slower, for we are so cramped for room, and we get up at four-forty A.M. so as to get away by seven A.M. Two of us have to stand outside the tent at night until things are squared up inside, and we find it cold work. Hunger grips us hard, and the food-supply is very small. My head still gives me great trouble. I began by wishing that my worst enemy had it instead of myself, but now I don't wish even my worst enemy to have such a headache; still, it is no use talking about it. Self is a subject that most of us are fluent on. We find the utmost difficulty in carrying through the day, and we can only go for two or three more days. Never once has the temperature been above zero since we got on to the plateau, though this is the height of summer. We have done our best, and we thank God for having allowed us to get so far.

January 6—This must be our last outward march with the sledge and camp equipment. Tomorrow we must leave camp with some food, and push as far south as possible, and then plant the flag. Today's story is 57° of frost [−25° F.], with a strong blizzard and high drift; yet we marched 13¼ geographical miles through soft snow, being helped by extra food. This does not mean full rations, but a bigger ration than we have been having lately. The pony maize is all finished. The most trying day we have yet spent, our fingers and faces being frost-bitten continually. Tomorrow we will rush south with the flag. We are at 88°7′ South tonight. It is our last outward march. Blowing hard tonight. I would fail to explain my feelings if I tried to write them down, now that the end has come. There is only one thing that lightens the disappointment, and that is the feeling that we have done all we could.

It is the forces of nature that have prevented us from going right through. I cannot write more.

January 7—A blinding, shrieking blizzard all day, with the temperature ranging from 60° to 70° of frost. It has been impossible to leave the tent, which is snowed up on the lee side. We have been lying in our bags all day, only warm at food time, with fine snow making through the walls of the worn tent and covering our bags. We are greatly cramped. Adams is suffering from cramp every now and then. We are eating our valuable food without marching. The wind has been blowing eighty to ninety miles an hour. We can hardly sleep. Tomorrow I trust this will be over. Directly the wind drops we march as far south as possible, then plant the flag, and turn homeward. Our chief anxiety is lest our tracks may drift up, for to them we must trust mainly to find our depot; we have no land bearings in this great plain of snow. It is a serious risk that we have taken, but we had to play the game to the utmost, and Providence will look after us.

January 8—Again all day in our bags, suffering considerably physically from cold hands and feet, and from hunger, but more mentally, for we cannot get on south, and we simply lie here shivering. Every now and then one of our party's feet go, and the unfortunate beggar has to take his leg out of the sleeping bag and have his frozen foot nursed into life again by placing it inside the shirt, against the skin of his almost equally unfortunate neighbor. We must do something more to the south, even though the food is going, and we weaken lying in the cold, for with 72° of frost, the wind cuts through our thin tent, and even the drift is finding its way in and on to our bags, which are wet enough as it is. Cramp is not uncommon every now and then, and the drift all round the tent has made it so small that there is hardly room for us at all. The wind has been blowing hard all day; some of the gusts must be over seventy or eighty miles an hour. This evening it seems as though it were going to ease down, and directly it does we shall be up and away south for a rush. I feel that this march must be our limit. We are so short of food, and at this high altitude, 11,600 ft., it is hard to keep any warmth in our bodies between the scanty means. We have nothing to read now, having depoted our

little books to save weight, and it is dreary work lying in
the tent with nothing to read, and too cold to write much
in the diary.

January 9—Our last day outwards. We have shot our bolt,
and the tale is latitude 88°23′ South, longitude 162° East.
The wind eased down at 1 A.M., and at 2 A.M. were up
and had breakfast. At four A.M. started south, with the Queen's
Union Jack, a brass cylinder containing stamps and documents
to place at the furthest south point, camera, glasses and
compass. At nine A.M. we were in 88°23′ South, half running
and half walking over a surface much hardened by the recent
blizzard. It was strange for us to go along with the nightmare
of a sledge dragging behind us. We hoisted her Majesty's
flag and the other Union Jack afterward, and took possession
of the plateau in the name of his Majesty. While the Union
Jack blew out stiffly in the icy gale that cut us to the bone,
we looked south with our powerful glasses, but could see
nothing but the dead white snow plain. There was no break
in the plateau as it extended toward the Pole, and we feel
sure that the goal we have failed to reach lies on this plain.
We stayed only a few minutes, and then, taking the Queen's
flag and eating our scanty meal as we went, we hurried back
and reached our camp about three P.M. We were so dead
tired that we only did two hours' march in the afternoon
and camped at five-thirty P.M. The temperature was minus
19° Fahrenheit. Fortunately for us, our tracks were not obliterated by the blizzard; indeed, they stood up, making a
trail easily followed. Homeward bound at last. Whatever regrets
may be, we have done our best.

The Last March

CAPTAIN ROBERT FALCON SCOTT

The bare facts are simple enough. There were five men in the final assault party: Scott, Wilson, Bowers, Oates, and Edgar Evans.° They reached the South Pole on January 18, 1912, only to discover that Amundsen had arrived there a month before. They traveled 721 staggering, awful miles on the last march back, and died 177 miles from their winter quarters.

But the facts alone provide only the outline of the story. The following is an extract from the diary kept by Captain Robert Scott, which has about it the nobility of literature. Scott had first been singled out to lead the British National Antarctic Expedition of 1901–04; he returned for his last expedition in 1910–12.

In the age of heroic polar exploration, these men, too, were heroes. Inscribed on the memorial cross erected by other members of the expedition were Tennyson's words of a heroic age:

> *"To strive, to seek, to find, and not to yield . . ."*

SUNDAY, *February* 18—R. 32. Temp. —5.5°. At Shambles Camp. We gave ourselves five hours' sleep at the lower glacier depot after the horrible night, and came on at about three today to this camp, coming fairly easily over the divide. Here with plenty of horsemeat we have had a fine supper, to be followed by others such, and so continue a more plentiful era if we can keep good marches up. New life seems to come with greater food almost immediately, but I am anxious about the Barrier surfaces.

Monday, February 19—Lunch Temp. —16°. It was late (past noon) before we got away today, as I gave nearly eight

---

° There were two men named Evans in Scott's expedition: Petty Officer Edgar Evans, who accompanied Scott on the final push to the pole and subsequently died; and Lieutenant Edward Evans, R.N., who was a member of one of the supporting parties. Lieutenant Evans survived and later became Admiral Sir Edward Evans.

hours sleep, and much camp work was done shifting sledges and fitting up new one with mast, etc., packing horsemeat and personal effects. The surface was every bit as bad as I expected, the sun shining brightly on it and its covering of soft loose sandy snow. We have come out about 2′ on the old tracks. Perhaps lucky to have a fine day for this and our camp work, but we shall want wind or change of sliding conditions to do anything on such a surface as we have got. I fear there will not be much change for the next three or four days.

R. 33. Temp. —17°. We have struggled out 4.6 miles in a short day over a really terrible surface—it has been like pulling over desert sand, not the least glide in the world. If this goes on we shall have a bad time, but I sincerely trust it is only the result of this windless area close to the coast and that, as we are making steadily outward, we shall shortly escape it. It is perhaps premature to be anxious about covering distance. In all other respects things are improving. We have our sleeping bags spread on the sledge and they are drying, but, above all, we have our full measure of food again. Tonight we had a sort of stew fry of pemmican and horseflesh, and voted it the best hoosh we had ever had on a sledge journey. The absence of poor Evans is a help to the commissariat, but if he had been here in a fit state we might have got along faster. I wonder what is in store for us, with some little alarm at the lateness of the season.

Monday, February 20—R. 34. Lunch Temp. —13°; Supper Temp. —15°. Same terrible surface; four hours' hard plodding in morning brought us to our Desolation Camp, where we had the four-day blizzard. We looked for more pony meat, but found none. After lunch we took to ski with some improvement of comfort. Total mileage for day seven—the ski tracks pretty plain and easily followed this afternoon. We have left another cairn behind. Terribly slow progress, but we hope for better things as we clear the land. There is a tendency to cloud over in the S.E. tonight, which may turn to our advantage. At present our sledge and ski leave deeply ploughed tracks which can be seen winding for miles behind. It is distressing, but as usual trials are forgotten when we camp, and good food is our lot. Pray God we get better traveling

as we are not fit as we were, and the season is advancing
apace.

Tuesday, February 21—R. 35. Lunch Temp. —9½°; Supper
Temp. —11°. Gloomy and overcast when we started; a good
deal warmer. The marching almost as bad as yesterday. Heavy
toiling all day, inspiring gloomiest thoughts at times. Rays of
comfort when we picked up tracks and cairns. At lunch we
seemed to have missed the way, but an hour or two after
we passed the last pony walls, and since, we struck a tent
ring, ending the march actually on our old pony tracks. There
is a critical spot here with a long stretch between cairns. If
we can tide that over we get on the regular cairn route,
and with luck should stick to it; but everything depends on
the weather. We never won a march of 8½ miles with
greater difficulty, but we can't go on like this. We are drawing
away from the land and perhaps may get better things
in a day or two. I devoutly hope so.

Wednesday, February 22—R. 36. Supper Temp. —2°. There
is little doubt we are in for a rotten critical time going home,
and the lateness of the season may make it really serious.
Shortly after starting today the wind grew very fresh from the
S.E. with strong surface drift. We lost the faint track immediately, though covering ground fairly rapidly. Lunch came
without sight of the cairn we had hoped to pass. In the
afternoon, Bowers being sure we were too far to the west,
steered out. Result, we have passed another pony camp without
seeing it. Looking at the map tonight there is no doubt we
are too far to the east. With clear weather we ought to
be able to correct the mistake, but will the weather get clear?
It's a gloomy position, more especially as one sees the same
difficulty returning even when we have corrected the error.
The wind is dying down tonight and the sky clearing in
the south, which is hopeful. Meanwhile it is satisfactory to
note that such untoward events fail to damp the spirit of
the party. Tonight we had a pony hoosh so excellent and
filling that one feels really strong and vigorous again.

Thursday, February 23—R. 37. Lunch Temp. —9.8°; Supper
Temp. —12°. Started in sunshine, wind almost dropped.
Luckily Bowers took a round of angles and with help of
the chart we fogged out that we must be inside rather than

outside tracks. The data were so meager that it seemed a great responsibility to march out and we were none of us happy about it. But just as we decided to lunch, Bower's wonderful sharp eyes detected an old double lunch cairn, the theodolite telescope confirmed it, and our spirits rose accordingly. This afternoon we marched on and picked up another cairn; then on and camped only 2½ miles from the depot. We cannot see it, but, given fine weather, we cannot miss it. We are, therefore, extraordinarily relieved. Covered 8.2 miles in seven hours, showing we can do ten to twelve on this surface. Things are again looking up, as we are on the regular line of cairns, with no gaps right home, I hope.

Friday, February 24—Lunch. Beautiful day—too beautiful— an hour after starting loose ice crystals spoiling surface. Saw depot and reached it middle forenoon. Found store in order except shortage oil—shall have to be *very* saving with fuel— otherwise have ten full days' provision from tonight and shall have less than seventy miles to go. Note from Meares who passed through December 15, saying surface bad; from Atkinson, after fine marching (2¼ days from pony depot), reporting Keohane better after sickness. Short note from Evans, not very cheerful, saying surface bad, temperature high. Think he must have been a little anxious. It is an immense relief to have picked up this depot and, for the time, anxieties are thrust aside. There is no doubt we have been rising steadily since leaving the Shambles Camp. The coastal Barrier descends except where glaciers press out. Undulation still but flattening out. Surface soft on top, curiously hard below. Great difference now between night and day temperatures. Quite warm as I write in tent. We are on tracks with half-march cairn ahead; have covered 4½ miles. Poor Wilson has a fearful attack snow-blindness consequent on yesterday's efforts. Wish we had more fuel.

Night came R. 38. Temp. —17°. A little despondent again. We had a really terrible surface this afternoon and only covered 4 miles. We are on the track just beyond a lunch cairn. It really will be a bad business if we are to have this pulling all through. I don't know what to think, but the rapid closing of the season is ominous. It is great luck having the horsemeat to add to our ration. Tonight we have had a

real fine "hoosh." It is a race between the season and hard
conditions and our fitness and good food.

Saturday, February 25—Lunch Temp. —12°. Managed just
6 miles this morning. Started somewhat despondent; not relieved
when pulling seemed to show no improvement. Bit by bit
surface grew better, less sastrugi, more glide, slight following
wind for a time. Then we began to travel a little faster.
But the pull is still *very* hard; undulations disappearing but
inequalities remain.

Twenty-six Camp walls about two miles ahead, all tracks
in sight—Evans' track very conspicuous. This is something in
favor, but the pulling is tiring us, though we are getting into
better ski drawing again. Bowers hasn't quite the trick and
is a little hurt at my criticisms, but I never doubted his
heart. Very much easier—write diary at lunch—excellent meal—
now one pannikin very strong tea—four biscuits and butter.

Hope for better things this afternoon, but no improvement
apparent. Oh! for a little wind—E. Evans evidently had plenty.

R. 39. Temp. —20°. Better march in afternoon. Day yields
11.4 miles—the first double figure of steady dragging for a
long time, but it meant and will mean hard work if we can't
get a wind to help us. Evans evidently had a strong wind
here, S.E. I should think. The temperature goes very low at
night now when the sky is clear as at present. As a matter
of fact this is wonderfully fair weather—the only drawback
the spoiling of the surface and absence of wind. We see all
tracks very plain, but the pony-walls have evidently been
badly drifted up. Some kind people had substituted a cairn
at last Camp twenty-seven. The old cairns do not seem to have
suffered much.

Sunday, February 26—Lunch Temp. —17°. Sky overcast at
start, but able see tracks and cairn distinct at long distance.
Did a little better, 6½ miles to date. Bowers and Wilson
now in front. Find great relief pulling behind with no necessity
to keep attention on track. Very cold nights now and cold
feet starting march, as day footgear doesn't dry at all. We are
doing well on our food, but we ought to have yet more.
I hope the next depot, now only fifty miles, will find us with
enough surplus to open out. The fuel shortage still an anxiety.

R. 40. Temp. —21°. Nine hours' solid marching has given

us 11½ miles. Only forty-three miles from the next depot. Wonderfully fine weather but cold, very cold. Nothing dries and we get our feet cold too often. We want more food yet and especially more fat. Fuel is woefully short. We can scarcely hope to get a better surface at this season, but I wish we could have some help from the wind, though it might shake us badly if the temp. didn't rise.

Monday, February 27—Desperately cold last night: −33° when we got up, with −37° minimum. Some suffering from cold feet, but all got good rest. We *must* open out on food soon. But we have done seven miles this morning and hope for some five this afternoon. Overcast sky and good surface till now, when sun shows again. It is good to be marching the cairns up, but there is still much to be anxious about. We talk of little but food, except after meals. Land disappearing in satisfactory manner. Pray God we have no further setbacks. We are naturally always discussing possibility of meeting dogs, where and when, etc. It is a critical position. We may find ourselves in safety at next depot, but there is a horrid element of doubt.

Camp R. 41. Temp. −32°. Still fine clear weather but very cold—absolutely calm tonight. We have got off an excellent march for these days (12.2) and are much earlier than usual in our bags. Thirty-one miles to depot, three days' fuel at a pinch, and six days' food. Things begin to look a little better; we can open out a little on food from tomorrow night, I think.

Very curious surface—soft recent sastrugi which sink underfoot, and between, a sort of flaky crust with large crystals beneath.

Tuesday, February 28—Lunch. Thermometer went below −40° last night; it was desperately cold for us, but we had a fair night. I decided to slightly increase food; the effect is undoubtedly good. Started marching in −32° with a slight northwesterly breeze—blighting. Many cold feet this morning; long time over footgear, but we are earlier. Shall camp earlier and get the chance of a good night, if not the reality. Things must be critical till we reach the depot, and the more I think of matters, the more I anticipate their remaining so after that event. Only 24½ miles from the depot. The sun shines brightly, but there is little warmth in it. There is no doubt the middle of the Barrier is a pretty awful locality.

Camp 42. Splendid pony hoosh sent us to bed and sleep happily after a horrid day, wind continuing; did 11½ miles. Temp. not quite so low, but expect we are in for cold night (Temp. −27°).

Wednesday, February 29—Lunch. Cold night. Minimum Temp. −37.5°; −30° with northwest wind, force 4, when we got up. Frightfully cold starting; luckily Bowers and Oates in their last new finnesko; keeping my old ones for present. Expected awful march and for first hour got it. Then things improved and we camped after 5½ hours marching close to lunch camp—22½. Next camp is our depot and it is exactly thirteen miles. It ought not to take more than 1½ days; we pray for another fine one. The oil will just about spin out in that event, and we arrive three clear days' food in hand. The increase of ration has had an enormously beneficial result. Mountains now looking small. Wind still very light from west —cannot understand this wind.

Thursday, March 1—Lunch. Very cold last night—minimum −41.5°. Cold start to march, too, as usual now. Got away at eight and have marched within sight of depot; flag something under three miles away. We did 11½ yesterday and marched six this morning. Heavy dragging yesterday and *very* heavy this morning. Apart from sledging considerations the weather is wonderful. Cloudless days and nights and the wind trifling. Worse luck, the light airs come from the north and keep us horribly cold. For this lunch hour the exception has come. There is a bright and comparatively warm sun. All our gear is out drying.

Friday, March 2—Lunch. Misfortunes rarely come singly. We marched to the (Middle Barrier) depot fairly easily yesterday afternoon, and since that have suffered three distinct blows which have placed us in a bad position. First we found a shortage of oil; with most rigid economy it can scarce carry us to the next depot on this surface (seventy-one miles away). Second, Titus Oates disclosed his feet, the toes showing very bad indeed, evidently bitten by the late temperatures. The third blow came in the night, when the wind, which we had hailed with some joy, brought dark overcast weather. It fell

below −40° in the night, and this morning it took 1½ hours
to get our footgear on, but we got away before eight. We lost
cairn and tracks together and made as steady as we could N.
by W., but have seen nothing. Worse was to come—the surface
is simply awful. In spite of strong wind and full sail we have
only done 5½ miles. We are in a *very* queer street since there
is no doubt we cannot do the extra marches and feel the cold
horribly.

Saturday, March 3—Lunch. We picked up the track again
yesterday, finding ourselves to the eastward. Did close on ten
miles and things looked a trifle better; but this morning the
outlook is blacker than ever. Started well and with good breeze;
for an hour made good headway; then the surface grew awful
beyond words. The wind drew forward; every circumstance
was against us. After 4¼ hours things so bad that we camped,
having covered 4½ miles. (R. 46) One cannot consider this a
fault of our own—certainly we were pulling hard this morning
—it was more than three parts surface which held us back—
the wind at strongest, powerless to move the sledge. When
the light is good it is easy to see the reason. The surface,
lately a very good hard one, is coated with a thin layer of
woolly crystals, formed by radiation no doubt. These are too
firmly fixed to be removed by the wind and cause impossible
friction on the runners. God help us, we can't keep up this
pulling, that is certain. Amongst ourselves we are unendingly
cheerful, but what each man feels in his heart I can only
guess. Pulling on footgear in the morning is getting slower
and slower, therefore every day more dangerous.

Sunday, March 4—Lunch. Things looking *very* black indeed.
As usual we forgot our trouble last night, got into our bags,
slept splendidly on good hoosh, woke and had another, and
started marching. Sun shining brightly, tracks clear, but surface
covered with sandy frostrime. All the morning we had to pull
with all our strength, and in 4½ hours we covered 3½ miles.
Last night it was overcast and thick, surface bad; this morning
sun shining and surface as bad as ever. One has little to hope
for except perhaps strong dry wind—an unlikely contingency
at this time of year. Under the immediate surface crystals is
a hard sustrugi surface, which must have been excellent for
pulling a week or two ago. We are about forty-two miles from

the next depot and have a week's food, but only about three to four days' fuel—we are as economical of the latter as one can possibly be, and we cannot afford to save food and pull as we are pulling. We are in a very tight place indeed, but none of us despondent *yet,* or at least we preserve every semblance of good cheer, but one's heart sinks as the sledge stops dead at some sastrugi behind which the surface sand lies thickly heaped. For the moment the temperature is on the —20°—an improvement which makes us much more comfortable, but a colder snap is bound to come again soon. I fear that Oates at least will weather such an event very poorly. Providence to our aid! We can expect little from man now except the possibility of extra food at the next depot. It will be real bad if we get there and find the same shortage of oil. Shall we get there? Such a short distance it would have appeared to us on the summit! I don't know what I should do if Wilson and Bowers weren't so determinedly cheerful over things.

Monday, March 5—Lunch. Regret to say going from bad to worse. We got a slant of wind yesterday afternoon, and going on five hours we converted our wretched morning run of 3½ miles into something over nine. We went to bed on a cup of cocoa and pemmican solid with the chill off. (R. 47.) The result is telling on all, but mainly on Oates, whose feet are in a wretched condition. One swelled up tremendously last night and he is very lame this morning. We started march on tea and pemmican as last night—we pretend to prefer the pemmican this way. Marched for five hours this morning over a slightly better surface covered with high moundy sastrugi. Sledge capsized twice; we pulled on foot, covering about 5½ miles. We are two pony marches and four miles about from our depot. Our fuel dreadfully low and the poor Soldier nearly done. It is pathetic enough because we can do nothing for him; more hot food might do a little, but only a little, I fear. We none of us expected these terribly low temperatures, and of the rest of us Wilson is feeling them most; mainly, I fear, from his self-sacrificing devotion in doctoring Oates' feet. We cannot help each other, each has enough to do to take care of himself. We get cold on the march when the trudging is heavy, and the wind pierces our warm garments. The others, all of them, are unendingly cheerful when in the tent. We mean to see the game through with a proper spirit, but it's tough work to be pulling harder than we ever pulled in our lives for long hours, and to feel that the progress is so slow. One can only say 'God help us!' and plod on our weary way, cold and very miserable, though outwardly cheerful. We talk of all sorts of subjects in the tent, not much of food now, since we decided to take the risk of running a full ration. We simply couldn't go hungry at this time.

Tuesday, March 6—Lunch. We did a little better with help of wind yesterday afternoon, finishing 9½ miles for the day, and twenty-seven miles from depot. (R. 48.) But this morning things have been awful. It was warm in the night and for the first time during the journey I overslept myself by more than an hour; then we were slow with footgear; then, pulling with all our might (for our lives) we could scarcely advance at rate of a mile an hour; then it grew thick and three times we had to get out of harness to search for tracks. The result is something less than 3½ miles for the forenoon. The sun is shining now and the wind gone. Poor Oates is unable to pull, sits on the sledge when we are track-searching—he is wonderfully plucky, as his feet must be giving him great pain. He makes no complaint, but his spirits only come up in spurts now, and he grows more silent in the tent. We are making a spirit lamp to try and replace the primus when our oil is exhausted. It will be a very poor substitute and we've not got much spirit. If we could have kept up our nine-mile days we might have got within reasonable distance of the depot before running out, but nothing but a strong wind and good surface can help us now, and though we had quite a good breeze this morning, the sledge came as heavy as lead. If we were all fit I should have hopes of getting through, but the poor Soldier has become a terrible hindrance, though he does his utmost and suffers much I fear.

Wednesday, March 7—A little worse I fear. One of Oates' feet *very* bad this morning; he is wonderfully brave. We still talk of what we will do together at home.

We only made 6½ miles yesterday. (R. 49.) This morning in 4½ hours we did just over four miles. We are sixteen from our depot. If we only find the correct proportion of food

there and this surface continues, we may get to the next depot
[Mt. Hooper, seventy-two miles farther] but not to One Ton
Camp. We hope against hope that the dogs have been to Mt.
Hooper; then we might pull through. If there is a shortage of
oil again we can have little hope. One feels that for poor
Oates the crisis is near, but none of us are improving, though
we are wonderfully fit considering the really excessive work
we are doing. We are only kept going by good food. No wind
this morning till a chill northerly air came ahead. Sun bright
and cairns showing up well. I should like to keep the track to
the end.

Thursday, March 8—Lunch. Worse and worse in morning;
poor Oates' left foot can never last out, and time over footgear something awful. Have to wait in night footgear for
nearly an hour before I start changing, and then am generally
first to be ready. Wilson's feet giving trouble now, but this
mainly because he gives so much help to others. We did 4½
miles this morning and are now 8½ miles from the depot—
a ridiculously small distance to feel in difficulties, yet on this
surface we know we cannot equal half our old marches, and
that for that effort we expend nearly double the energy. The
great question is, What shall we find at the depot? If the dogs
have visited it we may get along a good distance, but if
there is another short allowance of fuel, God help us indeed.
We are in a very bad way, I fear, in any case.

Saturday, March 10—Things steadily downhill. Oates' foot
worse. He has rare pluck and must know that he can never
get through. He asked Wilson if he had a chance this morning,
and of course Bill had to say he didn't know. In point of
fact he has none. Apart from him, if he went under now, I
doubt whether we could get through. With great care we
might have a dog's chance, but no more. The weather conditions are awful, and our gear gets steadily more icy and
difficult to manage. At the same time of course poor Titus is
the greatest handicap. He keeps us waiting in the morning
until we have partly lost the warming effect of our good
breakfast, when the only wise policy is to be up and away
at once; again at lunch. Poor chap! it is too pathetic to
watch him; one cannot but try to cheer him up.

Yesterday we marched up the depot, Mt. Hooper. Cold

comfort. Shortage on our allowance all round. I don't know that anyone is to blame. The dogs which would have been our salvation have evidently failed.* Meares had a bad trip home I suppose.

This morning it was calm when we breakfasted, but the wind came from W.N.W. as we broke camp. It rapidly grew in strength. After traveling for half an hour I saw that none of us could go on facing such conditions. We were forced to camp and are spending the rest of the day in a comfortless blizzard camp, wind quite foul. (R. 52.)

Sunday, March 11—Titus Oates is very near the end, one feels. What we or he will do, God only knows. We discussed the matter after breakfast; he is a brave fine fellow and understands the situation, but he practically asked for advice. Nothing could be said but to urge him to march as long as he could. One satisfactory result to the discussion; I practically ordered Wilson to hand over the means of ending our troubles to us, so that anyone of us may know how to do so. Wilson had no choice between doing so and our ransacking the medicine case. We have 30 opium tabloids apiece and he is left with a tube of morphine. So far the tragical side of our story. (R. 53.)

The sky completely overcast when we started this morning. We could see nothing, lost the tracks, and doubtless have been swaying a good deal since—3.1 miles for the forenoon—terribly heavy dragging—expected it. Know that six miles is about the limit of our endurance now, if we get no help from wind or surfaces. We have seven days' food and should be about fifty-five miles from One Ton Camp to-night, 6×7=42, leaving

---

* For the last six days the dogs had been waiting at One Ton Camp under Cherry-Garrard and Demetri. The supporting party had come out as arranged on the chance of hurrying the Pole travelers back over the last stages of their journey in time to catch the ship. Scott had dated his probable return to Hut Point anywhere between mid-March and early April. Calculating from the speed of the other return parties, Dr. Atkinson looked for him to reach One Ton Camp between March 3 and 10. Here Cherry-Garrard met four days of blizzard; then there remained little more than enough dog food to bring the teams home. He could either push south one more march and back, at imminent risk of missing Scott on the way, or stay two days at the Camp where Scott was bound to come, if he came at all. His wise decision, his hardships and endurance are recounted by Dr. Atkinson in Vol. II., 'The Last Year at Cape Evans.'

us thirteen miles short of our distance, even if things get no worse. Meanwhile the season rapidly advances.

Monday, March 12—We did 6.9 miles yesterday, under our necessary average. Things are left much the same, Oates not pulling much, and now with hands as well as feet pretty well useless. We did four miles this morning in 4 hours 20 min.—we may hope for three this afternoon, 7×6=42. We shall be forty-seven miles from the depot. I doubt if we can possibly do it. The surface remains awful, the cold intense, and our physical condition running down. God help us! Not a breath of favorable wind for more than a week, and apparently liable to head winds at any moment.

Wednesday, March 14—No doubt about the going downhill, but everything going wrong for us. Yesterday we woke to a strong northerly wind with temp. −37°. Couldn't face it, so remained in camp (R. 54) till two, then did 5¼ miles. Wanted to march later, but party feeling the cold badly as the breeze (N.) never took off entirely, and as the sun sank the temp. fell. Long time getting supper in dark. (R. 55.)

This morning started with southerly breeze, set sail and passed another cairn at good speed; half-way, however, the wind shifted to W. by S. or W.S.W., blew through our wind clothes and into our mits. Poor Wilson horribly cold, could not get off ski for some time. Bowers and I practically made camp, and when we got into the tent at last we were all deadly cold. Then temp. now midday down −43° and the wind strong. We *must* go on, but now the making of every camp must be more difficult and dangerous. It must be near the end, but a pretty merciful end. Poor Oates got it again in the foot. I shudder to think what it will be like tomorrow. It is only with greatest pains rest of us keep off frostbites. No idea there could be temperatures like this at this time of year with such winds. Truly awful outside the tent. Must fight it out to the last biscuit, but can't reduce rations.

Friday, March 16 *or Saturday* 17—Lost track of dates, but think the last correct. Tragedy all along the line. At lunch, the day before yesterday, poor Titus Oates said he couldn't go on; he proposed we should leave him in his sleeping bag. That we could not do, and induced him to come on, on the afternoon march. In spite of its awful nature for him he struggled on and we made a few miles. At night he was worse and we knew the end had come.

Should this be found I want these facts recorded. Oates' last thoughts were of his Mother, but immediately before, he took pride in thinking that his regiment would be pleased with the bold way in which he met his death. We can testify to his bravery. He has borne intense suffering for weeks without complaint, and to the very last was able and willing to discuss outside subjects. He did not—would not—give up hope to the very end. He was a brave soul. This was the end. He slept through the night before last, hoping not to wake; but he woke in the morning—yesterday. It was blowing a blizzard. He said, 'I am just going outside and may be some time.' He went out into the blizzard and we have not seen him since.

I take this opportunity of saying that we have stuck to our sick companions to the last. In case of Edgar Evans, when absolutely out of food and he lay insensible, the safety of the remainder seemed to demand his abandonment, but Providence mercifully removed him at this critical moment. He died a natural death, and we did not leave him till two hours after his death. We knew that poor Oates was walking to his death, but though we tried to dissuade him, we knew it was the act of a brave man and an English gentleman. We all hope to meet the end with a similar spirit, and assuredly the end is not far.

I can only write at lunch and then only occasionally. The cold is intense, —40° at midday. My companions are unendingly cheerful, but we are all on the verge of serious frostbites, and though we constantly talk of fetching through I don't think anyone of us believes it in his heart.

We are cold on the march now, and at all times except meals. Yesterday we had to lay up for a blizzard and today we move dreadfully slowly. We are at No. 14 pony camp, only two pony marches from One Ton Depot. We leave here our theodolite, a camera, and Oates' sleeping bags. Diaries, etc., and geological specimens carried at Wilson's special request, will be found with us or on our sledge.

Sunday, March 18—Today, lunch, we are twenty-one miles from the depot. Ill fortune presses, but better may come. We have had more wind and drift from ahead yesterday; had to stop marching; wind N.W., force 4, temp. —35°. No human being could face it, and we are worn out *nearly*.

My right foot has gone, nearly all the toes—two days ago I was proud possessor of best feet. These are the steps of my downfall. Like an ass I mixed a small spoonful of curry powder with my melted pemmican—it gave me violent indigestion. I lay awake and in pain all night; woke and felt done on the march; foot went and I didn't know it. A very small measure of neglect and have a foot which is not pleasant to contemplate. Bowers takes first place in condition, but there is not much to choose after all. The others are still confident of getting through—or pretend to be—I don't know! We have the last *half* fill of oil in our primus and a very small quantity of spirit—this alone between us and thirst. The wind is fair for the moment, and that is perhaps a fact to help. The mileage would have seemed ridiculously small on our outward journey.

Monday, March 19—Lunch. We camped with difficulty last night, and were dreadfully cold till after our supper of cold pemmican and biscuit and a half a pannikin of cocoa cooked over the spirit. Then, contrary to expectation, we got warm and all slept well. Today we started in the usual dragging manner. Sledge dreadfully heavy. We are 15½ miles from the depot and ought to get there in three days. What progress! We have two days' food but barely a day's fuel. All our feet are getting bad—Wilson's best, my right foot worst, left all right. There is no chance to nurse one's feet till we can get hot food into us. Amputation is the least I can hope for now, but will the trouble spread? That is the serious question. The weather doesn't give us a chance—the wind from N. to N.W. and —40° temp. today.

Wednesday, March 21—Got within eleven miles of depot Monday night*; had to lay up all yesterday in severe blizzard. Today forlorn hope, Wilson and Bowers going to depot for fuel.

Thursday, March 22 *and* 23—Blizzard bad as ever—Wilson and Bowers unable to start—tomorrow last chance—no fuel and only one or two of food left—must be near the end. Have

* The 6oth camp from the Pole.

decided it shall be natural—we shall march for the depot with or without our effects and die in our tracks.

Thursday, March 29—Since the twenty-first we have had a continuous gale from W.S.W. and S.W. We had fuel to make two cups of tea apiece and bare food for two days on the twentieth. Every day we have been ready to start for our depot *eleven miles* away, but outside the door of the tent it remains a scene of whirling drift. I do not think we can hope for any better things now. We shall stick it out to the end, but we are getting weaker, of course, and the end cannot be far.

It seems a pity, but I do not think I can write more.

R. Scott.

For God's sake look after our people.

PETER FREUCHEN, Danish explorer and writer, was born in Nykobing Falster, Denmark in 1886. Freuchen spent over forty years living and trading with the Eskimos of Greenland, northern Canada, and Alaska. He was active in the Danish Underground from 1940–45 and was captured by the Germans, but escaped to Sweden and was later decorated by his native land. Freuchen lectured extensively in the United States until his death in 1957.

VILHJALMUR STEFANSSON, the arctic explorer, was born in Canada in 1879 of Icelandic parents. In 1906 he explored the Mackenzie River Delta, where he studied the Eskimos, one of his lifelong interests. His second expedition (1908–12) to the Mackenzie Delta was under the auspices of the American Museum of Natural History and the Canadian government. Stefansson led the Canadian arctic expedition of 1913–18, which mapped large areas of unexplored territory. He set up the first scientific station on a drifting ice floe in 1918. For eight months his party made regular observations of ice and tides while they floated in the Beaufort Sea. Stefansson was the author of many books about the Arctic. He died in 1962.

KATHARINE SCHERMAN grew up in Manhattan and has spent her adult life in that city working as an editor and journalist. With her husband, also city-bred, she spends most vacations in out-of-the-way places—the Arctic, the Alps, the Italian Dolomites, the Cascade Range in Washington.

WILLY LEY was born in Berlin, Germany in 1906, and attended the University of Berlin. He came to the United States in 1935 and was naturalized in 1944. One of our most popular writers, lecturers, and teachers, he divides his immense talents between astronautics and paleontology. He was one of the founders of the German Rocket Society, and from 1944–47 was a research engineer at the Washington (D.C.) Institute of Technology. Since 1947 he has been an information specialist for the Department of Commerce.

FELIX RIESENBERG, American writer and engineer, was born in Milwaukee, Wisconsin in 1879. He was a member of the Wellman polar expedition of 1906–07 and spent that winter in charge of the camp established on Danes Island, on the north shore of Spitzbergen, where the experience described in this book occurred. In 1907 he served as navigator of the airship *America* in the first attempt to fly over the North Pole by dirigible. Riesenberg, who was the author of many books, died in 1939.

FRANK DUFRESNE was born in 1896 and died in 1966. He was a young newspaperman when he went to Nome, Alaska in 1920. It was to be a visit, no more, but he stayed there for twenty-four years, first as field man for the old U. S. Bureau of Biological Survey, then as Director of the Alaska Game Commission. He helped write the original territorial game laws. In 1944 he became Chief of Information for the new U. S. Fish and Wildlife Service in Washington, D.C. He "retired" to become West Coast associate editor for *Field and Stream*. His book *No Room For Bears* is considered a classic of nature writing.

ABECUK PRICKETT, who was one of the members of Henry Hudson's expedition of 1610, was sent along as an observer by Sir Dudley Digges, one of the expedition's backers. He and the other mutineers returned to England and erroneously reported to the organizers of the expedition that the Northwest Passage had been found. Prickett brought back his diary, as well as the dial of his compass, and the information therein was published in a famous map by Hessel Gerritz in 1612. Hudson's original chart was evidently sent to his old friend Peter Plancus, who gave it to Gerritz to engrave and who probably supplied him with the information for explanation of the chart. Strangely, the mutineers were never punished for their crime. Prickett even became a member of the Northwest Company, and on subsequent expeditions he successfully influenced those in charge to avoid places where Hudson and his companions might have found shelter.

SIR JOHN FRANKLIN, British Arctic explorer, was born in 1786. In 1819 he commanded an expedition to cross America between Hudson's Bay and the Arctic Ocean, with the specific object of exploring the Coppermine River. The expedition, which proved successful, took three years. A second journey, 1825–26, took him down the Mackenzie River to the Arctic Ocean. The two expeditions surveyed 1200 miles of Canada's hitherto unexplored coast. In 1845 he was given command of the *Erebus* and *Terror* and sailed once more to explore the arctic waters. The ships were last seen at the entrance of Lancaster Sound. The fate of Franklin's expedition was finally made known in 1859 when his diaries were discovered. They revealed that he and all the other members of the expedition had died of cold and exposure in 1847.

ELISHA KENT KANE, M.D., polar explorer, was born in Philadelphia, Pennsylvania in 1820, and died in 1857. In 1850 he became senior medical officer of the *Advance,* a ship fitted out by Henry Grinnell to rescue the British polar explorer Sir John Franklin. He commanded the *Advance* on a second rescue expedition in 1853. This expedition reached a latitude of 80°35′ N, was forced to winter in what is now called Kane Basin and reached Upernivik, a Danish settlement in Greenland, after a 1300 mile journey by boat and sledge. Kane discovered a polar route later followed by many American explorers.

ADOLPHUS WASHINGTON GREELY, American army officer and Arctic explorer, was born in 1844 and died in 1935. In 1881–84 he led the Lady Franklin Bay expedition, which was to establish one of a chain of international circumpolar meteorological stations. Although he was without previous arctic experience, he and his party performed notable feats of exploration; many hitherto unknown miles along the northwest coast of Greenland were added to the map, Ellesmere Island was crossed to the west shore, and Lt. James B. Lockwood achieved a new northern record of 83°24′ N. Relief ships failed to reach Greely's party, which was overcome by starvation. When the third relief vessel arrived in 1884, all but Greely and six others had perished. Greely was made a major general in 1906.

FRIDTJOF NANSEN, the Norwegian arctic explorer and zoologist, was born at Store Froen, Norway in 1861. He was appointed Curator of the Museum of Natural History in Bergen in 1882. Nansen headed the first expedition to cross the ice fields of Greenland in 1888. In 1893 he let his ship *Fram* drift from the New Siberian Islands in the hope that it might reach the North Pole. Disappointed, he tried to reach the Pole by sleigh but had to turn back at 86°4′. In 1896 the *Fram* returned to its home port, but Nansen had proved the existence of a deep warm sea in the arctic area, an important clue to later explorers. He went on to devote himself to oceanography, diplomatic service, and humanitarian work. He was awarded the Nobel Peace Prize in 1927 and died in 1930.

ROBERT E. PEARY, the first explorer to reach the North Pole, was born at Cressan, Pennsylvania in 1856. A civil engineer by profession, he joined the U. S. Navy and in 1886 made a study of the west coast of Greenland. In 1891 he was given charge of an arctic expedition by the Philadelphia Academy of Natural Sciences. He crossed Greenland in 1892 and proved it an island. Further arctic expeditions in 1898 and 1902 led him to a latitude of 84°17′27″, the northernmost then reached. A journey on the *Roosevelt*, 1905–06, brought him to 87°6′ N. His life's work was finally crowned on April 6, 1909 when he, Matthew Henson and four Eskimos reached the Pole, 90° North. Peary later became a rear admiral and died in Washington, D.C. in 1920.

RICHARD EVELYN BYRD, polar explorer, was born in Winchester, Virginia in 1888, and graduated from the United States Naval Academy in 1912. Byrd became interested in aviation and in 1918 was appointed commander of U. S. Air Forces stationed in Canada. In 1921 he crossed the Atlantic in a dirigible and in 1926 flew over the North Pole with Floyd Bennett. He made his first antarctic expedition in 1928–30. Establishing a base, Little America, on the Bay of Whales, he flew for the first time over the South Pole. On his second expedition, 1933–35, he discovered *Edsel Ford Mountain* and *Maria Byrd Land*. As commander of the U.S. antarctic expedition of 1939 he claimed some antarctic territories for his country. In 1946–47 he made a special antarctic survey to study meteorology, test personnel and equipment, and scout for uranium deposits. He was made a rear admiral in 1930, and died in 1957.

COMMANDER WILLIAM R. ANDERSON was born in Bakerville, Tennessee in 1921, and graduated from the United States Naval Academy. He was commissioned in 1942 and served on submarines from 1942 to 1959. In August 1958, he commanded the first atomic submarine *Nautilus* when it made its historic crossing of the North Pole beneath the Arctic Icecap. Commander Anderson was awarded the Bronze Star, and the Legion of Merit, among other honors, and is now a vice president of the Freedom Foundation.

THOMAS R. HENRY was born in Boston, Massachusetts in 1893. After graduation from Clark University he started his long and varied newspaper career, becoming, in the twenties, science editor of the *Washington Star*. During World War II he was a correspondent in Africa, Iceland, and Europe. In the winter of 1946–47, Mr. Henry accompanied the Navy expedition "High Jump" under Admirals

Byrd and Cruzen to the Antarctic. He spent the winter of 1948–49 on a Navy icebreaker in the Arctic Ocean.

ROBERT BLACKWOOD ROBERTSON was born in Cairo, Egypt in 1913 of Scottish parents. He received his early schooling in Dundee—a port that is to Scottish whaling what New Bedford was to American whaling—and took his undergraduate and medical degrees at St. Andrews University. Dr. Robertson served as a military surgeon during World War II. In 1950 he received an appointment as senior medical officer to one of the largest antarctic whaling expeditions of that season.

ROBERT CUSHMAN MURPHY, American zoologist and Lamont Curator Emeritus of Birds at the American Museum of Natural History, was born in Brooklyn, New York in 1887. Dr. Murphy made his first field trip in 1912. Fresh out of college, he joined the whaler *Daisy* to begin his lifelong study of marine birds. Decade after decade he has represented the American Museum in remote corners of the world, and his far-seeing eyes have studied the flight of more marine birds than have those of any other human being.

CAPTAIN FINN RONNE, U.S.N.R., American antarctic explorer, was born in Horten, Norway in 1899. He was educated in Norway, came to the United States in 1923, and was naturalized in 1929. His father, Martin Ronne, was with Amundsen's historic South Polar expedition and later was a member of Byrd's first expedition. Finn Ronne was a member of Byrd's expedition of 1933–35. He was in command of East Base, U. S. Antarctic Service from 1939–41. In 1946–48 Captain Ronne organized and directed his own private antarctic expedition which discovered vast tracts of unknown territory, now named for his wife—Edith Ronne Land. He is now a consultant to the United States Department of Defense.

ROALD AMUNDSEN, the Norwegian polar explorer, was born in Borge, Norway in 1872. He navigated the Northwest Passage and fixed the position of the North Magnetic Pole in 1903–06. He reached the South Pole on December 14, 1911, after an eight-week trip across the icecap. On his return he discovered a 14,000-foot-high mountain range which he named after Norway's Queen Maud. In 1918–20 Amundsen sailed through the Northeast Passage. Together with Lincoln Ellsworth and Umberto Nobile he flew from Spitzbergen over the North Pole in the dirigible *Norge* in 1926. In June of 1928

Amundsen disappeared while on a flight to rescue Nobile who had been lost returning from the North Pole.

SIR DOUGLAS MAWSON, Australian antarctic explorer and scientist, was born in 1882. He took part in Shackleton's antarctic expedition of 1908. In 1911–14 he led the Australian expedition to Adélie Land. The expedition faced generally harsher weather conditions than any previous recorded expedition to the South Polar regions. In his historic book, *The Home of the Blizzard,* Mawson tells of storms in which the wind force exceeded one hundred miles an hour. It was during this expedition that he made the trip described in this book. The expedition is credited with having contributed more geographical and scientific discoveries than any previous antarctic expedition. In 1930 Mawson again visited Antarctica and explored in the vicinity of Enderby Land. He has been called by other explorers "the father of the modern scientific expedition." His studies won him worldwide fame, and he was knighted in 1914. Sir Douglas died in 1958.

SIR ERNEST SHACKLETON, British antarctic explorer, was born in Kilkee, Ireland in 1874. He trained to be a merchant marine officer while still a young boy. Shackleton served as Scott's lieutenant in the 1901–4 antarctic expedition. In 1908 he sailed south from New Zealand on the *Nimrod* and came within ninety-seven miles of the South Pole, an exploit that won him a knighthood. A third expedition, 1914–17, on the *Endurance,* discovered Caird Land. He died of influenza at South Georgia Island while commanding his last Antarctic expedition in 1922.

ROBERT FALCON SCOTT, British antarctic explorer, was born at Devonport, England in 1868, and joined the Royal Navy as a midshipman in 1882. He commanded the British antarctic expedition of 1897. From 1900 to 1904 he explored the Antarctic in the *Discovery,* finding King Edward VII's Land in 1902. In June 1910, backed financially by the British and Dominion governments, he commanded the antarctic expedition on the *Terra Nova.* Scott and four companions—Bowers, Oates, Evans, and Wilson began the Southern Sledge Journey to the Pole in November 1911. They reached the South Pole on January 18, 1912, about a month after Roald Amundsen's expedition. Captain Scott and his companions perished on the return trip as a result of bad weather and insufficient food. His records and diary were found by a search party in November 1912.

Seon Manley and Gogo Lewis, who are sisters, have collaborated on many books. This present collection comes from their particular interest in how man adjusts to different environments and how even polar heroes had to come to terms with climate and terrain. As associates of Manley Management and Marketing Services, they have worked on studies concerning the environmental requirements of electronics for the polar regions.

Mrs. Manley, in private life Mrs. Robert R. Manley, lives in Greenwich, Connecticut. Mrs. Lewis (Mrs. William Lewis) lives in Bellport, New York. Both are active conservationists, as are their children.

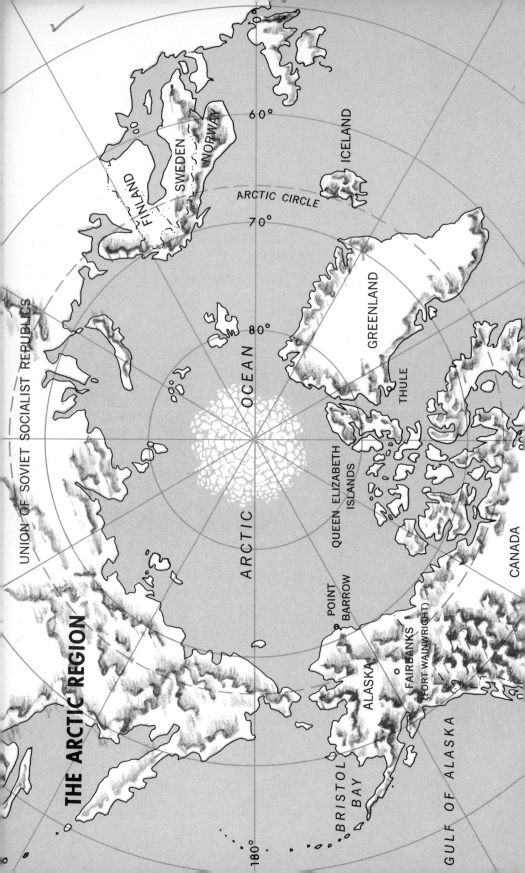

THE ARCTIC REGION

UNION OF SOVIET SOCIALIST REPUBLICS

FINLAND

SWEDEN

NORWAY

60°

ICELAND

ARCTIC CIRCLE

70°

80°

GREENLAND

THULE

ARCTIC OCEAN

QUEEN ELIZABETH ISLANDS

POINT BARROW

FAIRBANKS

(FORT WAINWRIGHT)

ALASKA

CANADA

BRISTOL BAY

GULF OF ALASKA

180°